# Ministry Among God's Queer Folk

# Ministry Among God's Queer Folk

## LGBTQ Pastoral Care

SECOND EDITION

**BERNARD SCHLAGER
and DAVID KUNDTZ**

CASCADE *Books* • Eugene, Oregon

MINISTRY AMONG GOD'S QUEER FOLK
LGBTQ Pastoral Care: Second Edition

Copyright © 2019 Bernard Schlager and David Kundtz. All rights reserved. Except for brief quotations in critical publications or reviews, no part of this book may be reproduced in any manner without prior written permission from the publisher. Write: Permissions, Wipf and Stock Publishers, 199 W. 8th Ave., Suite 3, Eugene, OR 97401.

Cascade Books
An Imprint of Wipf and Stock Publishers
199 W. 8th Ave., Suite 3
Eugene, OR 97401

www.wipfandstock.com

PAPERBACK ISBN: 978-1-5326-1711-9
HARDCOVER ISBN: 978-1-4982-4157-1
EBOOK ISBN: 978-1-4982-4156-4

*Cataloging-in-Publication data:*

Names: Schlager, Bernard, author. | Kundtz, David, author.

Title: Ministry among God's queer folk : LGBTQ pastoral care / by Bernard Schlager and David Kundtz

Description: Eugene, OR : Cascade Books, 2019 | Includes bibliographical references.

Identifiers: ISBN 978-1-5326-1711-9 (paperback) | ISBN 978-1-4982-4157-1 (hardcover) | ISBN 978-1-4982-4156-4 (ebook)

Subjects: LCSH: Church work with gays. | Gays—Pastoral counseling of. | Homosexuality—Religious aspects—Christianity.

Classification: LCC BV4437.5 M4 2019 (print) | LCC BV4437.5 (ebook)

Manufactured in the U.S.A.      01/18/19

# Contents

*Authors' Preface to the Second Edition* | vii
*Acknowledgments* | ix
*Introduction* | xi

**1** The Pastoral Care Relationship | 1
 —DAVID KUNDTZ

**2** The Functions of Pastoral Care | 38
 —DAVID KUNDTZ

**3** Pastoral Care in the Tough Times: An LGBTQ Perspective | 73
 —DAVID KUNDTZ

**4** Coming Out | 124
 —BERNARD SCHLAGER

**5** Creating Communities of Care for LGBTQ People | 153
 —BERNARD SCHLAGER

**6** Caring for LGBTQ People in Their Interpersonal and Family Relationships | 178
 —BERNARD SCHLAGER

*Epilogue: Thank You and Welcome* | 223
*Appendix: Sexual Rating Scales* | 225

*Resources* | 231
*Bibliography* | 253
*Index* | 261

# Authors' Preface to the Second Edition

THIS SECOND EDITION OF our book offers an updated handbook that covers the basic skills needed by religious caregivers and ministry students (of all sexual orientations and gender identities) to provide effective, enlightened, and supportive pastoral care to LGBTQ persons, the long-standard acronym for lesbian, gay, bisexual, transgender, and queer persons.

One obvious challenge for those writing about pastoral ministry to LGBTQ persons in 2017 remains the same as it was when we wrote the first edition back in 2007: the topic exists in a world still at odds about the basic rights of LGBTQ persons and/or the place of LGBTQ persons in communities of faith. Some readers will be attracted to our starting-point principles and convictions (listed in the Introduction below), while others will be repelled. Fundamentalists and traditionalists on one side, progressive and liberal thinkers on the other: we look out at each other over what seems an unbridgeable abyss.

Prospective readers, for example, might skim the Introduction to find out if it's the "right" kind of book for them. This deeply rooted dualism does not preclude a large "undecided" or "moderate" group in the center struggling for truth, wisdom, and practical advice about LGBTQ pastoral caregiving.

At the outset we want to make clear that we write for all pastoral caregivers, ordained or lay, who, in the name of God, a religious tradition, or spiritual identity, deal with, help, or otherwise minister to and with LGBTQ people. We especially write for students in Christian seminaries and theological schools as they prepare for their ministries.

We also include queer people's families and friends who are important in the whole pastoral care process, whether they benefit directly as readers interested in the spiritual welfare of their family members or friends, or indirectly though the effective pastoral caring of others. Our goal of being inclusive is related to our final goal, which is the spiritual good of lesbian, gay, bisexual, transgender, and queer people and their families. These are the people whom we hope will be the ultimate beneficiaries of this work, through the blessings of your ministry.

Our equally sincere hope is that the process of becoming a more effective minister to this important segment of God's people will help you to develop deeper skills of ministry in general and, in particular, bring abundant blessings to your self-understanding as a pastoral caregiver.

Our knowledge and experience are within the Christian tradition and it is out of that tradition and to that tradition that we write. We sincerely desire that our work may also be of use for those who minister within the Jewish faith and other non-Christian faith traditions.

The authors were motivated to write this book based on their own personal involvement in pastoral ministry with LGBTQ people of faith.

David became aware of the immense need for this book based on his lived experience as a gay man growing up in, and later serving for many years, churches in which queer people were not openly acknowledged, much less served. In addition, his teaching and counseling of clergy, seminarians, and lay people over the years has made him keenly aware of the ongoing pain and remarkable gifts of LGBTQ people who are too often separated unfairly and needlessly from their communities of faith.

Bernie enthusiastically agreed to join David in writing this book after many years of teaching church history and LGBTQ studies at Pacific School of Religion (PSR) and The Graduate Theological Union in Berkeley, California; and after several years as Executive Director of The Center for LGBTQ and Gender Studies in Religion (CLGS) at PSR. In addition, Bernie's ministry as Coordinator of the San Francisco Bay Area Coalition of Welcoming Congregations has helped him to understand more deeply some of the many challenges and rewards involved in building local communities of faith that are genuinely inclusive and affirming of queer people.

# Acknowledgments

WE WOULD LIKE TO thank two people, in particular, who have assisted us in preparing this second edition: Matt Wimer, the assistant managing editor at Cascade Books, and Justin Sabia-Tanis, DMin, PhD, for his careful, insightful, and generous reading and suggestions on the text. In the end, of course, we take full responsibility for what we have written.

# Introduction

ONLY SINCE THE LATTER years of the twentieth century have some religious bodies begun to develop a theology of pastoral care for sexual minorities—lesbian, gay, bisexual, transgender, and queer people (LGBTQ). The obvious reason is that people in these categories were considered sinners in need of judgment, condemnation, and punishment. Churches, synagogues, and other religious communities, no different from society at large, ignored our existence based on the theological and psychological suppositions that LGBTQ identity and behavior were both chosen and sinful. Indeed, religion has often been in the vanguard of anti-LGBTQ prejudice and discrimination.

Here we are, though, well into the twenty-first century: out of the closet, proud of our LGBTQ identity, and candidly vocal.

What a time to be in ministry with us!

While issues directly relating to LGBTQ people threaten to cause schism in some denominations,[1] we LGBTQ people are living our lives with the rest of humanity and often as members of the same denominations. All the while we are being discussed and analyzed, excluded and feared, vilified and damned, but especially judged by the society and the communities in which we live.

We don't have the luxury (and often not the patience) of waiting until our churches and synagogues pass from the debate stage to the decision stage about the moral acceptability of our queer lives and loves, whatever that might turn out to be for each denomination or congregation. No one knows how religious bodies will resolve the issues. Well-founded fears abound—on all sides.

---

1. See, for instance, The United Methodist Church, "Commission" for a description of the current conflict within the worldwide Methodist church over LGBTQ issues.

Within religious traditions there is a broad range of opinion in regard to LGBTQ people. Some Christian and Jewish denominations and movements support complete acceptance of LGBTQ people in their official doctrine and teaching; some have welcoming and affirming programs of congregational education and LGBTQ acceptance; others penalize or discipline member churches or synagogues for the welcome that they extend to queer people.

But LGBTQ people have to live their lives and make their decisions *in the present moment*, and they are doing so more and more publicly as "out" individuals who belong to dynamic queer communities. This is "a new thing" and they are doing it now. As we read in the book of Isaiah: "Behold, I will do a new thing; now it shall spring forth; shall you not know it?" (Isa 43:18–19)

The current work is an effort to contribute to the ongoing development of a pastoral theology and praxis for sexual minorities. We have written this book as a guide for pastoral ministry to LGBTQ people.

## PRINCIPLES AND CONVICTIONS

Below is a brief but critically important list of the theological and psychological convictions that ground this book. These convictions inform the principles from which we write and we hope that a clear and concise description of them here will help you, the reader, understand our approach.

### LGBTQ People as Gifts of God

God is the giver of life to people. This life is given in myriad ways, all of which reflect something of the nature of the Giver. Thus, God gives each of us our sexuality (one's sexual make-up), which includes our orientation (to whom one is sexually attracted) and our gender identity (the gender one knows oneself to be), as a part of our total gift of humanity. We see sexual orientation and gender identity as significant aspects of God's gift. We believe that "God affirms the embodiment of human sexuality in our relationships with one another and within the community of faith."[2] Along with this first principle is the assumption, based on the

---

2. Marshall, *Counseling*, 13. Marshall is summarizing the theological support for this statement by theologians Carter Heyward and James Nelson.

primacy of love, that all of us are loved by God and thus are lovable as we are.

The justice that flows from love is the basis for the equal treatment of all God's people. This justice-based-on-love gives rise to the oft-quoted but often ignored church phrase that "all are welcome." We also believe that authentic Jewish-Christian theology and contemporary psychology need to pay deep attention and respect to each other. Although ultimately truth is one, at any given moment one field of study will arrive at its door sooner than another. When they differ, we believe that we need to pay even deeper attention to the lived experience of the persons involved.

## Bible and Tradition

Many of the world's major religions are "Religions of the Book." A sacred text is their foundation. Some also hold Tradition with a capital "T" in a very high place of honor and power. While acknowledging these sources and fundaments of religion, the present work does not attempt to examine, exegete, or otherwise analyze them and their effects on LGBTQ people. We take this approach not because we think that these things are unimportant. On the contrary, they are so basic that our brief treatment could add nothing significant. More importantly, there are many who have already done this important work and still others who are continuing to do it. We commend you to their work.[3]

Most importantly, people of faith will no doubt continue to disagree strongly over interpretations of texts and traditions that are understood to refer to homosexuality and LGBTQ people. No matter what one concludes that the Bible or other sacred texts say or do not say about LGBTQ people, *we are still here*. We are in your churches and synagogues, a part of your communities, with needs, sufferings, gifts, and blessings, the same as everyone else. Here and now.

## Pastoral Care

Pastoral theology is practical, functional, and applied. Its bases are systematic, moral, and spiritual theology; its inspiration, the sacred texts, and often the traditions of the religious body. To maintain effectiveness,

---

3. See, for instance, Scoggs, *New Testament*; Helminiac, *What the Bible Really Says*; Rogers, *Jesus*; and Bellis and Hufford, *Science*, 76–77.

pastoral theology must also be organic, vibrant, developing, and a vehicle for dealing with an always changing people in an always changing world. It is the basis and source of pastoral care. Thus, pastoral care becomes the principal expression of pastoral theology and brings it to life; it is "doing theology" day by day.

Insofar as it is practical and relational, pastoral care in turn embraces the insights of the science of human psychology and weds the two sources, theology and psychology, in a unique and holistic service of care. Yet pastoral care is distinctive precisely because it is shaped by faith, and this shaping is not incidental but quite central to such care. This basis in faith gives birth to and permeates the whole pastoral care experience.

Please note that this work is expressly about pastoral *care*, not pastoral *counseling*. The two areas certainly overlap and some writers use "pastoral care" and "pastoral counseling" almost interchangeably. For our purposes, pastoral care, which certainly includes many skills used in counseling, is within the reach of all sufficiently trained ministers. In comparison, we consider pastoral counseling to be a form of psychotherapy which falls within the reach only of those educated in that discipline. We are aware that some of the examples we use could possibly be interpreted as crossing the difficult-to-define boundary into counseling. Thus, we urge pastoral caregivers, who naturally will have differing experience, skills, and expertise, to keep within their level of competence. (See chapter 1 on referral and rejection.)

Along these same lines, US states have differing laws on mandated reporting, that is, who is required by law to report child abuse (as well as, in some cases, threats of suicide or homicide). Some states include ministers of religion as mandated reporters. You will need to inform yourself of all applicable laws in this regard and we recommend that you also check with your own religious organization's administrative offices for up-to-date information on mandated reporting for ministers.[4]

We define pastoral care as the relationship of concern and service between the minister of religion and the people they serve within the context and motivation of religious faith.

Contextualizing pastoral care specifically for LGBTQ people is difficult. On the one hand, there is very little formal expression of it, and its most common characteristic has been negativity, denial of our presence,

---

4. For general information, see the Child Welfare Information Gateway, "Mandatory Reporters."

embarrassment at our existence, labeling us as evil sinners, and, at worst, aggressive pursuit and routing us out.

On the other hand, effective pastoral care of LGBTQ people has been going on for a long time. Often informally and quietly, in specific times and places, and by wise and often courageous ministers of care. Some of these caregivers who work within the context of specific religious traditions—Jewish, Christian, and others—would be called progressive; still others have become effective caregivers for LGBTQ people simply by following their pastoral instincts, their understanding of their faith message, and their own hearts.

## Heterosexual/Homosexual Rating Scales

We believe that sexuality is a fluid state that often confounds those who try to simplify it. Following from that, we assume that the Kinsey Heterosexual/Homosexual Rating Scale is fundamentally accurate and that the Klein Sexual Orientation Grid is also accurate in a more detailed way. These scales were developed by Dr. Alfred Kinsey and his associates in the early 1950s and by Dr. Fritz Klein in the 1970s. Both scales indicate a broad and flowing spectrum of sexual orientations.[5]

Instead of understanding sexual orientation as an exclusively "either-or" condition (either heterosexual or homosexual), Kinsey and Klein developed continuums: Kinsey's is based on the degree of sexual responsiveness people have to others of the same or different gender. Klein's scale is based on sexual attraction, sexual fantasies, emotional attraction, social attraction, lifestyle, and self-identification.

We recommend that all pastoral caregivers acquire an understanding of both scales. It is an understanding that will be helpful for your interactions with all people. (We have included an Appendix with a more complete exposition of these scales.)

## Choice/Variation

Further, we assume that most people *do* choose *how* they express their sexual orientation and/or gender identity. For example: some bisexual

---

5. See the Kinsey Scale and the Klein Sexual Orientation Grid in the Appendix. See also Klein, *Bisexual Option*.

people decide to live their lives one way to the exclusion of other ways. That, of course, is a choice, but people rarely choose to *be* bisexual.

Transgender people have to make many significant decisions, often over a long period of time, about how they want to live their lives. A lesbian may decide to choose a partner and both may then decide to live as an openly committed couple. A gay man might decide never to "come out" and thus live his life "in the closet." But *being* bisexual, transgender, lesbian, or gay is almost never a choice. Again, this is the same for all: human beings very rarely *choose* their sexual orientation or gender identity; possibly never.

As we've said, in this work we consider sexual orientation and gender identity as God-given gifts, which are good and holy variations of human sexuality.

## Unique

Another important conviction we share is that LGBTQ people are as capable of spiritual authenticity and holiness as anyone. Indeed, our lived experiences often lead us down spiritually challenging paths, frequently characterized by suffering; these are paths that others may never take. The spiritual territory we have traversed is often unique and unknown; thus our voices are also unique. We add significant new dimensions to the spiritual journey.

## Labels

Many do not like the restrictions imposed by sexual minority categories or labels, such as "gay" and "bisexual," and strongly resist using them for themselves and others. This is especially true of many younger members of today's LGBTQ communities. Still others consider lesbian, gay, bi, and trans to be social constructs that are distinctly modern. We respect both of these opinions but we believe for now, at this moment in our history, these categories are functional because so many people do, in fact, use them.

"Queer," a term that is considered offensive by some and empowering by others, is used to refer to sexual orientations, gender expressions, and gender identities that do not conform to predominant heterosexist societal norms. We use it here with the intention of inclusivity.

## A Positive Note

LGBTQ people are the way that we are because, simply put, we *are* the way that we are, just as everyone else is the way that they are.

We do not assume that sexual orientation and gender identity are conscious decisions that one makes at a certain point in life—even though there may be the rare individual who does that—or that they were chosen as one of several available options. Our assumption here is that for the vast number of LGBTQ people, *who* they are, as gendered and sexual beings, is an unchangeable given, as it is for heterosexual people.[6]

The debate and analysis of *why* any of us is the way that we are will continue for generations, maybe forever. We do not know in any complete way how human beings develop their sexual preferences or gender identity.[7] This, of course, is true of all human beings and all ways of being sexual. The assumption/belief/opinion that LGBTQ people should try to change their sexual orientation or gender identity to conform to what is seen as "acceptable" is itself one of the most serious problems that we face.

We hear more and more every day from LGBTQ people in North American societies—as well in other parts of the world—who feel no need to apologize about who they are. Rather, an increasing number use words like "gift" and "blessing" when referring to their orientation or gender identity.

Of course, all good-willed people can claim St. Paul's liberating proclamation of grace: "But by the grace of God, I am what I am and His grace toward me was not in vain." (1 Cor 15-10). Or can they? LGBTQ people of faith often find themselves in the awkward and painful position of having to make a particular point of including ourselves in the statement. While others are presumed to be full-fledged members of faith communities, we, very often, are intentionally excluded.

Thus, by circumstances out of our control, we are often coerced into a defensive stance because that is where prevalent forces in the popular culture would have us begin. We don't want to begin there—namely by defending LGBTQ people as we are examined and judged; we want to begin on a positive note.

---

6. See Isay, *Being Homosexual*, 20–21; and Weaver et al., *Counseling on Sexual Issues*, 191–92.

7. Money, *Gay, Straight, and In-Between*.

## Affirming Attitude

In this book we assume that you, the reader, share with us a positive and inclusive attitude toward LGBTQ people and our lives, that you treat LGBTQ people like you treat everyone else, hold them to the same standards, and give them the same breaks.

Certainly "people have a right to disagree on a matter as difficult and complex as human sexuality. Thousands of years of precedent should not be taken lightly but neither should the living presence of hundreds of thousands of people whose sexual orientation does not fit traditional boxes."[8]

We disagree with religious leaders and communities that deny that LGBTQ people can live holy, moral lives while at the same time giving healthy expression to their sexuality. Our position, which is far from unique or even unusual, is that those leaders and communities are simply wrong.

This is not an unreasoned position on our part as authors. Rather, we base our position on four foundations: (1) the Jewish and Christian value of welcoming the stranger and freeing the oppressed; (2) the support of the human lived-experience and testimonies of LGBTQ people of faith; (3) the overwhelming support of the scientific and psychological disciplines; and (4) the fact that, historically speaking, in literally *all* religious traditions, strong moral stances are often not immutable; they have changed.[9] "We must remember that we may change our position over time and still remain faithful."[10]

We do not deny that there are many historical causes for the negative positions of synagogues and churches. We simply believe that it is high time to move into the fuller truth from which we have been blocked. We also believe that communities of faith are wrong if they are homo-negative and, more broadly, that they err if they possess a fear of human sexuality that leads to an anti-sex stance which, in turn, so often becomes expressed in many damaging ways. People are suffering and many are dying because of these intransigent stances.

Furthermore, we believe that if one is unable or unwilling to reflect upon and revise in the light of faith those negative theological,

---

8. Greenberg, *Wrestling*, 32.

9. Over the centuries, Christian churches have changed their positions on such moral issues as usury, slavery, religious freedom, and marriage.

10. See Marshall, "Caring."

psychological, and social biases toward LGBTQ people that we all have absorbed from our queer-phobic society, then one should not undertake any ministry to them. However, if you are a minister, priest, or rabbi, for example, who wants to serve well the LGBTQ members of your congregation, then it is incumbent upon you to learn *how* to become a caregiver who ministers effectively and positively to LGBTQ persons.

To make our position even more specific (for those familiar with the sources), we endorse the fifth position as described by Jung and Smith[11] on the five possible moral positions in regard to homosexuality: "Homosexual orientations are natural; just, loving, and faithful homosexual behavior is good." We also endorse James Nelson's fourth option on the same question, which is described as "full acceptance."[12]

## FITTING IN? LEFT BEHIND?

Some readers will clearly know that they, as pastoral caregivers, fit comfortably into this positive and affirming group. Others will know that they do not.

But for those of you who, after considering the above assumptions, still have some doubts, still have questions about how your practice of pastoral care is consistent with your theological beliefs, we encourage you to give yourself the benefit of your doubt and plunge in. That doubt could well be a sign of your desire to be honest before God, with yourself, and in your ministry.

## PLAN OF THE BOOK AND AUTHORS

Chapter 1, "The Pastoral Care Relationship," is an exploration of the relationship between the pastoral caregiver and the care receiver. After defining this relationship and exploring issues such as homophobia and the caring intimacy required of pastoral caregivers working with LGBTQ people, this chapter examines the understanding and keeping of boundaries, transference/counter-transference, and other issues between caregiver and LGBTQ care receivers. The chapter ends with a treatment of the five goals of systemic pastoral care with examples from ministry among LGBTQ people.

11. Jung and Smith, *Heterosexism*.
12. Nelson, *Embodiment*.

Chapter 2, "The Functions of Pastoral Care," is built upon the six functions of pastoral care as presented by Howard Clinebell and their application to the lives of LGBTQ people: healing, sustaining, guiding, reconciling, nurturing, and prophetic pastoral care. It examines pastoral care with people of color and members of ethnic minorities, and presents a broad "Checklist for Pastoral Caregivers to LGBTQ People."

Chapter 3, "Pastoral Care in the Tough Times: An LGBTQ Perspective," deals with shame, anger, fear, and isolation. It also examines discrimination and stress in the lives of LGBTQ people. The caregiver's role is explored in terms of caring for LGBTQ people who are ill (physically or emotionally) and/or physically handicapped. Drugs/addictions, sex, and violence are also discussed. The chapter concludes with treatments of youth, aging, and "ex-gay" ministries.

Chapter 4, "Coming Out," explores this fundamental and pivotal experience in the lives of most LGBTQ people. After a consideration of some of the most common features of coming out of the closet, this chapter uses Eli Coleman's five-stage model as a framework to understand how many queer people of faith accept and embrace their gender identity and/or sexual orientation. The motif of journey is used to interpret the ongoing and life-affirming project that coming out can be for LGBTQ persons.

Chapter 5 is titled "Creating Communities of Care for LGBTQ People." Grounded in a study of nearly two dozen welcoming and affirming churches and synagogues, this chapter invites the reader to consider how congregations are working to become communities of care for LGBTQ people of faith. In addition, it offers concrete suggestions for congregations interested in creating genuine welcome, integrating queer people into synagogue and church life, and building alliances with LGBTQ persons and communities beyond the walls of the congregation.

Chapter 6, "Caring for LGBTQ People in Their Interpersonal and Family Relationships," invites the reader to consider the many ways in which queer people structure their relationships. Positing "Five Characteristics of Queer Relationships," this chapter includes case studies to illustrate how LGBTQ relationships and families are both similar to and different from their straight counterparts. Rather than assume that only those relationships and families based on the model of modern-day heterosexual marriage are morally acceptable for queer people, this chapter explores the variety of models that are found in many LGBTQ communities today.

*Introduction*

The work concludes with an Appendix on the rating scales of human sexuality, a Resources list (works cited, consulted and/or related to various topics, including books, web sites, and audio and video resources), a Bibliography, and an Index.

We have divided the chapters between us: David Kundtz wrote chapters 1, 2, and 3; Bernard Schlager wrote chapters 4, 5, and 6. Together we wrote the Introduction and the Epilogue. Please note that we have altered the examples and case studies in ways that protect confidentiality while keeping their essential significance.

We, the authors, are keenly aware of the similarities in our respective backgrounds and current social locations: both of us are white, gay, middle-class males who grew up as Roman Catholics and served for a time as official representatives of that church. Thus, we have consulted widely in our writing of the text. Since leaving the ordained ministry (David) and Catholic religious life (Bernie), we have continued to work in the fields of family counseling and seminar presentations (David), and seminary teaching and LGBTQ religious advocacy (Bernie).

## TERMINOLOGY

We use the word "minister" to refer to a person (ordained or lay) who in any way represents a religious faith tradition in a pastoral setting, whether as a professional or as a trained volunteer.

We use the term "pastoral caregiver" to mean the minister in the role of caring pastorally.

In referring to the recipients of pastoral care we most often use the terms "care receiver."

We use the word "congregation" frequently. With this word we refer to the gathering of believers in a local faith community. When we speak of a specific denomination or movement we name it.

Below are some definitions of terms regularly used in this work:

---

### A BRIEF DEFINITION OF TERMS

- "LGBTQ" refers to lesbian, gay, bisexual, transgender, and queer persons. A second "Q" in the acronym ("LGBTQQ") stands for "questioning." That is, it refers to people who are currently questioning their sexual orientation and/or gender identity.

- "Queer" is a broad term that can include all categories of people whose sexuality or expression of sexuality is non-normative. Sometimes expressed "genderqueer," which can refer to someone who identifies with traits of both male and female.
- "Lesbian" refers to female persons who are primarily or exclusively attracted to other female persons.
- "Gay" (or "gay man") refers to male persons who are primarily or exclusively attracted to other male persons. Sometimes "gay" is used in a broader way to mean both lesbian and gay or even all LGBTQ people.
- "Bisexual" refers to persons who are attracted to both genders, although not necessarily to the same degree. Sometime shortened to "bi."
- "Transgender" is "an umbrella term that refers to people who live differently than the gender presentation and roles expected of them by society."[A]
- "Transsexual" is "a term for people who seek to live in a gender different from the one assigned at birth and who may seek or want medical intervention (through hormones and/or surgery) for them to live comfortably in that gender. Transsexuals are the people who generally live full time as a different gender than the one they were assigned at birth."[B]
- "To come out (of the closet)" means to declare in some public way and to some degree (widely or narrowly) one's sexual orientation or identity.
- "Sexual orientation" refers to a person's innate sense of emotional, romantic, and/or erotic attraction to others (as opposed to "sexual preference," which implies a conscious choice.)
- "Sexual identity" refers to the gender one knows oneself to be.

[A]. National Center for Transgender Equality (NCTE), "Teaching Transgender."
[B]. National Center for Transgender Equality (NCTE), "Teaching Transgender."

# 1

# The Pastoral Care Relationship

### David Kundtz

Pastoral care is a relationship.

Beginning with the idea of relationship gets to the heart of all we deal with in this work. Pastoral care is the establishing and nurturing of a caring relationship between or among people, which is based on religious faith. Commonly it is between a minister of religion and member(s) of a religious congregation. More broadly, it is also the caring relationship between or among the members of the congregation, for we are all called to the ministry of pastoral caring.[1]

The specific pastoral care relationship, which is the focus of the present work, is between the ministering person of the religious community and its LGBTQ member(s). Often, the member is seeking some specific service or guidance: help with a major life transition, the baptism of a child, a bat mitzvah or confirmation, preparation for marriage, a consultation about their own or a family member's sexual orientation, a visit to a sick relative, making arrangements for a funeral service, consulting about a personal challenge, or a crisis in the family. Often, too, the relationship is simply what goes on between a minister of religion and the members of the congregation while interacting informally, such

---

1. Marshall, "Caring."

as a casual chance encounter between a Sunday school teacher and her student at the grocery store, rather than in designated formal settings.

The motivation and unique characteristic of pastoral care, especially in the caregiver, is religious faith combined with a primary concern for the wellbeing of the care receiver(s).

The coming together, in the context of religious faith, of caregivers and LGBTQ care receivers, both individuals and groups, creates the unique relationship of pastoral caring, which is our concern here.

The care relationship is also established between the ministerial representatives of the religious organization and any system that influences the queer care receiver. For example, a minister who is pastorally involved in the process of a young lesbian coming to terms with her possible life choices, by that very involvement is also relating in some way to her family, her girlfriend or partner, possibly to her school, her work, her neighborhood, and to all the broader societal and human-interaction systems of which she is a part.

What is distinctive about this book is that we focus solely on care receivers who are LGBTQ.

## THE RELATIONSHIP IS ALL-IMPORTANT

Every pastoral caregiver must have the professional qualifications and training that are necessary for pastoral ministry. With these skills and insights the caregiver is prepared to care effectively. Practically, however, in pastoral care, the relationship you build with your care receiver is the primary way these skills become fruitful and effective, especially at the beginning—the key moment in determining the nature and success of the relationship. Consider: a gay man in your congregation talks to you about the challenges he faces in coming out to his family. In that moment, what you have to offer him is yourself, in all your manifestations: your attention or lack of it, your smile or frown, your body language, your words, the common ground of your faith—that is, your willingness, your openness to begin a relationship of care. But the power and potential of that willingness can, and has, changed people's lives.

Many LGBTQ people, in previous pastoral encounters, have met with outright rejection at worst, and at best, a denial of care, or fear and incompetence masquerading as a denial of care. Many have encountered these attitudes so regularly in their faith communities that they might understandably test to see if the caregiver really cares. For example, they may ask questions, perhaps about your opinion on well-known gay or transgender celebrities, or find other ways of determining if you are going to be respectful of who they are, and safe to trust with the intimate details of their lives.

Recognize the possible "test" for what it most likely is: a natural instinct to avoid hurt and disappointment, and not a personal rejection or antagonism against you, the caregiver.

If, during any point within the ongoing work with your LGBTQ care receiver you are in doubt about how to proceed or what is called for, refocus on the relationship and do something that will strengthen or enhance it.

Pastoral relationships with LGBTQ people have three particular characteristics that merit attention. The balance of the chapter explores these areas from the point of view of what is specifically applicable to pastoral work with LGBTQ people: caring intimacy, clear boundaries, and awareness of systemic functioning.

## CARING INTIMACY

The first thing to note as you approach pastoral care with LGBTQ people is that you are establishing and building a *relationship* with a gay, lesbian, bisexual, transgender, or queer/questioning person or group. What is the model for that pastoral relationship? The common ground of faith leads us to the fact that religion itself involves a relationship, a caring intimacy between God and God's people. Thus, our goal: to imitate God's relationship with us. Granted, it is a goal beyond our reach, but nevertheless I believe it is an ideal to strive for.

In human terms, the divine goal is transformed into building an effective pastoral relationship, which creates a caring intimacy. This ideal stems in part from the expectations of people who seek pastoral care.

In a lecture on the differences between homoerotic and homosexual relationships, Robert Johnson, a straight Jungian analyst and writer, tells of a personal experience in India.[2] Johnson, a young, white man in search of his spiritual path, found himself unexpectedly alone in Calcutta. The poverty of the city depressed him and he felt desperate and needed help. At that moment he recalled an Indian tradition he had learned and

---

2. Johnson, "Study."

decided to try it; he would ask for help in a very specific way. He went to a public park and chose a middle-aged man, traditionally dressed, and seemingly educated. He approached the man and asked, "Do you speak English?" "Yes," was the answer. Then he looked into the stranger's eyes and asked, "Will you be the incarnation of God for me?" The man returned his earnest look, paused, and said, "Yes."

"Will you be God for me?" To our Western ears that sounds like an improbable question in an unlikely story. Johnson told of the experience as an example of how comfortable Indian people are, compared to Westerners, with intimacy between men; yet it also beautifully expresses the desire that underlies many of the expectations that queer people, like all people, bring to their pastoral caregivers all the time: a desire for God.

Johnson poured out his soul, his fears, and his feelings to this man. The man said very little. "I felt much better after that," reported Johnson. "It's just what I needed, someone to be with me and listen to what was going on for me. He did that." They never saw each other again.

When people are living through a time of stress, pain, or confusion, the relationship they find at the time—often the relationship with the pastoral caregiver—can enhance life or not, can be a moment of grace or not, can be an occasion of meeting God or not.

## AVOID FEAR AND ARROGANCE

Caring intimacy with LGBTQ people implies at least two specific attitudes in the caregiver, at different ends of a spectrum: one is an absence of fear and the other is an avoidance of a patronizing attitude. No fear, no arrogance.

A single, Latino male, about thirty-five, a successful lawyer, made an appointment with a priest who was director of seminary students for the local diocese. The next day he arrived on time and the first thing he said, with almost no introductory formalities, was that he was gay and he wanted to be admitted to the seminary. After these statements, he folded his arms and waited for a response, as if to say, "Let's see what you do with this one!" In other words, "Let's see if you care about me."

It turned out he had no lasting interest in the ministry. He was testing the degree of care in that particular minister of the church, and fairly or not, the care of the whole church, and even of God.

What he had was anger. Because he was "openly" gay, he assumed that he would have been rejected. He was angry at the hypocrisy he observed in the church. The caregiver, far from being fearful or patronizing, engaged him in a meaningful and respectful conversation about those very issues.

This caregiver solved no specific problems, but he was able to establish caring intimacy mainly because he showed no intimidation or fear of the care seeker's anger and directness. He expressed neither a patronizing attitude nor arrogance in assuming that he had all the answers. Though the presenting issues were not resolved (and the presenter's intentions probably less than straight-forward), this is an example of successful pastoral care because the person felt cared for and was invited into a pastoral relationship that could continue and grow.

Don't be afraid of LGBTQ people. The type of fear you might recognize, especially if you are not LGBTQ yourself (see below), is a fearful lack of confidence in dealing with LGBTQ people. You may think you don't understand them. Remember: LGBTQ people are people first and foremost. If there are specific issues that you do not understand, it is acceptable to admit to not understanding and ask the care receiver for clarification. If you are not LGBTQ, it's natural that there would be gaps in your understanding due to lack of personal experience. Don't try to fake sophistication or experience in the queer "world"; much better for the relationship is to admit what is unfamiliar or fearful to you and look for information and insight directly from the care receiver, from a competent consultant, or from your own reading and research.

Certainly all people are put off by a patronizing attitude, but queer people are perhaps especially sensitive to it simply because we so often encounter it, especially in religious bodies. Any attitude that implies a superiority based on not being LGBTQ is guaranteed to kill the care receiver's hope of achieving helpful pastoral care.

## DO YOU CARE ... OR NOT?

It's important to ask yourself from the very beginning: do I really care about this person? What exactly are my feelings toward this person? That self-knowledge is more important for the outcome of the pastoral care than any "solutions" you might provide or wise words you might offer.

In the great majority of pastoral care relationships, the caregiver is ready to care, anxious to care, and there is no doubt about the presence or degree of concern and positive feelings. Some situations, however, we don't like to acknowledge: what if you really don't care about this person and their problems for whatever reasons, justifiable or not, mature or not? Maybe the issue hits too close to home for you to maintain equanimity. Maybe you are going through a challenge in your own life similar to the one the care seeker brings to you. There are many reasons why you might not care the way you need to care.

As in any pastoral care situation, if you know you lack sufficient care for the person you're dealing with, or your negative feelings are too strong to overcome, there are two choices: postpone the encounter, or refer to another competent caregiver. Ideally, postponement and referral will be rare. However, I believe too many pastoral caregivers reject postponement and referral because it represents "weakness" or limitations. This lack of honesty is a set-up for a confusing and ultimately unsuccessful pastoral relationship. Much better to postpone or refer, especially if you have doubts about your preparedness.

## REFERRAL AND REJECTION

What is important to note in pastoral care with LGBTQ people is that postponement or referral might well be understood by the care receiver as rejection. Rejection is often a common experience of LGBTQ people as they encounter those with some kind of moral authority over them. Your act of postponement or referral will often feel like more of the same old thing. Indeed, these responses *are* a form of rejection. Be willing to acknowledge that and use caution in the process.

> **PASTORAL PERSPECTIVES**
>
> Postponement and Referral
>
> To mitigate the care seeker's possible feelings of rejection associated with postponement or referral, consider the following pastoral perspectives:
> - Talk about it. Consider the possibility of bringing up the subject of rejection with the care receiver, explaining that you realize that it might feel like you're passing them off or denying care, but in fact you believe this is best for the success of the pastoral care relationship. It tells care receivers that you want to be aware of their possible feelings.
> - If you postpone a session or meeting, set the time and date for the postponed meeting before the session ends.
> - If you postpone establishing a pastoral care relationship, never fail to follow up on the postponement as planned. This gives a clear sign that you have cared and continue to care.
> - If it seems appropriate and welcomed, pray with the care receiver. Prayer together is an excellent way to communicate your genuine care.
> - Take as much care and time in the referral as in the original intervention. Don't rush. Perhaps continue in the session a little longer than you ordinarily might by spending a few more moments; it can be a sign of care.
> - Perhaps you can find another way to involve the person in the life of the community in a way unrelated to the original issue: as a member of a committee? Asking for help on a project? Enlisting them in your efforts to influence some system of which they are a part?

Eleanor is a sixty-three-year-old, straight, white, married minister with many years of pastoral experience and a lovable disposition. She has led two congregations through the welcome-and-affirming process for LGBTQ people (see chapter 5).

One Sunday afternoon after services she found herself in her office with Chris, a pierced and punctured, dyed and denimed, spiked and unscrubbed, seventeen-year-old whose T-shirt proclaimed "Gender-Queer and Proud." Chris announced to her, "I want to join the church."

Eleanor was tired after the morning services and even though she philosophically fought it, she felt disdain for the person in front of her. She cared ideally and philosophically; practically and immediately she just could not get to real care.

If you were Eleanor what would you have done? Pause for a moment and consider.

Eleanor first tried to establish some kind of connection with Chris. None of her efforts worked; Chris remained monosyllabic and virtually non-responsive. Then this seasoned pastor summoned all her years of experience and suggested in careful terms that the church's youth minister would be able to help more than she. Chris agreed: "Yeah, I think you're right. That's cool."

This serves as another example of a successful pastoral encounter, even though the minister involved could not personally carry through on its fulfillment. The care seeker left feeling cared for and placed with someone within the community with whom a more productive relationship could be established.

An important characteristic of this referral is that the youth minister to whom Eleanor referred Chris was comfortable and knowledgeable about gender-queer and transgender youth. A basic element of good referral is to know the capacities, specialties, and competence of those to whom you refer. A mere "passing off" of someone to someone else is death to effective care.

Since many pastoral encounters occur in those in-between moments, it is helpful to compile and keep up to date a referral list containing the names, contact information, and competencies of other care-giving people. The list will include pastoral counselors, psychotherapists, psychiatrists, and other pastoral care ministers and colleagues who have a particular expertise. Maintaining such a list avoids delays and thus possibly losing the energy of the pastoral moment.

If you really do care, it will become evident, no matter if you engage, postpone, or refer the care receiver. If you really don't care, whatever your response, your lack of concern will be transparent.

## ARE YOU OPEN?

The second question, and almost as important as the first, is: are you really open to what the LGBTQ care seeker asks of you? Or do you have the assumption that your duty is to apply certain given teachings no matter the details of the situation? Do you have a predisposition toward the resolution of "this kind of problem?" If you have an open disposition, whatever someone brings to your care will elicit in your response a receptive mind and an open heart.

In this context, keep in mind that in many instances LGBTQ people are not working from any realistic moral guidelines or templates that they might have received from their religious traditions. Of course, they are included along with everyone else in the general moral principles offered, but when it comes to living a moral life as an LGBTQ person, churches and synagogues seldom offer much guidance.

Thus, queer people often forge ahead in the moral process on their own, discovering for themselves what is healthy, what is moral, what is life-giving and what is not. This is especially the case when LGBTQ people are trying to work out their relationships with other people: with friends, with family and those in authority, with peers, and, in particular, with possible romantic partners (see chapter 6).

Issues of living together, parenting, sexual expression, and participation in normal civil rights are some areas in which LGBTQ people make up some of the rules as they go along. The rules that they were taught often don't work for them; that is, they are not always life-giving, or moral, or intelligent, or even practical.

So this is what openness is about: willingness first to listen to the lived experience of the LGBTQ people with whom you work, and then to help them apply moral principles from their faith tradition that serve their needs.

I'll not easily forget a lesson I learned some years ago when I was an active member in a local PFLAG group (see Resources). One evening a young man came to the meeting who was, in my eyes, surly and unsightly. I remember wishing he had not come; I was embarrassed by him and not open to him. But the woman who served as leader of the group extended the same sincere and loving welcome to this young man as she had previously extended to me and would have extended to the most distinguished visitor. Under the loving care of this heterosexual, married leader, the young man thrived in the group and went on to become one of its leaders. Thus, I too was able to see what the caring leader had seen from the beginning: goodness, beauty, talent, and a generous spirit. But without that caring welcome (if the welcome he received were influenced by *my* sentiments), the results would not have been so good. It was a lesson for me in the transformative power of care that is truly open.

Think of these pastoral situations: a sixteen-year-old girl tells you she is "in love with my girl-friend and I want to just hold her and live the rest of my life with her, and, and . . . ! Oh what should I do?" A seventy-year-old man whose wife has just died comes to you for guidance and asks, "I would like to live with my male lover. How will this affect my relationship with the church? What do you advise?" A transgender woman applies for the opening that your congregation has posted for the director of education. Her qualifications are excellent. "I am a perfect fit for this work," she tells you. "It's exactly what I did in my former church for eight years." Are you open?

A simple application of existing and traditional rules to these cases might not be pastorally effective. Be open to the experience of the individual by: helping the young girl ask the right questions, by applying the right moral principles to her thinking and behavior without judging her and thereby closing the door to an ongoing pastoral relationship; understanding the man's dilemma of being old and alone and not having the moral alternatives of his straight counterparts—publicly accepted dating and marriage; hiring or not hiring the transgender woman based on her skills and qualifications, not on your discomfort or fears.

Ultimately, the goal is to help the person arrive at a satisfactory resolution of the issue, morally and practically. The most important means to that end is to sustain the pastoral relationship. Don't give up simply because there seems to be no way out; keep the relationship open and progressing. Truth and moral choices are often elusive and take time to achieve.

This approach does not belittle nor deny the importance of any religion's teachings and practice. But systemic or moral theology without the benefit of pastoral theology can become a weapon of destruction rather than a force for healing. We are all at different stages of ability to assimilate the implications of our experiences. Good pastoral care accepts us where we are without giving away the ageless wisdom of the faith tradition. By establishing a solid relationship with the LGBTQ care receiver, you open the way to countless possibilities and blessings, as you forego the immediate, but often ineffective, quick fix.

Even if your religious tradition does not officially accept homosexual behavior, which is the official position of many if not most religions, engaging pastorally with someone who is acting in contradiction to the official teachings of religious authorities is neither affirming nor condemning the behavior; it's relating to the person. This simple distinction continues to elude the resources and imaginative powers of many religious leaders who assume that even acknowledging LGBTQ people, much less serving and welcoming them, assumes that these pastoral acts will be seen as "affirming their behaviors." This attitude on the part of synagogues and churches also encourages double lives in its leaders and members: *whatever you do, whoever you are, just don't talk about it.*

Thus, the goal for every pastoral caregiver should be to establish a relationship with care receivers that is an effective vehicle for the skills, insights, and training that the caregiver brings to the moment, and to remain as open as possible to them and to their lived experiences. Here's a suggested pastoral practice: when you begin to engage with any LGBTQ person or group in a pastoral situation, think to yourself: *It's the relationship, it's the relationship! Be open!*

So much of the good that can be achieved in pastoral care is attained simply by the establishment, nurturing, and quality of the pastoral relationship. There need not be any "issue" or "problem" or "project" to deal with, although generally there is one. Simply the relationship with a pastorally based, caring person has remarkable power to heal and bless.

Thus, if at times you are not sure just what is the nature of your relationship with someone in or outside of your religious community, focus on and be grateful for the fact of the relationship rather than the specifics of it. Don't underestimate the simple power of the relationship itself. Keep it going, keep it fed.

## HETEROSEXISM/HOMOPHOBIA/TRANSPHOBIA

As pastoral caregivers, we need to be aware of the prejudice that is commonly called homophobia. In practice, it means the fear of—or more broadly, any kind of negative attitude toward—LGBTQ people and/or homosexuality in general. Transphobia is the same set of attitudes toward transgender people. These phobias are part of a broader and, in the long run, a more pervasive prejudice, which is heterosexism: a belief and assumption that male-female sexuality is the only natural, normal, or moral sexual behavior, or that it is superior to homosexuality.

Because of our current moment in history, it would not be surprising if a significant number of pastoral caregivers have some degree of heterosexism and its accompanying phobias. They are surprisingly agile prejudices that are shape-shifters—they often appear as something else—as well as long-time survivors in our culture. They can even sneak out of those of us who would consciously and philosophically disavow them.

Here is a snippet from a conversation in a church courtyard between Martha and Joe (a married couple), and Reverend James (their minister), speaking about a newcomer to the church, a woman whom they have just noticed is accompanied by a teen-aged boy.

Martha: Well, she's a lesbian, so she wouldn't have any children.

Joe: Of course, so the boy with her must be her brother, or maybe the son of a friend, or . . .

Rev. James: Martha, you shouldn't call her a lesbian! That's not fair.

Martha: But I'm quite sure she is. Her sister told me as much and I know there is no man in her life.

Rev. James: Yes, yes, but still . . . why would she be *here*?

Although the above text is brief, and out of a broader context it is clear that Martha and Joe and their minister need help with confronting heterosexism and homophobia; the minister possibly more so because he has an added responsibility in his role as pastor and pastoral caregiver to the people in the conversation, as well as possibly with the woman in question. They clearly believe that being lesbian is something negative.

Of this pastor we might ask: Is it "not fair" to name someone as lesbian—as if it were a prejudicial term, a type of name-calling? Even though for some it still falls into those negative categories, assuming it is so only affirms the prejudice, the homophobia, and the heterosexism. Of Martha and Joe we might ask: Is it really so that lesbians don't have children? The (assumed) knowledge that "there is no man" in a woman's life tells you nothing other than that apparent fact. While their attitude might be defended as simple ignorance, it would seem fair to expect most people to know better.

Heterosexism, homophobia, and transphobia are thorny prejudices and can show up in the most unexpected places, even in LGBTQ people. Internalized homophobia is the negative attitude that LGBTQ people have toward themselves and other queer people. Our whole society has internalized heterosexism to various degrees. The attitudes of these prejudices have been "internalized" from the prevalent attitudes of the wider society, the values of which people have made their own. Ultimately they are shame-based. Internalized homophobia can also be seen when one group within the LGBTQ community holds negative attitudes toward another of its groups.

I have often heard gay people say, "I just don't understand transgender people." The astute pastoral caregiver will diplomatically identify and help the person to see that there is nothing to "understand" about trans people any more than there is to "understand" about gay or lesbian or straight people. It's not a question of "understanding" but of believing and accepting their lived experience—or not.

## CLEAR BOUNDARIES

"Boundaries" refers to the person's physical, mental, or spiritual sense of self, or the "space" in which the person exists and holds as intensely personal and under the person's own control. Boundaries can differ from person to person in regard to their nature and strength. Respect for a person's boundaries directs the caregiver to recognize and acknowledge a person's limits as early as possible in the care relationship and not go beyond the parameters of the offered invitation.

Clear awareness of, and deep respect for, the boundaries of your LGBTQ care receivers is an important aspect of caring intimacy. At the same time, I believe incompetent handling of boundaries is the most common reason why pastoral caregivers get into trouble.

The goal of caring intimacy calls for constant balance: balance between respecting boundaries and challenging the person to extend boundaries where it is called for; between intimacy that leads to healing and intimacy that is inappropriate and leads to violations.

Boundaries are of particular importance when dealing with LGBTQ people for at least two reasons: first, because they are an intensely scrutinized, oppressed, and sometimes vilified sub-group of the culture; and second, because they are a people whose boundaries are often violated through false assumptions and misinformation.

In our context of offering pastoral care, the boundaries with which we are particularly concerned are the physical/sexual and the emotional/spiritual.

## Physical/Sexual Boundaries

Put simply, it is not permissible to have any kind of a physical/sexual relationship with anyone in your pastoral care. The reasons and implications of this are known and available in general compendiums of pastoral care. One of the principal foundations for this moral imperative is the inherent characteristic of power inequality in the pastoral care relationship. One must always understand this responsibility: the caregiver is assumed to have a moral power over the care receiver.

However, if it is possible to single out one group—besides children—for whom this prohibition is especially true, it is people who are identified by the general populace by their sexual orientation or their sexual identity: LGBTQ people. Our culture sees them primarily as sexual beings and often applies grossly inaccurate over-sexualized stereotypes to them. Of course, the stereotypes are no truer of LGBTQ people than of anyone else.

By violating this boundary the pastoral caregiver would, minimally, reinforce this too-narrow identity and affirm a skewed and inaccurate self-understanding in the care receiver, as well as gravely violate the trust they have been given.

In some situations, there might be a tendency in the care receiver to "come on" to the caregiver. In the majority of cases, it is important to see this not as a moral failure of the care receiver, but a failure of the social milieu in which the individual was nurtured; not the behavior of a moral degenerate, but the expression of a desire for care and acceptance by someone who has not learned other ways to express those feelings. In other words, this over-expressed behavior can be a normal stage of development in people who have been repressed.

Your response as caregiver? Understand this sexualized behavior as a developmental phase, have patience in the process, and always keep the balance between accepting and caring for the person and not allowing the behavior that would destroy the relationship and hurt the person. This is not a challenge for the unclear or weak-willed. To nurture the pastoral relationship while at the same time keeping the boundaries appropriate calls for a mature caregiver.

> **PASTORAL PERSPECTIVES**
>
> Respecting Physical/Sexual Boundaries
>
> - It is not permissible to have any kind of a physical/sexual relationship with anyone in your pastoral care.
> - There is an inherent inequality of power in the pastoral care relationship, for which the caregiver has the ultimate moral responsibility.
> - Getting too close physically is a gesture that might easily be misinterpreted.
> - Avoid making the assumption that LGBTQ people are sexual, asexual, hypersexual, or don't feel bound by prevailing sexual mores.
> - Don't assume that LGBTQ people are sexless, never had sex, never had sex with the opposite sex, were never married, or have no children.
> - Avoid any kind of presumptive touch (until you have established enough of a relationship that might allow this). This would include even a pat on the back, a hand on the arm, an arm around the shoulder and other similar touches, and certainly anything more overtly sexual.
> - Avoid putting the person in—or being with a person in—a cramped physical space.
> - Looking at the person in inappropriate ways; flirting/cruising glances are unacceptable.
> - Do not tell inappropriate jokes or stories or reveal personal experiences in the presence of the LGBTQ care receiver.
> - Within reason, do not make a comment, negative or positive, on the care receiver's appearance or clothing as this could be misinterpreted.
> - Avoid anything that would make a care receiver feel either singled-out or demeaned in any way.

## Emotional/Spiritual Boundaries

The emotional and spiritual boundaries of LGBTQ people can be the most challenging for the pastoral worker to recognize and respect. These boundaries are made up of feelings, convictions, and sentiments that are intensely personal and thus sensitive to any kind of negative invasion. Examples of invasions across these boundaries are: asking a too-personal question in regard to your care receiver's sexual history, or asking it too soon; assuming an intimacy of information between the two of you that is more than the care receiver is comfortable with; not recognizing fragile boundaries in someone who, for example, has just gone through a serious loss; asking transgender people personal questions about genitals, birth names, possible operations, etc.; assuming that a care receiver wants to pray aloud with you in regard to the issue at hand, or assuming that they don't: always ask.

As a result of our history as an outcast group in the larger society, LGBTQ people may have a tendency to be hyper-alert and sensitive to possible invasions of the emotional/spiritual boundary. When pastoral caregivers do get into trouble around boundary violations, it often starts with a problem in the emotional or spiritual area. It is regrettable that pastors and pastoral caregivers are often not well prepared for this set-up in their training. The "spiritual" and the "emotional" (both easily connected to the sexual) exist in all people simply as different facets of the same gem. They "reside" in the same spheres of the mind, in the same chambers of the heart. Often religious ministers are expected to delve into the spiritual realm with a great deal of intimacy, without a clear understanding that they are also entering another sacred realm: the emotional/sexual. Spirit and emotion: when you engage one, the other often responds as well.[3] Both the caregiver and care receiver are vulnerable at this point to moving into an interpersonal involvement that is a violation of the care receiver's boundaries. Forewarned is "fore-armed."

### Spiritual Boundaries: "Love the Sinner..."

One of the most significant boundary violations against LGBTQ people is based on the dictum, "Love the sinner, hate the sin." It primarily violates the spiritual boundary by injecting hate and sin upon the soul of a

---

3. Burke et al., *Religious and Spiritual Issues*, 102. See also the Faith Trust Institute, www.faithtrustinstitute.org.

person who is no more identified as sinner than anyone else and deserves no hate; it easily leads to emotional violations as well. This seemingly useful catch-phrase has done an immense amount of damage because at first it appears to be a logical and fair way out of a difficult question for some religious people: "What are we to do with LGBTQ persons?"

The reasons for its lack of validity are clear: on a practical level, it is extremely difficult to make the separation between "sinner" and "sin." What one hates, one works against, even destroys. It is difficult to hate an abstraction, such as sin, but easy to hate a person perceived as sinful. Hate always comes to land on the "sinner."

Sin, at least from a psychological point of view, does not possess a separate existence outside of human activity. There is no such thing as sin *per se*; only human acts that are considered sinful. So, ultimately, because we have no other "place" to put our hate, we hate those whom we perceive as sinners. Trying to love the sinner and hate the sin is, for this reason alone, impossible. The mentality of loving the sinner but hating the sin perpetuates hate, never gets to love, and must be challenged wherever it appears.[4]

## KEEPING CONFIDENTIALITY AND OUTING

Outing is making known someone's sexual orientation or gender identity, most often without their knowledge or consent.

Anyone in the public eye, like pastoral caregivers, is aware of meeting in public places people with whom they have a "professional relationship." In these social situations there is a certain degree of unease, based on the absence of an accustomed, and thus a safe, place. How the caregiver deals with these out-of-context situations is important to the integrity and success of the relationship.

When the lesbian parents of a girl in your religious education class see you at a neighborhood meeting, how you encounter them and introduce them to others is important to them—and noticed by others. When you see a gay member of your synagogue in the hardware store and say hello, and a friend asks you how you know each other, your answer is important to and influential in your pastoral relationship. Something as casual as saying to your friend, "Say 'hi' to Sally for me" when Sally is your

---

4. For a more complete treatment of "love the sinner, hate the sin," see Jacobson and Pellegrini, *Love the Sin*.

female friend's female partner could possibly be tantamount to outing your friend to others present; at the same time not saying it may be interpreted as dismissing or ignoring the relationship. Context and pastoral wisdom will determine your decision.

At issue is whose prerogative it is to make public knowledge that one is an LGBTQ person or the degree to which that person is out (see chapter 4). As a pastoral caregiver, it is your responsibility to know the importance of the information you have about your care receivers; other people may know that they are LGBTQ—or may not. To avoid unintentional outing, be aware of how you interact in public with them, what you say, how you introduce them. This, of course, also applies when speaking about them in their absence. So make it a point to ask your queer care receivers toward the beginning of your relationship to what degree they are out, and whether or not it is permissible to acknowledge it—to what degree, and to whom.

## LGBTQ TRANSFERENCE AND COUNTER-TRANSFERENCE

The field of psychoanalysis elucidates two relationship phenomena that are important for maintaining effective pastoral care boundaries: transference and counter-transference. Transference is the psychic process by which one transfers emotions, needs, or unresolved conflicts originally connected with one person and places them on another. Within the context of pastoral care, the feelings of the care receiver are often projected onto the caregiver. Frequently, but not always, the feelings in question were originally directed toward parents or some other authority figure, such as pastors or youth ministers who were mentors and role models and then became hostile or abusive when the person came out to them. Effective caregivers realize that they will often be placed, almost always unconsciously, in a parental/authoritative role. Because of the moral power that this transference of feelings often gives the caregiver, this is a good moment to recall that our underlying model for the pastoral care relationship is our relationship with the loving God. Be aware of your power and resolve to use it justly—and carefully.

The feelings involved in this process are often negative and thus you might receive the person's anger and frustration. By understanding the phenomenon of transference you will see that these attitudes are not personal toward you. Thus, to react to them personally would be incorrect, a response that could hurt the pastoral care relationship as well as hurt the care receiver. You are called on to "carry" these emotions with care, that is, to allow them to be "placed" on you (within reason, of course) without any negative or defensive reaction.

The feelings of care receivers might also be positive and involve emotional and sexual attraction to you; they could be bestowing on you the love they were never allowed to give to a parent, for example, or to an older sibling, or to a desired but unavailable partner.

Nor is it your direct responsibility as a pastoral caregiver to "lead LGBTQ persons in the working through of their feelings," since this is the work of a trained pastoral counselor or therapist. Nevertheless, your patience and understanding in the face of some "undeserved" feelings will be a kind of "working through" of the feelings by your care receiver and certainly will enhance the effectiveness of your care.

In terms of emotional boundaries, one might say that in this case LGBTQ persons are violating *your* boundaries; whatever they are feeling for you is not really yours—you don't deserve it, good or bad. This is not a true violation, however: it is simply a reality of effective pastoral care.

Inherent to the pastoral care relationship, at least in most cases, is an imbalance of power. The caregiver generally has more power. There can be situations when this is not so clear: if the care receiver is a major donor, years older, or chair of the parish board, she might well have more, or at least a different kind of, power over the pastoral caregiver. If it ever were to become a question of a juridical action against the pastoral caregiver, however, one must assume the power will be construed to reside in the caregiver. You have the responsibility to be both knowledgeable and able to carry what the receiver might need to place on you.[5] Like the power of a parent, this power is built into the role you have assumed and thus it is non-transferable.

Now put the shoe on the other foot: counter-transference is the emotional energy that you, the caregiver, place on the person who is the recipient of your care. Does the young gay man on the finance committee remind you of your neighborhood friend when you were a child? Or maybe of your estranged younger brother? Does the lesbian woman who heads your parish council have the same mannerisms as those of your first grade teacher? Or maybe she looks just like a woman you were in

5. For an understanding of the power imbalance in pastoral care ministry, see Gula, *Ethics*.

love with once? Does the care receiver who comes to discuss his bisexuality conjure up memories of your college psychology professor? And do you, in all those cases, project the feelings you had for those people from your past onto the present care receiver?

These counter-transference feelings happen to us all the time and will have an influence on how you deal with the people involved; it's simply human nature. At these times you need above all to be *aware* of your counter-transference feelings, to be as conscious of them as possible. Because awareness brings insight and safety, you will then be less likely to act on your feelings than on your knowledge, less likely to act from your heart rather than from your head.

Self-knowledge is an essential part of caregiving. We must know just where we stand personally, intimately, experientially, morally, and sexually with the issues that we deal with in others. The specific experience of dealing with LGBTQ persons can sometimes bring up for caregivers unresolved sexuality issues of their own. It is important that the caregivers first of all recognize what is happening within themselves, especially if these issues deal with orientation or identity, and then seek an immediate process of consultation with a trusted and competent advisor. This is not an uncommon occurrence and can become of moment of grace for the caregiver. Not to deal with issues of self-knowledge in this area can easily lead the caregiver into serious trouble with keeping appropriate boundaries. As Marshall gently states, "Clients and parishioners are most helped when caregivers are not caught in their own moral struggles at the same moment in which they are trying to assist . . . their . . . congregations."[6]

Outside a fiduciary relationship, teachers within the Christian church, for example, have used transference in a positive way, urging people to see others as Christ (Matt 25:40, 4). In other words, one is urged to project onto others the same feelings and attitudes one feels toward Jesus. In a way, this concept refers to the beginning of the chapter where the caregiver was encouraged to know their feelings toward the care seeker.

The patronizing attitude mentioned above in the section "Caring Intimacy" is also important to mention here in the context of the feelings that the caregiver and care receiver might have for each other. On the one hand, the caregiver's patronizing attitude might be, "I am the religious leader and I know best what is good for you." While as a trained pastoral caregiver you do have special information and knowledge, this attitude is

---

6. Marshall, *Counseling Lesbian Partners*, 4.

the patriarchal and futile attitude of authority having all the knowledge and the rest of humanity coming to get it.

On the other hand, it is possible to hear from your care receiver: "Look, I am the bisexual person here and I know what it's like; you have no idea!" If that's what's said to you, whether you "know what it's like" or not, a simple invitation might be in order: "Then please help me understand so that we both can know." Getting defensive will not help. In any case, don't allow yourself to be manipulated through guilt, suffering, or any other guise.

Acknowledging one's own limits is often very effective. "No, I don't know what it's like to be transgender, but I would like to know more and I hope you will help me understand." Always remember, when you're not sure of a response to an LGBTQ care receiver, consider: what can I say or do that will keep the relationship going and growing?

## CONTENT AND PROCESS

Of significant help in keeping appropriate boundaries with LGBTQ people is to analyze what's happening in the pastoral relationship from the point of view of the content and from the point of view of the process. The content is what you're actually dealing with: a stressful situation at the person's work, a death in the family, a problem with an aging parent, working on a problem with a fellow committee-member, and so on. Content is very important.

The process is different. It's what is happening on an interpersonal level between (or among) you and the person (people) you're dealing with, no matter what the content is. The process is the ongoing state of the relationship between you, the caregiver, and the care receiver(s).

Process, not content, is often the first aspect of the pastoral care relationship to which your LGBTQ care receivers will react.

For the gay male couple that has come to you to talk about baptizing their infant daughter, the details of the baptism (content) are important, but not as important as the tone and feeling of how you are all relating to each other (process). For the transgender woman who is looking for a deeper spiritual life (content), how she feels about the session as she leaves (process) is what will largely determine if she returns. Understanding the difference between these two aspects of the relationship is fundamental.

Without this understanding, the relationship has little chance of success; with it, little risk of failure.

Make an attempt to keep in mind both these points of view within the pastoral care relationship as you are experiencing it. This two-level approach will give you clarity in your interventions. Your thoughts might run something like this: is what she just said (or her tone of voice, or her choice of words) primarily about the subject we're talking about? Or is it more about what is going on between her and me?

## GAY AND STRAIGHT, IN AND OUT

Effective pastoral care takes into account the sexual identity and orientation of both the caregiver and the care receiver. Two combinations are possible: the first is that both the pastoral caregiver and the care receiver are LGBTQ. This sets up a very different dynamic from the other possibility: a caregiver who is "straight" (not LGBTQ). The point in specifying these combinations is to emphasize the need to understand the dynamic set up between the parties; it will influence the success of the pastoral care. Taking into account the degree to which parties are "out" adds further possible combinations of energies.

### Caregiver and Care Receiver Are Both LGBTQ

When the caregiver and care receiver are both queer, the ideal is for both to know who both are in as natural a way as possible. At times you may be dealing with someone who does not immediately come out, someone who does not reveal their sexual orientation or identity to you at first. In these cases keep in mind the following:

- Never presume to know a person's sexual orientation or identity; "playing dumb" is ineffective as well.
- If the situation calls for information about the person's sexuality or gender identity in order to be complete and successful, inquire as needed, as in any other situation.
- Always begin with belief and acceptance of what the care receiver tells you. If you have basis for doubts as to the accuracy or truth of the information that care receivers give you, proceed slowly and with care.

## The Pastoral Care Relationship

The pastoral caregiver being in the closet sets up a possible additional tension mostly centered on the question of "who knows what?" which can be a serious distraction from the ultimate purpose of the relationship: the good of the care receiver. Generally speaking, I recommend that the pastoral caregiver be as transparent in this regard as possible and thus have their sexual orientation or identity commonly known. In reality, this is often not the case, nor even possible or desirable in some circumstances. When the pastoral caregiver is in the closet, keep in mind the following:

- It is possible that the care receiver will "have a hunch" or "suspect" that the caregiver is LGBTQ. Thus, the tension that this "knowledge" might add to the relationship must be acknowledged, at least internally, by the caregiver, to ascertain what kind of influence it might have.

- Keep integrity and honesty as your primary focus when, as caregiver, your closet door is kept closed.

- In the long term, consider possible ways in which you, the LGBTQ caregiver, could successfully come out within the context of your denominational identity and pastoral position. While this question has a myriad of ramifications, I believe it must be at least considered in a serious way for the sake of personal integration and the broader LGBTQ cause.

- Seek competent, affirming, and knowledgeable support for yourself on an ongoing basis, whatever your decision about coming out.

In fairness, and particularly at this moment in the history of religious communities, it is important to acknowledge the significant challenges that face LGBTQ pastoral caregivers, who in some religious organizations work within a structure that not only fails to recognize their sexual orientation but also officially disparages or denies it.

Pastoral care for queer pastoral caregivers is especially important and necessary since they are vulnerable both to the anger of the LGBTQ community *and* to the reprimand or rejection of the religious community that they love. Personal integrity is a consistent challenge. At the very least, LGBTQ caregivers working within these oppressive bounds should find one another—and those caregivers within less oppressive communities of faith—for support, prayer, friendship, and to seek ways to lead their faith communities to grace. Because your work is so important and necessary, and the pressures on you are stronger than on many others, I would strongly encourage all queer pastoral caregivers to seek camaraderie in the ministry in some way, perhaps by participation in a support group.

One hears more and more often of pastoral ministers coming out in public and in responsible ways. Invariably and necessarily, they have good support systems in place before they do so.

---

**PASTORAL PERSPECTIVES**

Real-Life Pastoral Caregivers Coming Out[A]

Rev. Janie Adams Spahr: Janie was ordained a Presbyterian minister in 1974 and began her "out" liberation work very soon after. She is one of the founders of the Spectrum Center for Lesbian and Gay Ministries in San Rafael, California. Because of her sexual orientation, she was denied a call to a pastorate by the denomination's highest court in 1992. The next year another Presbyterian church invited Janie to become their evangelist to spread the good news by "personing the issue" and challenging exclusive church policies. Janie has traveled throughout the country, educating and informing Presbyterians and others working on behalf of greater inclusiveness for gay, lesbian, bisexual, and transgender people.

Fr. Warren Hall was removed as campus minister of Seton Hall University in 2016 after endorsing a controversial group that advocated for LGBTQ people. He was torn between remaining in the closet or coming out and being forced out of active priestly ministry. "Priests want to be good priests, they want to do their job," said Hall, who was reassigned to a parish. "More priests are rightfully more concerned about homelessness versus getting caught up in something about sex. We should be more concerned about those issues [like homelessness] that are impacting people."

---

A. Spahr, "Profile"; and Boorstein, "I'm Gay."

My own process of coming out as a gay man began with a pastoral relationship with a young man in the parish where I was assistant pastor. He came to me specifically for help in dealing with being gay. Some initial stumblings, fears, doubts, and self-searchings gradually gave way—first to supportive help for the care receiver, and ultimately to enthusiastic espousal, not only of him and his process but of LGBTQ causes and of my own process of coming out. My specific journey of coming out began when I realized I wanted to imitate the courage of that care receiver. What wonderful gifts our care receivers often have for us!

## Caregiver Is Straight, Not LGBTQ

In this scenario the possibility for tension is also lessened when both parties know the other party's orientation and agree that it is a non-issue.

When the non-LGBTQ pastoral caregiver does not know the sexual orientation of the care receiver at the beginning of the relationship, it most likely will be revealed if it is significant to the issue at hand. If not, there should be no need to clarify.

If, through observation and intuition, the caregiver believes that the sexual orientation of the care receiver is not being acknowledged *and* is a problem or an issue for that care receiver, always create safety first and establish your unqualified support. Then proceed with caution to seek more information. Always be prepared to be wrong. Always believe what care receivers tell you about their sexual orientation. Even if you have doubts, act as if you believe what they say. It establishes trust and confidence and frequently creates welcoming ground for openness and truth.

There are particular challenges when dealing with these "gay/straight, in/out" issues with transgender people. First, the general awareness of transgenderism—and gender identity in general—is still relatively recent and many people, including many caregivers, are still in the process of acquiring sufficient experience and accurate information to feel some competence in dealing with the issue, let alone in being helpful. Thus, the importance of up-to-date information and awareness.

Second, the processes through which trans people progress in their gender transition generally have extended stages and several variations in their progression. Some trans people never physically transition. Note too that transgender people may have any sexual orientation and thus fall under the general categories of LGBTQ in more than one way. This adds to the need for openness, frankness about limits, accepting where they are in their process, and willingness to learn on the part of the caregiver.

Though one's sexual orientation and one's gender identity always influence how one responds to anyone in life, the goal is that the sexuality of both caregiver and care receiver be a "non problem," and to have each one be appropriately transparent to the other in as natural a way as possible.

If the pastoral care relationship is specifically about a sexual issue of the care receiver, it is even more important for the combinations and distinctions mentioned here to be understood and acknowledged.[7]

## SYSTEMIC FUNCTIONING: THE PASTORAL RELATIONSHIP WITH SYSTEMS AFFECTING LGBTQ PEOPLE

In the systemic care of LGBTQ people, pastoral caregivers concern themselves not only with a relationship with the individual LGBTQ people within their purview, but also extend that concern to a relationship with the interconnecting and broader systems and social power arrangements that shape their lives or have some influence on them. These systems include significant others, spouses/partners, family, workplace, social groups, neighborhood organizations, schools, communities of faith, political groups, societal matrices, cultural assumptions and forces, and extend even to the eco-centric system of our planet earth.

The psychosystemic approach to pastoral care and the categories of care that I use in this section are based on the work of Larry Kent Graham.[8] The term "psychosystems" is a combination of psyche, which "delineates the soul... which is formed in relation to God, self and the world in which one lives," and systemic, which "indicates that the elements of reality are regarded in religious terms as the interlocking dynamic forces of the natural and social forces."[9] Think of a psychosystems approach to pastoral caretaking as primarily based on the philosophical, ecological, and religious precept that we are all interconnected with each other and with the world; the actions of the one affect the many and the actions of the many affect each one.

Psychosystemic pastoral care is especially relevant to the care of LGBTQ people. It acknowledges that pastoral care with the faith-based values of justice and charity, for example, which are given to a person, might not stand up to the influence nor match the power of the many

---

7. See, for example, Weaver et al., *Counseling on Sexual Issues*, and Marshall, *Counseling Lesbian Partners*.

8. Graham, *Care of Persons*.

9. Graham, "Prophetic," 53.

secular systems that advance different, even contradictory, values and constrictions on that same person. Systemic care also acknowledges that some secular systems of service are more clearly based on justice and charity than are some of their religious counterparts; many LGBTQ refugees from religious communities find excellent care in social centers, PFLAG, and other welcoming secular groups.

Effective pastoral care means cultivating an awareness of and challenging the systems in which people live. It involves broadening and deepening the pastoral caregiver's vision and sphere of influence from the exclusivity of this one person or congregation to the expansive matrices of relationships that the world contains. Psychosystemic care "sees" the broad implications and struggles of the individual in their world as it is, whether secular, sacred, or somewhere in between. Frequently it begins with and stems from a local, close-to-home occasion of pastoral care.

Religious communities and their pastoral care representatives have unprecedented opportunities in the first quarter of the twenty-first century to exert their influence for the just and fair treatment of LGBTQ people. Especially because of the outspoken nature of the more vocal, organized, reactionary (and often religious) groups who work in opposition to LGBTQ people, any expression of care and enlightened wisdom from a religious community-based voice will be heard, perhaps more clearly than expected, simply by being different from the often-anticipated response from religion.

Following Graham's framework, here are descriptions of the five goals of psychosystemic pastoral care. After the explanation of each goal, I present brief examples or suggestions for the application of that goal to the ministry of the pastoral caregiver with LGBTQ people. Not intended to be a complete listing of opportunities, these are merely samples or possibilities of the living out of psychosystemic pastoral ministry. They ask the question: if pastoral caregiving were to embody the values and goals of the psychosystems approach, what are some examples of what pastoral interventions might look like?

Note that a "psychosystems approach to ministry" does not imply an either/or choice but an attitude, an understanding, a vision that can enhance everyone's pastoral ministry, whether carried out in the church office, in the town square, or on the internet. The psychosystemically aware pastoral minister will always remember: we're all in this together and what we each do influences everyone else.

Note too that all five of the goals of the psychosystems approach to ministry involve movement—movement from a state of pain and injustice to a state of fairness and joy; from a place of suffering to a place of peace; from transgression to grace.

The five goals of psychosystemic pastoral care are to encourage movement:[10]

1. From being organizations that hurt to becoming organizations that help.
2. From the unfair balance of power to the fair balance of power.
3. From destructive conflicts over values to mutual understanding of values.
4. From creativity kept powerless to creativity that blossoms.
5. From being stuck in "no" to getting to "yes."

## BECOMING ORGANIZATIONS THAT HELP

The goal here is to see and respond to societal structures, groups, and organizations that are flawed and thus do harm to people, and to engage with those broken structures in the real world where they operate. The following are brief examples that present opportunities for the psychosystemic pastoral caregiver to be aware of and respond to harmful structures that influence LGBTQ people.

### Contemporary Feminist Concerns

I begin with the rights of women for two reasons: first, I believe that the interests of women are similar in important ways to the interests of LGBTQ people and both are the interests of all.[11] Rabbi Steven Greenberg says, "We cannot address the question of homophobia without also addressing the question of misogyny."[12] My statements are based on the assumption that homophobia and sexism come from the same antifeminist attitudes.

---

10. Graham, *Care of Persons*. For purposes of simplicity and clarity, I have changed some of Graham's wording of these categories while making every effort to retain his meaning.
11. See Pharr, *Homophobia*.
12. Greenberg, *Wrestling*, 14.

It is the effeminacy of gay men and the masculinity of lesbians that often make them the target of hatred. Second, the way the world, including many of its religious bodies, treats women as second-class people must be at the forefront of all pastoral concern. The pastoral caregiver will recognize and engage these flawed systems, from local social service agencies and employers to national and international organizations. Any system that mistreats women is based on what Gallo and Peck call the "wrong relationships of domination, exploitation, and dehumanization."[13]

## Opening the Closet Door

The psychosystemic caregiver will not only care about the congregant who is in the process of coming out, but will move from that single experience into the reality of the societal-based LGBTQ closet throughout the congregation, town, city, and broader world. Many organizations, for various reasons of apparent self-interest, strive to keep closet doors closed. Life in the closet creates in the ones involved attitudes that run counter to any wholesome religious experience and mature living in general and often increases the possibility of substance abuse.[14] The closed door of supposed safety and stagnation must give way to the open door leading to the wholesome promise of inner freedom. The pastoral caregiver becomes the careful and caring advocate of opening LGBTQ closet doors, and a helper in the process, to members of schools, religious congregations, the military, social groups, the government, and so on.

## The LGBTQ Person's Family of Origin

When a family rejects a gay son or lesbian daughter, a transgender parent, or bisexual uncle simply because of their sexual orientation or gender identity, the flawed structures that created that family become immediately apparent. Centuries of influence by broad-based social structures of which the family is a part (the local congregation, for example), and deeply influential channels of authority are brought to bear on that family to create their counterintuitive attitude of rejection. The caregiver here

---

13. Peck and Gallo, "JPIC," cited in Graham, *Care of Persons*, 204.

14. See, for instance, Peregoy et al., "Society Identity," on the relationship between closeted living and "negative health and mental health outcomes, including substance abuse, suicide, depression, and high risk behaviors."

has an opportunity to examine these structures and influences with this particular family and possibly with the broader communities involved.

## ESTABLISHING A FAIR BALANCE OF POWER

Another way to state this goal: there's a powerful energy loose in human culture that affects the ways that power is distributed. The pastoral goal is to wrestle with the energy and bring access to power into a mutually satisfying and fair balance, while respecting and using power justly. Here are four brief examples of areas in which pastoral care can help create movement to fairness for LGBTQ people.

### Women in Society

Again, one of the primary and most obvious power imbalances is between the overarching power of world patriarchy on the one hand and the power of women, and by association, the power of LGBTQ people on the other. Pastoral care workers will see that the values of patriarchy have been well embedded in the structures of religious organizations and thus they are called to become prophetic voices for wholeness (and holiness) within the context of their denominations.

### LGBTQ Ethnic Groups

Black, Latinx, Asian, First Nations, and other ethnic minorities have their own proportionate percentages of LGBTQ members, although a recent Gallup poll indicated that percentage-wise, non-whites are more likely to be out of the closet than whites.[15] People in these populations struggle under two oppressions, both based on the prejudices and denial of power to them by the dominant groups in society. Psychosystemic care holds the religious ideal of equality as a constant template against which to see human interactions. Does it exist in this situation? Why not? What needs to be done here and now? (See chapter 2 for more on pastoral care with ethnic minorities.)

---

15. Gates, "In US, More Adults Identifying as LGBT."

## The AIDS-Related Power Imbalance

The HIV/AIDS epidemic created a power imbalance from the moment it hit the human community. From denial of access to care and drugs, to becoming ostracized from society for perceived causes, people living with HIV/AIDS (especially women and people of color) have been and in some cases even continue to be kept from the sources of power. To which organizations can you add your voice and power in the fight for fair and just treatment of people living with HIV/AIDS? The psychosystemic caregiver knows the truth of the saying proposed by World AIDS Day: "We all have AIDS . . . If One of Us Does."[16]

## LGBTQ Homeless and Marginalized

Because the impaired social structure of the family is so often prejudiced against the LGBTQ member, a disproportionate number of homeless youth are LGBTQ, having been disowned or physically thrown out by their families. Many of these children end up on the streets. Make no mistake: this still happens on a regular basis. Urban-based pastoral caregivers should be available to cooperate with agencies that care for street kids, bringing a values-based dimension of pastoral care to the challenge.[17]

### MUTUAL UNDERSTANDING OF VALUES

This goal of psychosystemic care acknowledges that the virtues of love, kindness, and care are thwarted at every level of society and never seem to win, at least not at first, not easily, and not generally for the benefit of the poor and powerless. Psychosystemic care recognizes the presence of conflict in human values on all levels and is ready to cast its lot and its influence with the values it brings from its faith tradition. Examples of embodying this goal:

---

16. For the historical background of the saying, "We all have AIDS," see Davis, "Evolution." See also Kramer, *Tragedy*.

17. An example of this kind of ministry is Covenant House, which provides shelter and other services to homeless and runaway youth.

### Harmonizing Conflicting Values: LGBTQ Marriage

Even though the US Supreme Court ruled in June 2015 that same-sex marriage is a constitutional right, meaning that all fifty states must allow it and that all existing bans are invalid, it still seems to be an unsettled issue, with a significant minority of the population vocally intent on overturning the ruling. It is also clear that religiously based teachings and convictions have influenced the opinions of the majority of people who oppose it, and perhaps less often, ironically, those who support it. Psychosystemic care, no matter the individual caregiver's current opinion—personal, political, or other—will be engaged in this ongoing struggle and always seek the values of justice and truth and eschew avoidance of the issue.

### Legal Protections for LGBTQ People

Many religious leaders oppose anti-discrimination laws or hate-crime laws which are based on sexual orientation and gender identity. Are there opportunities in your pastoral care to point out these discrepancies between faith and action? Are there opportunities to join your voice to those who work against this type of inequality?

### LGBTQ Self-Acceptance in a Non-Accepting World

Perhaps the most fundamental LGBTQ issue, self-acceptance and self-love, is at the heart of all pastoral care with the LGBTQ community. There are many forces out there that continue to foster non-acceptance, which is expressed too frequently by name-calling, taunting, bullying, gay-bashing, and even murder. Questions for the caregiver include: What and who are the forces for such harm? How can synagogues and churches confront and transform them effectively, especially when they happen in your own town or city?

### Keeping LGBTQ People from God

It is no secret that a significant percentage of queer people are angry at communities of faith and at religion in general. This anger is primarily based, I believe, on personal experience and on the anti-gay stances upheld by many religious communities. Notwithstanding claims by some communities of faith that they are not anti-gay, LGBTQ folks stay away from churches and synagogues in droves. At the same time a significant percentage are actively engaged with their churches.[18] Homophobic/transphobic religion interferes with the ability of LGBTQ people to form healthy and meaningful relationships with God and with communities of faith, and, like everyone, they have a right to those relationships. Rather than avoid the discomfort, psychosystems-based caregivers will deliberately place themselves at the intersection of these groups, helping to clarify conflicting and misapprehended values.

## Discounting LGBTQ Experience: The Double Standard

The double standard is a common way to thwart values. With LGBTQ people it is expressed in the proclivity of many faith communities not to accept the simple truth and validity of the lived experience of queer people, while at the same time accepting the truthfulness of non-LGBTQ people's lived experiences. Representatives of these religious traditions often seem to say that they know what LGBTQ people experience better than they do; for example, the assumption that the goal for LGBTQ people should necessarily be quiet assimilation. The pastoral caregiver finds in this contradiction a rich opportunity for the voice of prophetic truth.

### PROMOTING A CREATIVITY THAT BLOSSOMS

This goal recognizes that social matrices often intersect in such a way that human creativity is discouraged, unrecognized, or kept underground. The challenge for the pastoral caregiver is to support its liberation. For example:

## Keeping LGBTQ Social Roles Rigid

Frequently society says "no" to LGBTQ people: in many cases, they can't adopt children or (in many places in the world) join the armed forces as out individuals. In some places and times they are not allowed to teach

18. See Tigert, *Coming Out*; Balka and Rose, *Twice Blessed*; and "U.S. Transgender Survey, 2015."

children. Some schools will not accept them as students; most religious bodies will still not ordain them. Many civil jurisdictions do not include them in non-discrimination policies. Many employers reject them. All that creativity, service, and life is denied to the world; all those opportunities to serve and create are lost to the individuals. These are great occasions for the systems-based pastoral caregiver to work to free creative forces that are kept down.

## Creating Rules and Norms for Moral Relationships

Because LGBTQ people are not encouraged by society in general to have intimate or romantic relationships, at least not "legitimate" ones, they have to create their own rules, customs, and standards as they form these relationships. Insightful pastoral caregivers will see an opportunity to explore with their care receivers how and if traditional moral standards might fit with these new moral realities. They will also learn from these experiences and apply these "new" ways of human relating to the creation of stronger intimate relations in general.[19]

## LGBTQ Grief

Grief is often a window to emotional awakening and creativity. Grief abounds as LGBTQ people, both young and old, develop and become more aware of what they are denied and how negatively they are often held in the public esteem. In recent decades, members of the queer community have experienced a devastating and cumulative grief from losses related to the AIDS pandemic. A common companion of grief is often, understandably, shame; one feels responsible in some way for the loss. And shame is a common road to addictions. Pastoral caretakers will seek opportunities to help LGBTQ individuals and groups deal with grief and shame, to emerge from these negative feelings with new life and, inevitably, with renewed creativity.

---

19. See Kosnik et al., *Sexual Morality*, 92: the characteristics of moral sexual acts are described as self-liberating, other-enriching, faithful, socially responsible, life-serving, and joyous.

## GETTING TO "YES"

At every level of human life there are forces that keep human beings from getting through to each other, that sabotage our communication, and that keep us from understanding each other's intended meaning, which is a primary human need. This is as true within the dyad of marriage as it is between and among countries at the United Nations. This goal of psychosystems pastoral care is to help open and keep open the lines of human communications. For example:

## LGBTQ Intergenerational Issues

The psychosystems caregiver will recognize one of the challenges for LGBTQ people, as for all people, is for the young to accept the old and *vice versa*. So much wisdom is lost in generation gaps. This especially applies to the LGBTQ minority insofar as it needs all of the creativity that it can muster to achieve equality and justice. Add to this the generation that has been decimated by AIDS. Bringing together young and old LGBTQ people is the challenge.[20] What better place than church and synagogue?

## The World of Religion and LGBTQ People

On a broader basis, initiating and influencing the dialogue between LGBTQ people and their interests on the one hand, and the wide expanse of religion on the other, is a noble and urgent goal.[21] This service brings the wisdom of each within the understanding of the other: its eventual goal is harmony brought about by mutual understanding and appreciation. This can only be accomplished by actively destroying impasses that separate, and by building bridges that unite LGBTQ people with their communities of faith.

---

20. For one example of LGBTQ intergenerational programming, see Parson, "Finding Common Ground." See also the resources available at the Queer Cultural Center (QCC), https://qcc2.org.

21. A practical example of an engaging systemic ministry that seeks to influence and heal transactional impasses between the LGBTQ world and religion is The Center for LGBTQ and Gender Studies in Religion (CLGS) at Pacific School of Religion in Berkeley, California (www.clgs.org/).

## LGBTQ and Non-LGBTQ Communities

The goal is to cause unity by removing the gap that exists between LGBTQ people and non-LGBTQ people. Queer culture is, in many ways, different from straight culture. An inevitable step along the way is bringing them together and encouraging them to listen to each other. Good pastoral experience shows that when that happens, attitudes begin to change. The psychosystems-based pastoral caregiver looks for opportunities to introduce LGBTQ persons to non-LGBTQ persons. On every level, human contact is a consistently transformative agent: it is more difficult to hate or fear queer people in general, when you know and like Vickie, a specific friend who is lesbian, or Colin, a known and respected colleague who is bisexual.

## THE POWER OF THE "STRAIGHT" VOICE

Here, at the conclusion of the section on systemic pastoral care of LGBTQ people, I want to call attention to a specific and often unrecognized source of power for the betterment of queer people and the systems that influence them: the supportive public voices of "straight" allies.[22]

Often non-LGBTQ caregivers do not seem to be aware of their power to influence the thinking of other non-LGBTQ people in regard to the issues that face the queer community. The power comes from a simple fact: "You (non-LGBTQ people) are not us (LGBTQ people)." "We" "have an agenda," which according to many is an undesirable agenda at best, and often is labeled much worse. "You" (non-LGBTQ people) don't have that agenda according to this kind of thinking.

If you are non-LGBTQ, your supportive comments tend to make many other non-LGBTQ people stop and think. These are people who might otherwise dismiss the remarks of any queer person as a self-serving example of the "gay agenda."

If you are a non-LGBTQ ally and pastoral caregiver, you are indeed a gift to all gay people. We need you! Please never stop thinking that our concerns indeed are your concerns and the concerns of all. Keep Pastor

---

22. PFLAG (originally also known as "Parents, Families, and Friends of Lesbians & Gays") is perhaps the best known and most influential of these voices. See www.pflag.org. Many synagogues and churches have organizations specifically devoted to supporting their LGBTQ members: some are recognized by the authorities of their denominations/traditions, while others are not. See Resources.

Niemöller's poem[23] in mind and never underestimate the power and influence of your supportive words.

More than any technique, intervention, or ability to solve problems, it is the strength and quality of the human relationship created within the context of faith-based pastoral care with LGBTQ people that enables the care seeker to move from the place of pain and challenge to the place of joy and resolution—and ultimately to peace. Pastoral care that affirms and strengthens the relationship, pastoral care that aims to heal the broad-based and interconnected systems within which LGBTQ people live, and pastoral care that ensures that the relationship remains open for future rekindling—such pastoral care indeed partakes of the divine.

---

23. Niemöller, "First They Came."

# 2

# The Functions of Pastoral Care

### David Kundtz

THE FUNCTIONS OF PASTORAL care bring the applications of all theology down to earth, down to the daily ins and outs of ministry to human beings. It's the nitty-gritty of theology which deals with the real, unpredictable, ever-changing, and often messy situations in which pastoral ministers find themselves. The functions of pastoral care tell us what it does; they are the types of services it provides to people, the kind of work it accomplishes.

In presenting the functions of pastoral care for LGBTQ people, I adopt the schema of Howard Clinebell as he has modified it from the work of Clebsch and Jaekle. Clinebell offers five functions of pastoral care: Healing, Sustaining, Guiding, Reconciling, and Nurturing. In addition, and based primarily on the work of Larry Kent Graham, I add the function of Prophetic Pastoral Care.[1] I consider each of these functions from the unique point of view of providing pastoral care for LGBTQ people.

---

1. Clinebell, *Basic Types*, 42–43; Graham, "Prophetic."

## HEALING

The function of healing, according to Clinebell, "aims to overcome some impairment by restoring the person to wholeness and by leading him to advance beyond his previous condition."[2] Overcoming impairment: the impairments that present themselves first in most LGBTQ people are the wounds that are inflicted by the world into which they are born.

## Woundedness

In varying degrees of intensity, woundedness is one characteristic you can almost always count on in the LGBTQ people with whom you relate, and thus you will encounter a clear need for healing. Of course, LGBTQ people have all the wounds that are inherent in the human family. They do, however, tend to have a few battle scars that are particularly characteristic. With some people the scars are truly devastating; with others, there is less damage. I do not hesitate to use the word "always" in regard to the woundedness of LGBTQ people; there is indeed always some woundedness. It would seem close to impossible to have avoided it given the history that has produced the predominant attitudes toward queer people in the early twenty-first century.

## Wounds Inflicted by Faith Communities

Too frequently the wounds have been inflicted by the religious community, directly or indirectly. If that is the case, it is essential that the pastoral caregiver keep in mind that these care receivers are engaging with the very reality that wounded them. The process might well feel risky and make them feel vulnerable anew. You as caregiver represent both the power and the responsibility of the faith community. Both power and responsibility might well involve an acknowledgment of the wounds and perhaps an apology.

A comment as simple as, "You know, I'm really sorry for how the religious community has hurt you," can be an effective way to begin a process to undo decades of pain and enter into a healing relationship.

---

2. Clinebell, *Basic Types*, 42. Clinebell is quoting from Clebsch and Jaekle, *Pastoral Care*. Stewart Hiltner, Wayne Oates, and others have contributed to the development of these functions.

It seems to me there is no better place, no better community than the church or synagogue to make up for the pain that it had a role in creating. Thus, the healing of LGBTQ people will involve making the specifically healing elements of church life as easily available as possible. For sacrament-based churches this clearly involves sacraments, all the sacraments. For all, it involves making access to worship and fellowship not only available, but easy and welcoming (see chapter 5).

Most religious communities are blessed with people who have the gift of affirmation; they are the enthusiastic and sincere supporters of people and good causes. Imaginative pastoral care will find ways to unite your hesitant care receivers and these loving, affirming people.

### Family of Origin Wounds

Most LGBTQ people leave their family of origin with some wounds, wounds that have been directly or indirectly inflicted.

Reason and experience tell us that all wounded people can be unpredictable and isolated, and understandably so. They have reasons not to trust; they have experience that tells them they will be hurt, and scars to remind them. Thus, some LGBTQ people have been worn down by wounds inflicted deeply and early in life by those who should have loved them most, and they might have either retreated into unfriendly isolation or become aggressive and defensive. With the eyes of pastoral care, we can see through the hard exterior into the bright souls hoping for healing.

I have already mentioned internalized homophobia as something to watch for in your LGBTQ care receivers. In the same vein are shame-based attitudes of self-denigration or low self-esteem. An aware pastoral care provider will notice these isolated individuals, no matter the cause, and act to heal by facilitating their incorporation into the broader community of faith. One frequently encounters this woundedness in both older and younger LGBTQ people who make assumptions that indicate they do not expect or think they deserve anything better than "the back-of-the-bus" and "don't ever talk about it" treatment that our culture has traditionally offered them.

One Sunday morning several years ago, after the last service, I asked a fellow pastoral worker, "Did you notice that kid in the last row? He always seems to be alone." We all had noticed him. It turns out that he was a thirteen-year-old white boy from a large, poor, un-churched, local family that was literally being destroyed by an alcoholic and rage-aholic father. The youngster had come to our church because it was the closest one to his home and just sat in the back row every Sunday morning, arriving late and leaving early. One morning the director of religious education corralled him in her unique and loving way and that was the beginning of a long, complex, but ultimately redemptive saga of a whole family and a small-town church. Fortunately for him, he had a winning personality and an indomitable spirit and, in time, the whole parish sort of adopted him.

His father had identified him at ten years old as "a faggot kid" (the father's words). The details he revealed of his father's violence, his mother's helplessness, and his siblings' avoidance and fears startled all who heard them. He at first easily acknowledged (to anyone who would listen) that he was gay, coming out later in life as transgender, and is now living, happily partnered, as a woman.

This kid's sitting alone in the back of a church was initially the sole impetus for whatever limited healing the family eventually achieved. This particular young person expressed an exceptional personality by reaching out and by having a rich imagination. Most kids in that situation are not blessed with these gifts and end up on the streets of the nearest large city and may have very short lives.

The point for pastoral caregivers: don't miss the subtle cries for help, especially in the old and young. Don't underestimate the depth of the wounds that a family is capable of bestowing.

## Trading Places

As a pastoral caregiver to wounded people, especially if you are not LGBTQ, learn to develop the virtue of understanding, and specifically of trying to put yourself in their place. In other words, "Walk a mile in their shoes." Such an attitude will go a long way in allowing your care to be effective.

For a moment, imagine living in a world in which what seems like your very being is questioned and found wanting—if not downright evil. Such a response would have a strong effect on anyone. The "closet" seems safe, quiet, and peaceful by comparison. The problem, of course, is that it is also dark, hidden, and lonely—and ultimately not a healthy choice. (See "Queer for a Day: An Exercise for Non-LGBTQ Caregivers" in chapter 3.)

The healing of wounds takes time and care. Recall the centrality of the relationship you have with care receivers. It is within the context of your relationship that much of the healing will take place, whether you are relating to your people in the context of worship, working together on a committee, or eating supper together at the parish picnic.

## Healing Systems

Woundedness exists not only in individuals but also in the organizations they create. The seasoned pastoral sense of Leonard, a sixty-eight-year-old, African American, retired pastor-emeritus, led to some broad changes in the whole geographic region of his church.

Leonard's story begins with a casual conversation with a sixty-three year-old member of the church, Helen, who told him tearfully that she did not know how she would get along now that "my friend Sarah is moving away." What Leonard noticed were the tears and the strong emotional response that Helen's statement brought out in her. He followed up, inquiring more deeply into her experience.

What he found out over a period of caring follow-up to that conversation was that Helen, who was African American, and Sarah, Irish American, had shared a life and a home for twenty-one years and were indeed life partners. Sarah needed to live at a medical care facility because of her health and Helen was not eligible to go with her. Leonard became not only Helen's supporter in the church community but her advocate with the care facility, which eventually allowed the two women regular extended and private visits. Leonard also influenced the facility's administration to extend this policy of recognizing same-sex relationships to its other facilities in the region. Equality and justice for LGBTQ seniors became the focus of ministry for this straight, widowed, retired minister.

This wide-ranging series of healings, both individual and psychosystemic, began with a moment of noticing—with Pastor Leonard's noticing in her seemingly casual announcement to him that Helen was deeply upset. He didn't miss it!

## SUSTAINING

Sustaining is "helping a hurting person to endure and transcend"[3] circumstances that in all probability will not change.

The circumstances of the function of sustaining can range from a general need for encouragement in the face of angry and mean-spirited politicians, to trying to deal with the very personal problems we share with everyone else. The function of sustaining recognizes that the world offers few supports for LGBTQ people.

At the beginning of the twenty-first century what do LGBTQ people have to endure and transcend?

## Being Queer

The place to begin is perhaps so obvious that it is easy to miss: We are LGBTQ people who live in an often unfriendly or belligerent world; although improving, that is not going to change any time soon. Many LGBTQ people, certainly not all, need encouragement simply to be who they are in a proud, dignified, and self-accepting way. The yearly "Gay Pride" event celebrated in most cities is a celebration of all things LGBTQ. No matter one's political or cultural appraisal of these events, for many, such a celebration was the first time we felt affirmed, celebrated, and happy to be who we are. No small moment.

LGBTQ people have different experiences based on where they live—and whether or not they are out. Those in the urban centers of North America often have the advantages of numbers, resources, and generally more enlightened attitudes in the population. Thus, they will often not have the same kinds of needs as those in rural and isolated regions. Typically, there is little acceptance and understanding of queer people in many, although not all, rural areas and often there are dangerous levels of ignorance and homophobia. Pastoral caregivers in these less populated areas are called to develop a special sensitivity to their LGBTQ peoples' needs, which might not be so readily expressed.[4]

The affirming and accepting pastoral caregiver will deepen and broaden this life-giving sense of self-worth in whatever ways possible, but probably most effectively by day-to-day interactions of care and joy

3. Clinebell, *Basic Types*, 42.

4. Four resources: Gray et al., *Queering the Countryside*; Fellows, *Farm Boys*; Murray, *Farm Family*; and Smith and Mankoske, *Rural Gays*.

with their LGBTQ congregants. These low-key, ordinary-seeming pastoral interventions can be "high-key" in terms of effectiveness.

The power of affirmation is often remarkable. Ask members of Parents, Families and Friends of Lesbians and Gays (PFLAG)[5] what it was like for them to march in their first gay pride parade and many will tell you it was "life-changing." Ask those LGBTQ people who cheer them along the parade route what it's like to see parents and friends marching and you'll hear, "I can't explain to you how much it means to me to see parents out there supporting us!"

## Under Siege

Even acknowledging the significant recent gains, presently LGBTQ people are still under siege in many cultures and countries. Our very legitimacy is often questioned in a public and vociferous way, and we are consistently under public scrutiny. The fact that we are the subject of an emotionally charged news story weekly, if not daily, is enough to tell you that we are a population that could use some help to "endure and transcend."

Arguably, the institutions that are debating the status of LGBTQ people the most loudly and argumentatively are churches and political parties. I hope you see this as an opportunity, not as a roadblock. Your sustaining pastoral care in the form of support and encouragement can indeed bear immediate and abundant fruit.

Anyone under siege is likely to have strong feelings. I have referred before to the anger and frustration that many LGBTQ people hold toward some churches and synagogues in particular and religion in general. The sustaining pastoral caregiver will accept the anger and then find ways to help them sublimate these feelings into constructive and fulfilling channels of activity or interest. Frequently the most effective response is to enlist these strong-feeling people into the ranks of the reformers, the rebels, and others working for justice and equality.

## LGBTQ Relationships

Since June of 2015, same-sex marriage is the law of the land in the United States. Even so, it still remains one of the hot issues of our times.

---

5. See PFLAG for local contact information (www.pflag.org/).

Everyone weighs in with a particular insight, a unique approach, or a critical comment. And, of course, the number of churches that will marry a same-sex couple remains relatively small. However, above and beyond those variables, the simple reality remains that gay people form romantic relationships—whether or not they are sanctioned (see chapter 6). This is another example of our not being willing to wait for the world to decide who we are and what we can and cannot do. We live now. It would be both unreasonable and unhealthy to put one's life on hold until some religious or civil authority finally makes up its collective mind. Good pastoral care will help LGBTQ people sustain healthy, life-giving relationships now, like Carolyn did.

Carolyn, an Asian American, is the new, young, recently married assistant minister to the congregation. Martin, the Latino care seeker, is forty-five, in an almost-two-year relationship with Paul, white, forty-three, who has tested positive for the HIV virus. Martin is distraught and reports that his family and many friends are urging him to get out of the relationship. Carolyn mostly just listens carefully to Martin as he relates at some length the elements of his story, his feelings, and his worries. Caregiver Carolyn believes she hears, mostly between the lines, that Martin does not want to leave Paul, that he loves him, and he believes that it is mutual. Carolyn says as much to Martin.

Martin in turn responds with relief: "What I need is someone to encourage me and not to think I am crazy to stay. I love Paul deeply and I am willing to go through the challenges that surely await us together."

It is worth noting that the reason Martin chose Carolyn as a pastoral caregiver—rather than the LGBTQ-affirming, older male pastor—was because of her quiet, contemplative nature. In turn, Carolyn recognized in her care receiver a religiously-motivated desire for virtue and sacrifice which, she believed, offered a good probability of success. She was eager to work with Martin.

An important part of Carolyn's sustaining pastoral care would, of course, be follow-up and continuing involvement in the challenges that may be part of this family's life.

## Illness and Suffering

Another clear application of the sustaining function is caring for people affected by sickness, especially HIV/AIDS, and any other ongoing suffering. This topic is discussed in chapter 3.

## GUIDING

Guiding is "assisting perplexed persons to make confident choices between alternative courses . . . affecting . . . the state of the soul."[6] Guidance is a wonderful gift, especially when received at just the right time. It involves several elements: educating your care receivers in the implications and ramifications of their possible choices; educating the young who are exposed to many confusing choices; reminding the elderly of what might have faded from mind in forgetfulness; serving as the well-grounded guide, asking the right questions, and encouraging virtuous responses.

### Competence with LGBTQ Issues

Often ministers of religion give in, or fear being perceived as giving in, to the cultural stereotype which says that "if I know too much about gay issues or if I seem too well acquainted with gay people I am somehow 'tainted' or *one of them*," or some other such unreasonable conclusion. Part of pastoral competence for *all* caregivers is to understand the basic issues of being both LGBTQ and religious in contemporary society; this knowledge says nothing about anyone's sexuality.

Those who are confident give the best advice; guidance by committee or by consultation is often ineffective. Confidence is not arrogance. It is born of preparation, care, study, and experience.

Johnny is a quiet, polite fifteen-year-old member of a large Reform Jewish congregation. One evening after a youth group meeting he asks to see Rachel, the rabbi who serves as youth director. During their session he tells her he's gay. "I've known it for a long time now and I just want everyone to know" he says smiling and confident. "I've just told my parents. They're pretty bummed but they'll get over it because they're really liberal."

---

6. Clinebell, *Basic Types*, 42.

To this announcement, Rachel, forty-ish, straight, married, mother of two, generally quick-witted and ready with a retort, responds with a stunned silence. She has been taken by surprise and she does not know what to say.

"So anyway, thanks," says Johnny, leaving. "I gotta get going. See you soon and thanks again."

Rachel is left sitting there, feeling very unsettled.

Early the next morning Rachel gets a call from Johnny's father. "We want to see you as soon as possible," he says. "Can we come over right away?"

The first thing to say about this case is that Rachel, as an ordained rabbi and youth minister of a congregation, has the responsibility to know what do in this situation. The fact that she was surprised is a sign of how ill-prepared many pastoral caregivers are when it comes to being LGBTQ-aware, knowing facts, understanding implications, and simply feeling confident and competent to deal with LGBTQ issues and persons. (Another reality that this case demonstrates is that kids are coming out younger than ever before. This topic is treated in chapter 3.)

Johnny and his parents need guidance. They need someone who knows the territory, the questions to ask, the dangers to watch for, how to relate to a fifteen-year-old gay boy, someone who has the skill to help with the parent-child relationship, advice for limit-setting and guidelines for companionship, someone who knows the referrals to make, and especially the referrals not to make. Too frequently people who come out young are forced by their parents' abandonment of them to take over their own parenting (very often with poor results) or they receive only censures, rejections, and thus years of unnecessary pain.

After a rocky start, Rachel fulfilled her role as pastoral caregiver and guide for Johnny and his family. Indeed, she became a strong voice for LGBTQ issues. Non-LGBTQ religious leaders who express public advocacy for queer people often explore a lonely and uncharted territory that takes courage and dedication, and sometimes a tough skin.

What Rachel realized as she moved into the situation that confronted her is that she indeed had the skills needed: after all, she would have known what to say and do if the situation were of a heterosexual nature. What she had to overcome was her feeling of being in unknown territory where she felt incompetent. She began a crash-course in self-education. Of course she could be helpful, insightful, and knowledgeable in this situation! Why couldn't she?

As a pastoral caregiver who gives guidance to LGBTQ people (as well as to all), you need to have a broad, general knowledge of human sexuality. Without it, you can actually add to the challenges of those seeking your care, rather than helping them. I mention this issue of awareness simply because it is frequently passed over in training. If someone says she's femme or butch, he's into leather or he's a bear, would the blank, uncomfortable look on your face immediately tell them to look elsewhere? Since education in sexuality is not the purpose of this work, I recommend you to consult (1) the Resources list at the end of this book, (2) your favorite search engine (exercising caution), and (3) a sexually educated and aware friend, and/or local resources, contacts, colleagues, and authorities who can educate you.

## Public Guidance

Another way to provide guidance for your LGBTQ people is by public statement. This is also a systemic application of guidance.

When the topic of LGBTQ rights becomes a locally hot issue, consider writing an encouraging op-ed piece in your local newspaper, giving a radio interview, or penning a commentary of support in your religious community's bulletin. Such actions might seem risky, but think not only of the LGBTQ people in the area who would receive guidance, encouragement, and pastoral care through these kinds of communication, but keep in mind as well the other readers or listeners who might have their assumptions challenged and their boundaries expanded in the direction of understanding and compassion.

## The "Sins" of Omission

If you find that you do not have the information that you feel is necessary, don't be afraid to ask the care receiver for the information you need. Also, don't hesitate to inquire more deeply into an issue if your pastoral instinct tells you to do so, always, of course, with care. I believe that more poor pastoral caregiving is the result of *not* doing than of doing poorly. It's often what you did not ask and did not suggest that leaves your care seeker unfulfilled. LGBTQ issues, although much more "out" and "dealt with" than just a decade ago, can still cause embarrassment, shame, and shyness in both the caregiver and care receiver.

Proactive guidance or confrontation is something most of us don't like, whether we are the receivers or the givers. It can lead to anger and resentment. Your function as a source of guidance, however, sometimes demands it. Confrontation of LGBTQ people can be challenging, especially if the one confronting is a representative of the church. The caregiver might be hesitant to confront the care receiver for several reasons. Unfamiliarity with the territory and fear of being seen as unsympathetic with a minority are two excuses that come to mind. My advice: plunge in with care. Responsibility demands that we challenge LGBTQ people just as we would challenge any other people if they are seeking advice or acting irresponsibly and unwisely.

## Moral Guidance; Exploring Options

Often, people will approach the pastoral caregiver seeking moral guidance in regard to a practical situation in their lives:

- A man in your church is HIV-positive and living healthily with anti-retroviral therapy. However, he wants to talk to you about the future possibility of ending his life if he should become very ill.
- A young, interracial lesbian couple is considering artificial insemination and asks about the moral implications of what they are planning.
- A sixteen-year-old high school boy in your youth group tells you he is gay and he has been "asked out on a date" by a twenty-two-year-old college student. He is confused and seeks guidance from you.
- A transgender woman considering surgery comes to you and asks about church teaching on the morality of such surgery.
- A twenty-five-year-old woman asks you if it is a sin to be involved in a lesbian sexual relationship.
- A sixty-five-year-old married woman consults you with the question, "Do you think that people can really be bisexual?"

These, of course, are just a few of the very real moral dilemmas and questions that face LGBTQ people all the time. I believe the first response in all these situations is not to give an immediate and definite "answer," and certainly not to make a pronouncement. True pastoral care and guidance call you to explore the options, examine the moral implications and their meanings, clarify the moral principles involved, and get to know your care receiver. Joretta Marshall puts it succinctly: "The important thing in pastoral care with people facing moral crises is neither to pretend we can be morally neutral nor to pronounce moralisms; rather, it is to discern with people as they engage their life issues. We must not deny our moral stand nor should we insist that others stand where we do."[7]

## Talking About It

Over the years I have taught classes to mid-life clergy persons. I always ask how many have ever mentioned LGBTQ people in a sermon or homily during worship. Typically one (or none) had done so, and that one was often in a negative way. The point is to talk about LGBTQ people and their issues in some kind of positive light and in some kind of public way, the same way you mention straight persons—such as in the weekly sermon or homily or other occasion of teaching. Even mentioning LGBTQ people as one group in a grouping of several, or as an example, will teach your congregation to be more aware. By never mentioning LGBTQ people and issues, one makes a powerful negative statement and further renders them "invisible."

In addition to talking about queer issues publicly, there's just plain talking about sex in general. It's no secret that sex is a difficult subject to talk about in our culture. It is considered off-limits in many circumstances and off-putting in many others. Yet, there remains a tremendous need to talk about it. Nothing takes the place of sharing information and feelings honestly, carefully, and kindly in a safe place. People inevitably grow in understanding, appreciation, and wisdom from such "holy conversations."[8] How can you further that goal?

## Spiritual Direction

A long-time staple in the Catholic spiritual repertoire, spiritual direction has found popularity in much broader spiritual circles in the last twenty years. I understand spiritual direction to be a person of faith accompanying a co-religionist in a supportive and encouraging way on the journey of faith in order to clarify and understand its challenges and issues and

7. Marshall, "Caring."
8. See Oliveto et al., *Talking About Homosexuality*.

move closer to God. I endorse the approach of James Empereur, SJ, who emphasizes the giftedness of being gay and its centrality in the process of spiritual direction with queer people.[9]

Offering spiritual direction to LGBTQ people in your congregation, people who have so frequently been kept at a distance from the rich and refreshing waters of the spiritual well, will bring welcome rewards.

## RECONCILING

If there is one function that stands out as urgent in dealing with the LGBTQ community, it is reconciliation. This is the function that "seeks to re-establish broken relationships"[10] among persons, and between persons and God. I will add: also between persons and the religious community. The exodus of LGBTQ people from synagogues and churches continues to be steady and widespread. The stereotypical process is for an individual to reach teenage years or young adulthood, come out, and leave the church or synagogue. Statistics on queer membership in faith communities are understandably hard to come by, but experience and casual surveying indicate that the number of older LGBTQ people leaving or not participating is also significant. Leanne Tigert's *Coming Out While Staying In* is a good history and analysis of LGBTQ participation in churches.[11]

### Alienation/Reconciliation

Alienation currently is the dominant relationship mode tendered to LGBTQ people in most communities of faith, with few but notable exceptions.[12]

---

9. Empereur, *Spiritual Direction*.

10. Clinebell, *Basic Types*, 42.

11. Tigert, *Coming Out*. See also Murphy, "Lesbian"; James et al., "2015 U.S. Transgender Survey"; and Halkitis et al., "Meanings."

12. There are churches that make welcoming and affirming LGBTQ people an official part of their teaching. Among them are the United Church of Christ, the Metropolitan Community Church, the Unitarian Universalist Association, and the Religious Society of Friends (Quakers). For a guide to welcoming synagogues of different affiliations, see the online "Equality Guide" sponsored by Keshet, www.keshetonline.org/guide.

Consider, when you approach queer people, that they are, in all probability, alienated to some degree from this church or synagogue, in particular, or from faith communities in general. Even if they are active members, I believe on some level that no one who is LGBTQ can escape the pervasive energy of alienation that currently divides so many denominations. The basis of that feeling of alienation is the depth of the rejection, the breath of the avoidance, the power of the revulsion, and the overall enormity of the negative energy that emanates from so many religious people toward their LGBTQ neighbors. It can be overwhelming.

Most LGBTQ people over the age of eighteen, and probably many under, have been struck by the force of the enmity that often comes at us. We know, on some level, that we have become, unfairly, the scapegoats of some dark and alien representation of "otherness"; that rather than being seen as "gifted by otherness,"[13] we are damned because of it.

## Religion/Spirituality

Many LGBTQ people have joined with others in contemporary society in the practice of separating spirituality from religion. It's a step that excludes involvement in the church or synagogue and the community they offer, while keeping clear and open the way to God and religious values. It seems to be a more and more common choice. On the one hand, it deprives the person of being part of a rich and long tradition and a member of a supportive faith community; on the other hand, given the circumstances, it allows spirituality to flourish and grow and be part of one's life.

Currently, the category of "none" is often considered the fastest growing group in religious affiliation—or lack of it. They are the ones who check "none of the above" in identifying religious identity. In 2016, the Pew Research Center found that "the share of Americans who do not identify with a religious group is surely growing:[14] while nationwide surveys in the 1970s and '80s found that fewer than one-in-ten US adults said they had no religious affiliation, fully 23 percent now describe themselves as atheists, agnostics, or "nothing in particular."[15] The Pew study comments that many interpret this high statistic simply as more people

---

13. See Countryman and Ritley, *Gifted by Otherness*, for a positive understanding of being LGBTQ from a faith perspective.
14. Pew Research Center, "America's Changing Religious Landscape."
15. Smith and Cooperman, "Factors."

being honest about their lack of religious affiliation, because it is more socially acceptable.

LGBTQ people in the "spiritual but not religious" category would seem to be the most promising for reconciliation. Many have, or had, a commitment to the spiritual life. Can you, as pastoral caregiver, offer reconciliation in which that spiritual life would be enhanced and affirmed for queer people by becoming members of your religious community?

## Sacramental Reconciliation

Churches with a sacramental system—Roman, Anglican, and Orthodox Catholics, Lutherans, and others—have a wonderful opportunity for reconciliation in the sacrament of the same name. But how available is this sacrament to your LGBTQ people? It's a complicated issue but one also ripe for pastoral creativity. Consider these pastoral perspectives as you contemplate LGBTQ people participating in the sacrament of reconciliation:

- LGBTQ people who are not celibate are excluded in some churches from communion, a source of unity in the church, and from reconciliation.
- Why should people who are excluded from the sacraments of unity and reconciliation be expected to participate in the life of the church? As with the divorced (and remarried) in some denominations, LGBTQ people are, in practice if not in theory, treated as second-class members.
- From the point of view of LGBTQ people of faith, the exclusion is based on living out one's unchangeable identity, of being and acting who one was created to be by God. Exclusion and judgment hardly embody the ideals of a Christian sacramental theology.

These reflections and questions bring me to the last and perhaps most important consideration in regard to the pastoral function of reconciliation with LGBTQ people.

## "In the Meantime..."

What you actually do in situations when you don't know what to do, and when the consulting of laws, customs, and precedents does not help, is often referred to as the "pastoral solution." It always favors the person over the rules. A pastoral solution emphasizes God's loving kindness, not cut-and-dried regulations and laws.

Sometimes reconciliation seems quite impossible between LGBTQ people and the faith community. The differences are too clear and too strongly held to give way to compromise and reconciliation. What's the solution when there seems to be none? When both parties are left in the pain of isolation, frustration, and probable defeat? The experience of Steven Greenberg, a gay rabbi, serves well as a response.

As he came out of the closet as a "gay Orthodox Jewish rabbi," these are some of the comments Rabbi Greenberg received from other representatives of his faith: "You're an absurdity . . . an oxymoron, a dangerous perversion of truth." "Change is possible and homosexual desire is a test. God has given us a spiritual challenge to struggle with same sex desire and defeat it with abstinence." Your choice is to choose your faith or "be gay and leave the community."[16]

These are the kinds of comments many of us hear when we take our pain to our communities of faith and they surely represent a reconciliation impasse. Or do they?

I cite the example of Steven Greenberg and his supporters because of their refusal to make an either/or choice but perpetually to move toward what seems to be an impossible reconciliation of faith and same sex love. After years of struggle, pain, and ongoing doubt and conflict, Rabbi Greenberg is a living example of reconciling the seemingly irreconcilable simply by not giving up, by not ending the process, by becoming comfortable with doubt. As Greenberg says, "There is great hope in a tradition that loves good questions even more than good answers, a tradition that teaches that God listens to the deliberation of the sages in order to know"[17] the Jewish law.

Rabbi Greenberg simply *is*. His existence is a powerful statement; his presence a constant symbol of trust.

And there is no refuting that! Just how will it all work out? Well, paraphrasing the words of one of his supporters, "We'll just have to see what God wants us to do about this. Sooner or later we'll know; in the meantime we do what we can."[18]

16. Greenberg, *Wrestling*, 12.

17. Greenberg, *Wrestling*, 23.

18. This is a paraphrase (my wording) of Daniel Boyarin, Professor of Talmudic Culture at the University of California, Berkeley, during his public response to a

Here is an example of "reconciliation-in-waiting," or "refusal to give up," or "perpetually ongoing reconciliation." Here's an example of a "pastoral solution." Nothing has been definitely resolved but—and this is an important point of pastoral care of LGBTQ people—nothing has been ended, no one has been abandoned; the process is ongoing, forever, if necessary.

It's not perfect. There are probably still many who reject Steven Greenberg. It's an open-ended, ongoing, faith-based reality that he, his partner, and their supporters live daily.

## NURTURING

Clinebell notes that nurturing has always "been a persistent motif in the history of the church" and defines it as enabling "people to develop their God-given potentialities throughout the journey of life with all its valleys, peaks, and plateaus."[19] In some times and places it is referred to as sanctification, the process of becoming holy/whole.

I see the most important application of the function of nurturing to queer people in its systemic sense; that is, in helping to create structures and systems that deal with LBGTQ people justly, fairly, and with acceptance and affirmation. In other words, seek opportunities to nurture systems. The previously mentioned case of Leonard, the retired pastor, influencing the retirement care system is a good example of this function. Here's another:

### Nurturing Exposition

Claire, white and German born, is the pastor of a progressive suburban parish of an eastern city. She is lesbian and lives with her partner in the parish-owned parsonage. Allen, one of their close friends and a member of the church, is bisexual and out. Through her friendship with Allen, Claire has learned much about being bisexual. Over the period of a year and in various ways—preaching, mentioning it in conversation, writing about it in the church bulletin, reading up on current books on

---

lecture by Rabbi Greenberg sponsored by The Center for LGBTQ and Gender Studies in Religion (CLGS) at Pacific School of Religion in Berkeley, California, on April 12, 2005.

19. Clinebell, *Basic Types*, 42.

the subject—Claire has brought bisexuality into the consciousness of her church community. As a result, both she and her partner and their bisexual friend have noticed a heightened and more enlightened awareness of the subject.

Thus, through a nurturing exposure of the reality of being bisexual, the system—in this case the church community—can become more understanding, more conversant, and thus more accepting of bisexuality.

## Human and Faith Development

There is an important application of the nurturing function to LGBTQ people on a more individual level as well. It deals with the characteristic way that we tend to develop as human beings. Or don't. Developmental patterns, both in faith and society, are not clear-cut, of course; but while some non-LGBTQ people may have developmental gaps, many LGBTQ people do, and it tends to be the same one: we characteristically get stuck around the stage of securing our identity and moving on to intimacy.

LGBTQ people follow the familiar stages described by Erikson and others,[20] sometimes with one exception: when it comes time to advance to the stage of maturity that resolves the conflicts around social development (the Eriksonian adolescent stage), some LGBTQ people get stuck because there seems to be nowhere to go.

The reason for this developmental fixation is that the intimacy we naturally seek is not allowed by the systems that have the strongest influence on us: family, community of faith, and school. Normally this occurs in teenage years and thus most are not sufficiently independent or self-reliant to go against the systems. So we stop developing in that area and often find a substitute area on which to concentrate. Unfortunately, the substitutes are not always the healthiest.

As a pastoral caregiver, please take this stoppage into consideration with your LGBTQ people. Taking care not to be invasive, notice, for example, when a member of your congregation seems to be overly absorbed in an isolating activity or sinks too deeply into work/school to the exclusion of all else. Both behaviors might attract pastoral care notice to the area of problematic development.

---

20. See Erikson, notably *Childhood and Society*; also Levinson, *Seasons*; Fowler, *Stages of Faith*; and Green, *Psychological Development*.

Parallel to stages of social development are stages of faith development. Frequently there are parallel stoppages. In terms of Fowler's schema the LGBTQ person can get stuck between Stage Three, Synthetic-Conventional Faith, and Stage Four, Individuative-Reflective Faith.[21] The gap is possibly a result of leaving childhood communities of faith as an adolescent (when coming out, for example) and never benefitting from adult spiritual formation because of trans/homophobia on the part of faith communities.[22]

If there is enough compartmentalization going on with the individual (that is, they can keep the different aspects of their lives separate from each other; in a sense, they lead a "double life"), it is possible to skip a stage and continue through the progression of the faith stages.

But in order to do this, the person must clearly isolate these two areas of life: development in social intimacy and development in faith. There are many adult religious people who have done just that. Of course, it is not the ideal; it can result in an immature faith and awkward social skills.

It is important to note that women and people of color were generally not included in the development of these theories of human development and thus their usefulness and general application is limited (see Shelia Green's *The Psychological Development of Girls and Women*). I present the forgoing discussion primarily so that pastoral caregivers can become aware of the developmental process, recognize when it possibly becomes problematic in a member of the congregation, and thus become a supportive, nurturing presence in the process.

On a positive note, even if one misses a stage in development, one can generally go back and catch up, so to speak. It's not the same, but it can work. A forty-year-old going through some of the squirrelly processes of adolescence and learning intimacy is often not an easy challenge. The support of a nurturing pastoral caregiver and a supportive community, and, of course, a good sense of humor, are big helps.

---

21. Fowler, *Stages of Faith*, 151–84.
22. I am grateful to Justin Sabia-Tanis for this observation.

> **PASTORAL PERSPECTIVES**
>
> Pastoral Interventions for Nurturing in the Developmental Gap
>
> - Cultivate the practice of noticing the lives of your people from a developmental point of view.
> - Recognize in them the presence of delayed development, perhaps helping them recognize and accept it (and thus be able to do something about it).
> - Refer them to a pastoral counselor or other therapist, when appropriate, to more efficiently and quickly resolve developmental issues.
> - Patience and understanding are the needed virtues here.

## Noticing

The function of nurturing calls forth an important trait of good pastoral caregiving: noticing. So many of our human pleas for help go unnoticed by those around us. The caregiver who notices these signs—the tone of voice, the drooping shoulders, what people don't say, the look in their eyes, the subject of conversation, the attitude of mind—is the caregiver who is in a position to nurture. Noticing means that you are aware of what is going on between the lines in your people's lives. It is frequently this space that holds the most important meanings.

## PROPHETIC PASTORAL CARE

Here is where psychosystemic pastoral care (see chapter 1) and prophetic/ecological awareness come together. As in the psychosystems part of chapter 1, here too I am indebted to the work of Graham and Clinebell.[23]

For the most part, the pastoral caring tradition that we have inherited has been what Graham terms the "existentialist-anthropological model of care."[24] That is, it focuses on individuals, their problems, and

---

23. Graham, "Prophetic"; Clinebell, *Ecotherapy*.
24. Graham, *Care of Persons*, 14.

their ultimate happiness within a context of self-realization. This type of pastoral care, which has achieved a tremendous amount of good, assumes a certain distance or disconnectedness between the person and the larger realities of the world and its cultures. Also, "in spite of many positive outcomes, the pastoral caretaking enterprise has become increasingly isolated from many of its communal and religious roots, and from the formative experience of the oppressed in our culture—especially women, non-whites, and gay persons."[25]

Prophetic pastoral care is thus more communal than individualistic and primarily based on the fact that we all live and move and have our being within a wide variety of systems that are continually influencing us, and upon the lived experiences and values of oppressed groups in our culture. The ultimate system that we must care for, of course, is the earth, our home.

The joining of these bases with two characteristics from the ancient prophetic tradition of Israel give us the foundation for prophetic pastoral caring. From the prophets: "First . . . they provide a critique of what is currently dominant. Second, they offer a direction toward health, salvation, shalom, justice and fulfillment."[26] In other words, the prophets were always talking about the hottest topics of the day and, despite many differences in style and circumstances, they called the people to work for the "welfare of the nations and of the created order."[27]

Bringing the elements together we can say that prophetic pastoral care is:

- Speaking out in justice and compassion, in one way or another . . .
- to the people and systems of our communities and of our world . . .
- for the healing of the people, especially the oppressed, and the right relationship of all on earth with each other and with God.

Prophetic pastoral care has deep roots in process theology, liberation theology, feminist theology, ecology[28] (and ecotherapy[29]), family systems theory (psychology), and certain aspects of personality theory.

---

25. Graham, "Prophetic," 50.
26. Graham, "Prophetic," 50.
27. Graham, "Prophetic," 50.
28. Graham, "Prophetic," 52.
29. See Clinebell, *Ecotherapy*.

This is not to say that prophetic pastoral care is anything new to contemporary eras. People like Albert Schweitzer, Dorothy Day, Martin Luther King, Jr., Mother Teresa of Calcutta, Mahatma Gandhi, and others long before and after them have raised prophetic voices from within the religious world; and not only on the world stage have these voices cried out. Often we have to look no further than the church or synagogue around the corner to find strong prophets raising their voices in righteous anger toward the injustices of the world's blindly accepted systems. Often, too, those prophetic voices emanate from unexpected places, like PFLAG; what a wonderful example for all churches this world-wide organization gives for loving and affirming our children, not rejecting them; and GLSEN, which "strives to assure that each member of every school community is valued and respected regardless of sexual orientation or gender identity/expression."[30] For those with ears to hear, prophetic pastoral voices can be heard all the time and anywhere.

The need for specific application of prophetic care to LGBTQ people is clear, especially since the queer experience is central to its development. One can easily make a case for LGBTQ people needing all the help possible in trying to deal with the systems of the world. For example, the relationship of LGBTQ people to the military, to all levels of government, to educational institutions, and especially to all religious institutions, offers fertile ground for the contemporary prophet.

### Imagination

I end this section on the prophetic dimension of pastoral care with the issue of the human imagination, a sure sign of the effective prophet, and as a reminder that no one can come out of the closet as queer, embrace their own identity, or proclaim it to their world unless they are first able to imagine themselves doing and being all those things; the imagining must precede the reality of the actual procedure.

Thus, your prophetic pastoral care has a more specific application as well. Your interventions with LGBTQ people who are solidly closeted and suffering from it might be along the lines of, "What would it be like if . . . ?" "Can you imagine yourself . . . ?" "How might that happen . . . ?" or "What might prohibit its happening . . . ?" Develop ways to encourage their imagining themselves out and free. So often one hears from queer

---

30. See PFLAG (www.pflag.org) and GLSEN (www.glsen.org).

people of all varieties and ages, "I can't even imagine being out to my father (mother, family, etc.). It's totally impossible. It's not even thinkable." These remarks indicate the depth and power of the locks on some closet doors. Freedom from the closet must begin in the imagination of the person. If you cannot imagine it, you probably cannot achieve it.

## PASTORAL CARE WITH PEOPLE OF COLOR

The first idea to note here is that this entire work, in all of its chapters and parts, includes *all* LGBTQ people as both caregivers and recipients of pastoral care, whether members of a specific minority or not. It excludes no one. However, there seem to be enough particularities to being a member of a minority in our North American culture to warrant, in addition, some specific treatment.

The plan in this section is first to identify several key issues that I believe are common to LGBTQ members of minority groups, then to name some specific characteristics in the areas of religion and tradition, and, lastly, to present general guidelines and a few insights for the pastoral caregiver. For more references, see "People/Communities of Color" in the Resources list; these originate, for the most part, with LGBTQ members of the specific minority.

I use the word "minority" here to mean what I believe is still the general meaning that many North American people give it: a part of a population, frequently smaller in numbers from the majority, who identify with a particular national or racial culture or identity (both of which can include a religious dimension) and are often subjected to unfair and prejudiced treatment. These demographics change rapidly. It is also useful to note that at this point in our national history, the words "majority" and "minority," when referring to cultural groupings, are fast becoming obsolete. Thus, please keep in mind that, although I use the terms because of a lack of any better terminology, I also acknowledge that they might not always be exactly accurate.

### Key Issues

I believe that the key challenging issues for LGBTQ members of minority communities are the same ones as for the majority culture, but to differing degrees of strength and emphasis. Thus, I would identify religion, tradition, work, family, and peer pressure as the key social issues at play here; and shame and fear as the key personal issues. I believe these are always the ultimate sources of our pain, LGBTQ or not, minority or not, because they are the primary sources of meaning in human life. Although these same sources of pain can serve as sources of ecstasy as well, it's the pain I am concerned with here.

## Religion and Tradition

Ethnic church communities have generally been much more than simply religious organizations. In many instances the church also serves the educational and leadership needs of the community and is the place where people learn their traditions and values. Because LGBTQ people grow up in those churches, they often also take on their homophobic assumptions.

"I Don't Mean to Offend, but I Won't Pretend" is the title of a perceptive essay by D. Mark Wilson.[31] In it he presents and examines the challenges for African American gay men in a specific church community in keeping the balance between the love, respect, *and* full participation in their church family (the "I-don't-mean-to-offend" part), while at the same time acknowledging their pride in being gay and all that it implies in their lives (the "but-I-won't-pretend" part). His essay offers helpful insight for pastoral caregivers into the delicate balance that many minority LGBTQ people are forced to maintain to ensure a life of equanimity.

A value for the African American is the validation of the individual by others, especially by the family, broadly understood. African American people also tend to be, as an ethnic grouping, more holistic than dualistic, self-knowledge being revealed through symbol and interpersonal relationships that are harmonious. Oral traditions are an important source of wisdom, humor, and insight.[32]

The church is central also to the Latinx experience. According to a CARA/Georgetown study, "There are approximately 30.4 million people in the United States who self-identify their religion as Catholic and their ethnicity as Hispanic or Latino/a. Some 16.4 million are native-born (54%) and 14.0 million are foreign-born (46%). Fifty-seven percent of

---

31. Wilson, "'Don't Mean to Offend.'"
32. Lee, *Introduction*. 78–79.

adult Hispanics self-identify as Catholic."[33] Most of the others are members of Protestant denominations and some fewer follow other religious groups. So the vast majority of Latinx people are influenced by a church. Latinx LGBTQ people have a rough road to travel since almost all of their church affiliations will teach them that living openly as an LGBTQ person is sinful, excludes you from family, and jeopardizes your eternal soul. Rejection by one's family is especially debilitating to LGBTQ Latinx people because of the key importance of the family relationship to the identity of the individual and its general place of honor and reverence in the culture.

Especially for members of Latinx communities, loyalty to the family is highly valued. *Compadres* is a significant category and often include close friends, god-parents, and others by choice. They are often considered to be as close and important as family. Probably through the historic influence of the Catholic Church, Latinx people have a strong sense of the direct connection between the events of life and the power of God, which may appear at times as fatalism.[34]

Many Asian North Americans (the Asian minority identity often includes Filipinos and Pacific Islanders) are influenced by the values and teachings of Confucianism, Buddhism, and Taoism, as well as Christianity. Thus, values that are common in many Asian cultures are harmony, emotional restraint, and indirect communication, the last being a trait different from the more blunt and direct style of Western discourse and something that effective pastoral caregivers need be especially aware. Tao spirituality, for example, emphasizes the balance of yin and yang, the female and male, the dark and the light, the passive and the active.[35]

For Asian Americans, the needs of the group often take precedence over the needs of the individual and thus their religious identity or affiliation will tend to be favored and followed, even at times when it might be in the person's benefit that it not be favored.[36] The Confucian ideal of filial respect and obedience to authority is strong in many. Some LGBTQ Asian North Americans also may remain in the closet within their ethnic community while being very open and out in all of the other parts of their lives. The power of the possible stigmatization by rejection can be

33. See CARA, "Fact Sheet."
34. Lee, *Introduction*, 92.
35. Lee, *Introduction*, 102, 108.
36. Lee, *Introduction*, 104.

strong, especially with parents of LGBTQ persons. Some parents—and this would seem to apply to *all* parents—may well know about an LGBTQ identity in their child but expect it never to be named explicitly. This of course sets up a different kind of pressure and stress in the LGBTQ child, but no less strong.

In many Native American tribes in the United States and in many First Nation communities of Canada, general acceptance of homosexual behavior may or may not be somewhat more historically accepted than in most other cultural identities. Thus, members of this ethnic minority who are aware of this tradition may have fewer inhibitions to live an LGBTQ life. The Two-Spirit tradition would seem to be an affirming LGBTQ identity among North and South American ethnic minorities. Traditionally referred to as berdaches, some among the First Nations and Native Americans reject the term because of negative and non-native associations. The Berdache[37] is a person who is born male but lives and is often raised female in all roles, even as a sexual partner to the men of the community. In some Indian nations, but not in all, this practice has been accepted as normal and useful to the community. A more acceptable term currently among North American native people is the term "Two Spirit," a term originating in 1990 but generally believed to be based on ancient traditions.[38]

However, many American (North and South) natives have been deeply influenced by European-based religion and culture and thus many of the traditions have been largely lost for decades. Recently, the Two Spirit tradition has had a resurgence of popularity. There are historical native terms for Two Spirit individuals in several Native American and First Nations languages.[39]

Frequently, ethnic minority cultures will have a different interpretation of gender roles than those operative in the dominant white culture. For example, the stereotypes of *machismo* within Latinx cultures, and of studiousness among Asians, even though they are stereotypes (which means that they are frequently inaccurate), still hold sway to a degree in both the minority and majority cultures. With Asian Americans, relationships are often defined by roles and thus these care receivers may be

---

37. Williams, *Spirit and the Flesh*;. Lee, *Introduction*, 149.
38. See Pullin, "Two Spirit"; and Jacobs, Thomas, and Lang, *Two-Spirit People*.
39. Jacobs, Thomas, and Lang, *Two-Spirit People*.

more comfortable placing the pastoral caregiver in a role of authority and be reticent to express a differing opinion or to correct.[40]

These cultural traits, however, can be almost completely lost within one generation. Careful evaluation and steering clear of any stereotypical assumptions will help you avoid harmful and sometimes insulting attitudes that can mortally damage the pastoral relationship.

In your pastoral care relationships with any group of people, ethnic minority or ethnic majority, I believe you will find that they will respond more enthusiastically and cooperatively the more personal and individual—and the less bureaucratic and formal—your approach.

---

**PASTORAL PERSPECTIVES**

Guidelines for Pastoral Caregivers to LGBTQ Members of Ethnic Minorities

- If you are from the majority culture and your care receiver is from a minority;
- Or, if you are from a different minority from your care receiver;
- Or, if you are from a minority and your care receiver is from the majority culture:
  - Never pretend to "understand" someone's experience within any culture that is not yours. Assuming the "attitude of a beginner" is an asset.
  - Always defer to the care seeker's lived experience and understanding of his or her cultural beliefs and customs.
  - Ask the care receiver for any important information about cultural assumptions, etc. that you feel you need to know. There is little wrong with not knowing. There can be much wrong with guessing.
  - Consult with professional colleagues of the particular minority in question. Use resources (books, articles, videos, etc.) created by members of the minority group in question.

---

40. Lee, *Introduction*, 93, 108–11.

- On the one hand, try not to underestimate the power and influence and difference of the minority experience. On the other hand, it would be irresponsible to play naïve when it comes to being aware of obvious cultural differences.
- Be very careful of cultural stereotyping. It can be a strong temptation because of the oversimplifications and typecasting of popular culture, but it is very often wrong and offensive, and rarely or never helpful.

## Double Stress

All LGBTQ persons who are part of an ethnic minority are doubly challenged. For the pastoral caregiver, it is urgently important to understand the force of this double stress. There is the stress that comes from being a member of the queer community and there is the stress that comes to one as a member of a minority.

Both of these pervasive life realities can produce unrelenting stress. The double becomes triple and beyond when you consider the identity groups to which these individuals have to relate: the dominant culture, their minority culture, and the LGBTQ cultures within both.

However, it is fundamentally important to understand that simply being queer and being a member of an ethnic minority are *not inherently stressful states in themselves*. The stress-related problems that people of color and LGBTQ people have to face are the direct result of the racism, heterosexism, homophobia, and transphobia that exist in the culture, *not* with color of skin, sexual orientation, or gender identity. This might seem a subtle or even an obvious point, but one that is often missed.

This crushing degree of stress often hits the person at adolescence and early adulthood, a most vulnerable time of life even if there are no additional stresses. Jason is an excellent example.

Jason was a young black man, about twenty-four, of gentle disposition and easy smile, college educated, who had just arrived in town from Chicago when he came to the church to register. At first shy, he only slowly and guardedly became part of the church community. As I got to know him, I learned the following things (among others of course) about Jason: He was gay, closeted (especially to his family in Chicago), had an "on-and-off" boyfriend twice his age and both of them kept each other hidden from their day-to-day lives, was unemployed and looking for work, was literally terrified of contracting the HIV virus, was brought up in a strict Catholic family but disillusioned with his church, was socially isolated outside of a limited "gay scene" in the city and formal contact with the church community, the members of which were mostly white and older, and when we would talk, he was often in tears from loneliness. Talk about stress. As the caregiver, all I could think about with Jason is *how can anyone, especially so young, bear such pressures?*

From a pastoral caregiver, Jason—or anyone in his situation—needed first and foremost an abiding and involved presence and accessibility, help in integrating the various elements of his life, encouragement, affirmation, and especially insight into arriving at a vibrant, fulfilling faith life within a community to which he can be known and valued for all he is. The affirming and caring presence and accessibility of the caregiver is the essential expression and incarnation of faith; it is the creating of the healing pastoral relationship that participates in divine grace.

If you are a caregiver from the cultural majority, please do not underestimate the power of ethnic identity on the LGBTQ person. This is, of course, no different than the power of ethnic identity on people of the majority. But simply because the majority is the majority, its members can often miss their common ties with all identities. This influence can be overwhelmingly powerful and reach to the very core of a person's identity, even to the point of allowing the individual to be and do things they would never be or do under normal circumstances. Examples often have to do with hiding and covering: a normally honest young man will lie about his sexual orientation; a grandmother will refer to her granddaughter's female partner as a husband when she talks about her; in conversation, a bisexual woman will deliberately omit reference to anything in her life that has to do with same-sex relationships; the brother of a transsexual woman will speak only in the most vague terms about her and avoid pronouns; a middle-aged man who regularly has sex with men would not even think of identifying as gay. All of these subterfuges, and many more, exemplify the basic problem: double lives.

On the other hand, be sure you do not overlook or blind yourself to the positive influences from the ethnic community. Often among them: a strong sense of identity, of belonging, of family; a pride of ethnic origin; customs, rituals, and celebrations that create community. These traits can be called on to support pastoral ministry by acknowledgement and affirmation.

## Inter- and Intra-Ethnic Issues

Just as there are issues and disagreements within the LGBTQ family of diversities, so are there differences within and among minorities. Pastoral theologian Archie Smith tells of attending a conference on embracing diversity. It was an "impressive" conference, he reports, but "we failed . . . as pastoral care providers to cross racial boundaries and address the painful issues of interethnic conflicts and violence. . . . None of us addressed the inter- and intra-ethnic pastoral care issues of gay, lesbian, transgendered, and questioning persons in our communities."[41] Ethnic identities clearly have rich traditions of building communities but many of them have been lost over time. Smith calls for the "recovery of certain traditions of subjugated knowledge (such as practicing non-violence, enacting justice, and showing unconditional respect for persons)."[42]

As a pastoral care provider, you have an opportunity to develop that sensitivity to the subtle signs of lost traditions within the ethnic groupings of your faith community and encourage their development and contemporary expression.

## Pastoral Care

Human caring in any form is a potent agent for growth, harmony, and peace. It not only says *I care about you*, it lives it out in practice, puts its money where its mouth is. *Pastoral* human caring, that is care springing from the bottomless well of faith, embodied with the most noble values and abundant generosity of faith, and practiced with love and humility within the context of faith, adds not only a new dimension of care, but the immense and mysterious, the gentle and transforming, the glorious and powerful dimension of grace.

Grace, of course, knows no limits and is a strong and wild energy. Thus, there's no telling the wonders it might achieve. Your pastoral healing, sustaining, guiding, reconciling, nurturing, and prophesying with God's LGBTQ children participates in that force, whether it's to the

---

41. Smith and Riedel-Pfaefflin, *Siblings By Choice*, 29.
42. Smith and Riedel-Pfaefflin, *Siblings By Choice*, 93.

communities of the world or to the community gathering this evening—and waiting for you—in your basement hall.

## Double Lives

This is a reality that *all* LGBTQ people know something about, not just minorities. Probably most of us, especially those who are older, have spent time keeping our gay lives separated from the rest of our lives. Because it is not so much separation as hiding, this process, by its very nature, produces shame. Of course, the ultimate goal when dealing with a double life is to evolve both parts into a single, integrated life.

Living "on the down low" is a popularized expression of this double life. Brought to public attention by J. L. King's book, *On the Down Low*,[43] being on the DL is when a man maintains a relationship with a wife/girlfriend/significant other while also maintaining a separate and hidden life that includes sexual/loving relationships with another man or men. The down low is a long way from being an exclusive characteristic of any ethnic minority. The current awareness of it, however, has been heightened by King's book, which explores the reality within the African American community.[44]

Insightful pastoral caregivers will see all of these subterfuges as variations on a single theme of the double-bind: a result of what seems to be an irresolvable conflict; an expression of an impossible-to-open closet door; a way to cope when there seems to be no other way; a resistance to choose when the choice is between family, friends, and cultural identity on the one hand, and an honest expression of who I am on the other. In other words, "Damned if you do—damned if you don't."

Ending this chapter on the functions of pastoral care on a messy, difficult-to-solve, and challenging situation is perhaps as it should be. It is a good reminder that effective pastoral care is more often a creative art than a cut-and-dried application of stored wisdom. To conclude and review, below is a checklist for caregivers.

---

43. King and Hunter, *On the Down Low*.
44. See also King and Carreras, *Coming Up*; and Boykin, *Beyond the Down Low*.

## A CHECKLIST FOR PASTORAL CAREGIVERS TO LGBTQ PEOPLE

1. *Examine Your Own Assumptions*
   - Be aware that being L, G, B, T, or Q may not be the problem that brings the person to seek pastoral care and normally is not a "problem" at all.
   - Be aware that religion may be the problem.
   - Be aware that your care receivers may not wish to explore their sexual or gender identity.
   - Be aware that, because of social pressure and fear, sometimes LGBTQ people avoid identifying themselves as LGBTQ or sharing that information with you.
   - Be aware that a person concerned about same-sex attraction may not be lesbian, gay, or bisexual.
   - Be aware that the meaning your care receiver assigns to words might have different meaning for you.
   - Be aware that roles in LGBTQ relationships may or may not run along the same lines as heterosexual relationships.
   - Be aware that bisexuals are just that and not merely or always going through a stage, a phase, or a transition to being gay.
   - Be aware that someone who is married to a person of another gender may be lesbian, gay, bisexual, or transgender.
   - Be aware that getting married to an opposite sex person is never a "solution" or a "cure" for homosexuality.
   - Be aware that children are in no more danger of suffering sexual abuse from LGBTQ people than they are from heterosexual people—and, in fact, possibly less.
   - Assume nothing about lesbian, gay, bisexual, or transgender behavior.
   - Be aware that care receivers may expect you (as a religious person) to be homophobic or transphobic and may be looking for signs to confirm this.

## The Functions of Pastoral Care

- Be aware that a transgender person, both male-to-female and female-to-male, may be gay, lesbian, bisexual, or straight, and thus there is an overlap of experience. Be aware that most transgender people hold that being transgender is innate, just as being gay is; one does not "become" transgender.

2. *Be Informed*

- Be informed about help lines, books, web pages, films, videos, pastoral and other counselors, etc.
- Be informed about the teachings and practices of the various religious denominations with regard to LGBTQ issues.
- Be informed about religious resources for LGBTQ people (see Resources list).
- Be informed in general; consider if there are aspects of any sexual minority about which you need to learn more, and do so.
- Be both informed and cautious in regard to the terms you use, especially in regard to terms referring to transgenderism and transsexuality. These terms can change in popular use and are sometimes used differently by different people.

3. *Be Self-Aware*

- Monitor your own attitudes and responses, regardless of your own gender identity and sexual orientation.
- Be aware of your reaction to having a pastoral care relationship with LGBTQ men and women and that there may be different dynamics from what you expect.
- Be clear about the limitations of what you can offer.
- Be clear on ways to quickly identify and contact possible referrals.
- Be clear about your own feelings toward your care receiver.
- Be clear on all the boundary issues in your pastoral care relationship.

4. *Respect*

- Respect your care receiver's orientation, identity, personal integrity, and cultural assumptions.

- Respect your care receiver's relationship by not asking inappropriate and non-applicable questions such as, *Who's the "man" and who's the "woman" in your relationship?*

- Respect your transgender care receiver by not asking inappropriate medical questions pertaining to possible surgery, possible physical changes or characteristics, etc.

- Respect and acknowledge the pain of those who struggle with their sexual orientation and/or gender identity when it conflicts with their religion or belief system.

- Respect and acknowledge the capabilities of your care receivers.

- Remember the possibility of a "pastoral solution"—don't close the door.

# 3

## Pastoral Care in the Tough Times
### An LGBTQ Perspective

### David Kundtz

Though LGBTQ people contribute an immense and diverse richness of gifts to the world and to communities of faith, though they commonly carry the gifts of joy and happiness, and frequently bear an active and fulsome faith, here I want to consider the painful and difficult things that they can also carry: shame, anger, fear, isolation, and all the stressful challenges that life presents. During these tough times, queer people will often turn to you and expect to be held in responsible, knowledgeable, and helpful hands.[1]

### SHAME

Perhaps the most common negative burden that LGBTQ people carry is shame. It is, of course, a common human burden, but for queer persons it is also a bestowed burden, one given by the cultures in which they have been raised and nurtured. Shame often comes with the territory of LGBTQ lives and for many the struggle to overcome it is lifelong.

1. With a nod to O'Brien's metaphor in his post-Vietnam novel, *The Things They Carried*.

Some years ago I read a potent description of shame: shame does not come when you understand that "I made a mistake"; shame settles in when you believe that "I am a mistake." Something essential is wrong with me, is the message that creeps into the young LGBTQ soul; it is something that they might not be able to change, perhaps ever. The effects remain even when shame is conquered and left far behind. By truly understanding this, you will be a more effective caregiver.

If you recognize some serious signs of shame in your care receiver, your calling attention to the burden of shame might help. Choose your time and place carefully and perhaps bring up the topic in the context of the shame to which all oppressed people, including LGBTQ people, fall heir. Calling shame by its name and perhaps recommending some reading can go a long way to achieve healing. Shame and internalized homophobia are closely related, the latter being an expression of the former. Carrying the feelings of hurt and anger are invariably companions of shame.[2]

As caregiver, your words and attitude can help heal and transform shame when its signs appear, for example, by reminding someone that "you are a well-beloved child of God; you are beautiful; your gifts are needed and appreciated; of course you're an integral part of this community, why wouldn't you be?"

Opportunities to offer these words are far from rare. Imagine: a lesbian member of your church who lives with her non-member partner, but is not out in any specific way at church, tells you, "Don't worry, Pastor, Alice won't be coming with me to the church picnic." How easy it is to say, "All right" or "Whatever you wish." But how healing are the words, "I wish Alice would come with you. Please bring her!" Of course, a whole set of realities must be in place within your congregation (as well as within your own heart) for you to be able to make such an invitation. The process has to start somewhere; why not here?

## ANGER

It would seem impossible for LGBTQ people *not* to feel some anger, given their status in many of the world's cultures: from being considered deserving of death, to being barely tolerated second-class citizens, or, in

---

2. Bradshaw, *Healing the Shame*.

limited locations, being simply tolerated.[3] In the United States, gay rights have taken great steps forward in recent years, even though there is still strong anti-gay sentiment in many parts of the country. In many other parts of the world, however, the picture is not so positive. At the time of this writing it is widely reported that the Russian territory of Chechnya is carrying out a brutal persecution of gay men, including kidnapping and torture.[4] Closer to home, currently there are the so-called the "bathroom bills" and "religious liberty" initiatives that would limit LGBTQ people's access to public accommodations and services. Religious people are on the forefront of pushing—and sometimes opposing—these laws/bills.

Combine that anger with the free-floating generic anger that many members of the populace feel today about their lives and the institutions that affect them, and you have a recipe for great anger. We all know it is important for well-developed adults to move beyond anger. For some this is a formidable task, especially overcoming anger at religion and religious institutions.

Here are two recommendations for you, the pastoral caregiver:

1. First, learn to recognize underlying anger. When anger is on the surface and expressed with little reserve, it is easier to identify and respond to. But when it is in hiding, it is more dangerous and difficult to identify both by the person involved and the observer. Underlying anger is anger indirectly expressed, for example, by passive-aggressive behavior, a surly attitude, intolerance, and inveighing against perceived enemies. Realize that giving up anger will feel like (and is) a loss. Something needs to take its place.[5]

2. Thus, secondly, once you have recognized the anger, try to find some way to help your care receiver to channel the anger, something to fill up the void left by anger. Channeling negative feelings into positive actions is the moral person's rule of life; it's what resourceful

---

3. In these countries homosexuality may be punished by death: Afghanistan, Iran, Mauritania, Nigeria, Qatar, Saudi Arabia, Somalia, Sudan, the United Arab Emirates, and Yemen, according to Bearak and Cameron, "Here Are the 10 Countries." For more information and current statistics on the punishment of homosexuality around the world, see OutRight Action International, www.outrightinternational.org.

4. Peter, "Chechen Police." For a more complete treatment of the issue see: Gessen, "Gay Men."

5. Passive-aggressive behavior can be described (non-clinically) as a pattern of negative attitudes and resistance in interpersonal or occupational situations along with non-acknowledgement of the behavior or even a claim of its opposite.

people do naturally, all the time. Ask yourself: toward what creative outlet can I encourage this care receiver to move their anger? Here is an opportunity for creative pastoral caring. Could they write to express their anger? Maybe letters to the editor, op-ed pieces, articles, or simply personal journaling? Is there some project of the congregation that needs a person of strong emotional energy to lead it? Will you help your angry care receivers to redirect their energies by joining an effort that is directed at righting the wrongs that anger them? Something as simple as classes in art, sewing, yoga, history, genealogy, and so forth, can act to channel the energy of anger. Be creative.

## FEAR

Many queer people are full of fear, some because of violence threatened or done to them personally or to people they know; all of us because we know violence to be an ever-present possibility. Gay-baiting, gay-bashing, gay-killing, and especially anti-transgender hate crimes of all sorts, including murder, happen all the time (see "Violence" below). Although most of the terms use the word "gay," the violence finds its victims in all the letters: L, G, B, T, and Q.

It is especially the young who carry the fear of rejection simply because of their youth and their age-appropriate fear that they cannot survive without the support, understanding, and acceptance of family and society. This is not paranoia but a reality-based fear, for, indeed, even at this advanced stage in the process of liberation, some parents, siblings, and friends still reject LGBTQ people when they come out. In particular, for anyone at any age, rejection based on a core identity can be devastating to one's sense of self, one's way of being in the world, and one's self confidence.

Effective pastoral caregivers will look for opportunities to stop possible rejection before it happens by undertaking sensitive intervention into family dynamics, by educating family members, by becoming advocates for LGBTQ people within the religious community, and by publicly expressing support, understanding, and appreciation of all members of the queer community.

## TEACH YOUR CONGREGATION

- Teach them the truths of LGBTQ experiences, after having researched them and learned for yourself, if necessary.
- Weave the experiences of your LGBTQ members into your preaching on such topics as justice, charity, and the universality of God's love.
- Provide for LGBTQ topics in your educational programs.
- Teach by including LGBTQ people in the liturgical, educational, administrative, and spiritual structures of the congregation.
- Make sure the youth programs include LGBTQ topics that teach understanding and full acceptance, and do not provide fertile ground for bullying.
- Teach about subtle, often non-physical forms of violence. Emotional violence (rage, degrading, shaming, denigrating, etc.) and spiritual violence (excluding from salvation, naming as sinner, keeping away from synagogue/church and religion, denying welcome, etc.) are probably more pervasive than the violence inflicted by fists and weapons.
- Finally, teach clearly: violence is never an appropriate response to people who are simply different.

For many caregivers, enlightened teaching will necessarily include an interpretation of your denomination's official teaching, which is often LGBTQ-negative. Such interpretation is commonplace and necessary. In addition to communities of faith that are officially LGBTQ-welcoming and affirming, I know of many specific congregations—Jewish, Lutheran, Presbyterian, Methodist, Catholic, among others—that create a safe, positive, and accepting welcome to LGBTQ members, notwithstanding queer-negative public stances or the official teachings of their denominations.

## ISOLATION

An understandable result of shame, anger, and fear is social isolation. Notice the member of the congregation who holds back, about whom no one knows very much, or who is always withdrawn. Train yourself to notice the most unnoticeable and find a way to care. (Chapter 5 explores in more detail how to create welcoming congregations.)

The first challenge for the pastoral caregiver is always to notice. Be on the lookout for shame, anger, fear, and isolation. Especially if you are not LGBTQ, it is understandably difficult to gear your sensitivity toward issues and attitudes that might not naturally come your way. You might try the Queer for a Day exercise below—or your own variation of it.

### "QUEER FOR A DAY": AN EXERCISE FOR NON-LGBTQ CAREGIVERS

1. Pick an average workday in your pastoral ministry and in your mind take on the identity of an L, G, B, or T person.

2. In every circumstance, from the moment you begin work in the morning to when you stop your work schedule at the end of the day, "become" that person in your own mind.

3. Assume that some are aware of your identity and some are not. If practical and appropriate (for example, with colleagues), tell them of your assumed identity.

4. Notice at every encounter with someone how your assumed identity affects what's happening to you and your sense of self.

5. Notice other effects on your life: how you might feel differently with different persons, during a meeting, in public, while alone.

6. How does this identity change your social life? Your spiritual/prayer life? Your emotional life?

7. Realize that what is role playing, "faking it" for you, is what some LGBTQ people have had to do, sometimes for a lifetime.

8. How might you integrate your experience into a Sunday homily or Sabbath teaching, or into an article for the congregational bulletin, or local publication?

You might have noticed something urgently important in all these negative things that we carry. The impetus for them originates outside of us; for the most part, we did not bring these burdens on ourselves.

One often hears about a so-called "gay agenda," a term that implies sinister machinations to overtake society and topple all moral values in the process. Such talk mostly comes from anti-gay sources. In fact, the only "agenda" the vast majority of LGBTQ people have is simply to be left alone and allowed to live their lives. Of course, LGBTQ people have as many internally generated problems as any other segment of the population; we carry those in addition to the ones handed to us at birth by the culture into which we are born. The LGBTQ community is not the only one to whom a negative birthday gift is given, however; life is stressful for each person in different ways.

## STRESS AND DISCRIMINATION

Stress is rightly a hot topic in the early twenty-first century with our stress soaring to levels not imagined in the relatively easy-going decades before and even following the Industrial Revolution.

For each person, stress is generated at a global level (by climate change, weather disasters, the unknowns of space exploration and cosmic events); at an international level (by wars, famines, politics, economics, terrorism); at a national level (by war, politics, party disagreements, deep social divisions over values and economic matters); at a local level (through politics, lack of affordable housing or jobs or adequate schools, disagreements with neighbors, keeping schedules); and at a personal level (because of work, money, racial discrimination, relationship challenges, and the normal give-and-take of family life).

(I am writing this just six months into a new presidential administration in the US, which is causing a great deal of stress for so many people in this country—and even throughout the world—for both those who object to the administration and those who support it.)

Is there a particular type of stress experienced by LGBTQ people? I think the only unique stress is the type generated simply by being LGBTQ in the world. The stress, of course, is not inherent to sexual orientation or gender identity as such, but rather is the result of the violence and intolerance of homophobic, heterosexist, and transphobic people toward queer people. But that stress is more than enough, especially when you consider that it is added to stress from all the other levels.

As a pastoral caregiver, be aware of the discrimination shown to LGBTQ people and their families by religious organizations and people and the discrimination evident in the areas of civil rights, employment, housing, and education.

In addition to the levels of stress we all carry around, many people are also affected by the groups or strata of society to which they belong, particularly if society holds their group in negative esteem. The term that researchers use for this phenomenon is "minority stress." Please don't underestimate or dismiss this reality. Recent research shows clearly its ongoing negative effects of the LGBTQ community.[6]

In North America, simply being a member of any of the following categories brings a degree of discrimination and stress. The more groups one belongs to, the more the stress. The categories are presented in no particular order and of course there are exceptions:

- Female
- Ethnic minority
- Foreign-born (some more than others)
- Single (non-married)
- Single (divorced)
- Single parent
- Non-English speaking
- Limited English speaking
- Having a foreign accent (some more than others)
- L,G,B,T, or Q minority
- Member of a minority religion
- Jobless/Unemployed
- Chronically ill
- Physically disabled
- Old
- Poor or homeless
- Addicted
- Mentally ill

---

6. For insight into loneliness among gay men today, see Hobbes, "Together Alone."

- Being overweight
- Victim of violence or crime
- Perpetrator of violence or crime

A quick perusal of the list reveals that there are many millions of people who belong to two or more of these categories. Indeed, the "person" (in the US) who remains is native born, white, male, married, mentally and physically healthy, of the majority/"acceptable" religion, straight, fully employed, financially stable, young or middle-age, clean living, and lucky. There are many in that group and reverse discrimination against them is by no means unheard of.

## Within LGBTQ Communities

Queer people have their own specific proclivities and challenges when it comes to prejudices and discriminations. Racial discrimination within the LGBTQ community has been justly noted and criticized in many places.[7] Misogyny and misandry exist not only in the straight world but in the queer world as well. Some people are "suspicious" or unaccepting of bisexuality, judging that it is merely (or always) a stage in coming out as gay or a way to semi-hide being gay. It seems that lesbian, bisexual, and gay people share a degree of the same prejudice and misunderstandings toward transgender people that the wider society shows. One also hears less than respectful terms glibly used about straight members of society. Like the broader society in which they exist, ageism and lookism are not hard to observe in LGBTQ communities.

Clearly, LGBTQ people are not without challenges when it comes to discrimination and prejudice. One might think that with people who have endured so much discrimination and prejudice these traits would be less prevalent. However, it is not untypical for oppressed groups to manifest bullying and a type of blindness to the group's own weaknesses. One hopes that the current communities within the larger LGBTQ

---

7. According to a recent survey by GMFA, a gay men's health charity in the UK, more than 7 in 10 black gay men experience racism in the LGBT community in Great Britain. All of the Arab men surveyed had experienced racism and believe that it is a problem. Among other ethnicities, 86 percent of South Asian gay men, 81 percent of South East and East Asian gay men, and 78 percent of gay men of mixed ethnicity said that they had experienced racism. By contrast, less than half (49%) of white gay men thought that racism was a problem. See Haggas, "Racism."

community are reaching a stage of development that accesses their own deeper wisdom and opens them to self-reflection and the wise and loving criticism of supportive others.

As a pastoral caregiver dealing with stress and discrimination:

- Consider stress reduction programs as ministry.
- Find ways to provide quiet, safe, and peaceful space, especially for members of the above categories.
- Find ways for people in these categories to find each other for mutual support, acceptance, and understanding.
- Some people operate both at staggering levels of stress and within numerous categories of stressfulness. Helping stressed people to recognize and identify those levels and categories can itself bring insight and welcome change.
- Often the most stressed ones among your people will have to be searched out.
- Teach by your example. The caregiver's self-care speaks louder than the caregiver's words.
- Don't hesitate to deal with the discrimination and prejudice you observe within the LGBTQ community. Encourage honest self-criticism and self-reflection, for these are signs that the "movement" has achieved a degree of maturity and is losing the shrillness of youth and inexperience.
- When dealing with anyone in regard to their prejudices, look first and steadily at your own.

## PHYSICAL ILLNESS: HIV/AIDS AND BEYOND

Much has happened in the field of HIV/AIDS between the publication of the first edition of this work in 2007, and the time of this writing, mid-2017. Viewed as a terminal disease just a decade ago, HIV/AIDS is now most often characterized as a chronic yet manageable disease that allows people to live normal or near-normal lives with normal or near-normal life spans. The reason for this improvement is the development of antiretroviral drug therapy.

However, many still face AIDS-related health and social issues that are frequently not acknowledged; one commentator has said that some people living with HIV/AIDS experience the same degree of PSTD (post-traumatic stress disorder) experienced by many returning from the Vietnam War.[8]

Here is a brief compendium of current information in regard to HIV/AIDS in the USA as of mid-2017:[9]

- Today there are more than 1.2 million people in the US living with HIV, the virus that causes AIDS, and one in eight of them don't know it.
- More than seven hundred thousand people living with AIDS have died since the beginning of the epidemic in 1981.
- From 2005 to 2014, the annual number of new HIV diagnoses declined 19 percent.
- HIV continues to have a disproportionate impact on certain populations. Gay and bisexual men, particularly young African American gay and bisexual men, are most affected and continue to be impacted at high rates.
- Antiretroviral therapy has substantially reduced AIDS-related morbidity and mortality and improved long-term outcomes for people with HIV. Treatment is advised as soon as one is diagnosed.
- The number of new HIV diagnoses in 2015: over 4,000; percentage of people infected with HIV who don't know it: 13 percent. As people are living longer with the disease, new infections continue to occur, and diagnoses surpass deaths each year.
- With possibly close to fifty thousand new HIV infections each year in the United States, and no cure or vaccine available, prevention is key.

Please note that this treatment does not provide exhaustive information for the pastoral caregiver who is dealing pastorally with congregation members living with HIV/AIDS; refer to the Resources list for more information or, better still, contact local agencies and professionals for further insight; this is a constantly developing field. It seems that the most up-to-date resources are online rather than in book form. One useful book,

---

8. Anderson-Minshall, "HIV Survivors."

9. For current statistics on HIV, see Centers for Disease Control and Prevention website (www.cdc.gov).

however, is *Voices in the Band: A Doctor, Her Patients, and How the Outlook on AIDS Care Changed from Doomed to Hopeful* by Dr. Susan Ball.[10] This book will give the reader a good overview of what the HIV/AIDS epidemic was like from about 1992 to 2015, and from a physician's point of view; the author is a very insightful, competent, and caring physician I might add.

It seems to me, at this point in the progression of the HIV/AIDS pandemic, the current focus of the caregiver will be on education, prevention, and ongoing support.

The pastoral caregiver who is prepared to minister to people living with HIV/AIDS should be aware of the following:

- In general, have a good knowledge of HIV/AIDS, its current status, future geographic and populace projections, and the most at-risk populations, especially if they fall within your pastoral purview.
- In regard to at-risk populations, one commentator notes: "As the disease has disappeared from the national consciousness, black gay and bisexual men are still contracting it at rates higher than those of any country in the world." It's "one of the most shameful public-health failures in the US today."[11]
- Know how the disease is transmitted, and how it is not.
- Understand the psychosocial issues facing people living with HIV/AIDS as it continues to transform from a death sentence disease to a manageable illness; also the psychological issues such as (in North America at least) being straight and having AIDS; finances; finding a system of support; religious stigma and relationship to religious community; and so on.
- Have a general knowledge of the current treatment protocols (antiretroviral drugs); be aware of PrEP (Pre-Exposure Prophylaxis), which is a preventative, anti-HIV medication intended to keep HIV-negative people from becoming infected. It is important to note that PrEP is not a vaccine and it is not a cure,[12] must be taken daily, within various parameters, and can be expensive (it costs about $1,300.00 per month without insurance).[13] The decision about whether or not

10. Ball, *Voices in the Band*.
11. Villarosa, "America's Hidden H.I.V. Epidemic," 38.
12. For more information on PrEP go to: https://www.cdc.gov/actagainstaids/basics/prep.html.
13. See Costa-Roberts, "8 Things You Didn't Know."

to use PrEP can weigh heavily on an individual; thus, your understanding and help in thinking it through can be especially helpful.

- Be aware of PEP, which stands for post-exposure prophylaxis. PEP may help prevent HIV infection after exposure to HIV. The following is from the website of the Centers for Disease Control: "PEP... means taking antiretroviral medicines (ART) after being potentially exposed to HIV to prevent becoming infected.... PEP must be started within 72 hours after a recent possible exposure to HIV, but the sooner you start PEP, the better. Every hour counts. If you're prescribed PEP, you'll need to take it once or twice daily for 28 days. PEP is effective in preventing HIV when administered correctly, but not 100%."[14]

### HIV/AIDS PASTORAL CARE—SOME GENERAL CONSIDERATIONS

- Don't assume anything about a care receiver's HIV status. This means, for example, not assuming that because he is a gay man he is HIV-positive, or because she is a straight woman, she isn't. Both are frequently not true.

- Assume a no-blame attitude and assume the reality-based attitude that illness is illness and there is no guilty illness or non-guilty illness. Notions of "lepers" and "pariahs" must be realities of the past.

- Be aware of the global reality of AIDS and that it is now especially a disease of the developing world in women, men, and children. AIDS in the US is identified as a "gay man's disease" (although not by any means exclusively) and men who have sex with men accounted for over 75 percent of new HIV cases in 2015.[A]

- Thus, it is extremely important to support the dissemination of information on prevention within at-risk communities. It is no secret that religious communities often do not deal well—if at all—with sex, which has caused many people to go underground with their sexual issues. Work to help all religious leaders deal with sexuality honestly and without fear.

---

14. For more information on PEP, see www.cdc.gov/hiv/basics/pep.html.

- Understand that there can still be a feeling of shame about seroconversion, especially among those "who should have known better." People really struggle with self-blame, which detracts from making healthy choices for early treatment.

- Grief, often unaddressed for years, about loss of previous partners and friends can last a long time and can have an ongoing impact on well-being in the present if the grief has been suppressed (maybe because the person was too busy as a caregiver at the time to attend to it).

- My final encouragement is to take care of yourself as a caregiver. Self-care involves getting enough sleep and rest, enough time off and away from work, support from colleagues, a relatively peaceful ambience in your ministering community, and whatever else you personally need to be an effective caregiver. Ministry to the ill and troubled is exhausting.

---

A. Statistics on HIV infection rates can be found at the Centers for Disease Control and Prevention website (www.cdc.gov).

With regard to pastoral care for LGBTQ people with other physical illnesses, much of what has been mentioned about care of people living with HIV/AIDS applies to non-AIDS-related illnesses as well. As of the time of this writing, there is a growing concern for the spread of the human papillomavirus (HPV). It is spreading among the population in general and the LGBTQ population specifically. The virus is spread by sexual contact and often "hides" from detection. There is a vaccine, but the use of it is somewhat controversial. Be sure to be fully informed before taking any action.[15]

In addition, work toward the following with all of your ill LGBTQ care receivers:

- Facilitate access to the ill person by spouses, partners, and family members, especially in hospitals and other care facilities. Religiously affiliated facilities may present particular challenges that you, as a pastoral caregiver, can help address.

---

15. For more information on HPV vaccines, see the website of Know HPV (www.hpv.com) and the website of the Centers for Disease Control and Prevention (www.cdc.gov). See also Sylvestre, "HPV."

- Arrange regular pastoral visits if the ill person desires.
- Seek out the ill among your LGBTQ members who might not be easily visible.
- Make an effort to understand some of the symptoms and characteristics of a person's illness. Your interest is likely to be appreciated and seen as caring.
- Be available to be the go-between with the ill person and their family, especially when there is estrangement between the LGBTQ person and the family, or divorce, or other common family challenges that create tension. Illness can often be a catalyst to healing family rifts.
- The chronically ill have special needs that can include but are not limited to: feelings of depression, discouragement, and frustration; the desire to make friends and be a part of a worshiping community; needs for transportation, for privacy, and appropriate surroundings for intimacy.
- Hospital chaplaincies and departments of pastoral care are almost always rich sources of enlightened and experienced pastoral care for the ill and their friends and families. Many chaplains today are nonjudgmental and comfortable dealing with LGBTQ people. Take full advantage of their services and expertise.[16]

## MENTAL ILLNESSES

Although one might think it unnecessary to state this well into the twenty-first century, I believe that it still is: being LGBTQ is *not* a mental illness, nor an emotional problem, nor an addiction, and never has been—despite having been commonly considered such for decades. The American Psychological Association (APA) removed homosexuality from the list of mental illness over forty years ago.[17] The placing of LGBTQ people in the categories of mental illness stems from an era when the ordering of such information, understandably for the times, fell within the purview

---

16. See the resources available from ACPE, The Association for Clinical Pastoral Education (www.acpe.edu), and CAPPE, The Canadian Association for Pastoral Practice and Education (www.spiritualcare.ca/).

17. See the website of Group for the Advancement of Psychiatry (www.ourgap.org); and Bellis and Hufford. *Science, Scripture*, 41–45.

of both medicine and religion. Today it is clear that there simply are no symptoms present in being LGBTQ that would indicate a diagnosis of a mental illness, an emotional problem, or an addiction.

In regard to transgender individuals, there has been a change in attitude in the psychological community. The most recent edition of the mental health manual used by psychiatrists and other mental health professionals to diagnose disorders, the *Diagnostic and Statistical Manual of Mental Disorders, Fifth Edition*, (DSM-5) shows a clear change in thinking on gender identity.

In the current edition, the now-replaced diagnosis of gender identity disorder (GID) has been given a new name: gender dysphoria, which also reflects a more accurate understanding.[18] This shift in attitude is recognition that the disagreement between birth gender and identity are not pathological if that disagreement does not cause the individual distress.

LGBTQ people are, of course, subject to all of the same mental illnesses and emotional challenges that all human beings are. Being LGBTQ, however, can add other layers of stress to those challenges and illnesses. Three disorders in particular, I believe, are important to look at when considering the challenges of any oppressed minority in the first quarter of the twenty-first century: depression, obsessive-compulsive disorder, and manic-depression.

## Depression

If you see signs of depression in your care receiver, don't hesitate to take action. First of all, recognize the signs of depression (see box below). If symptoms are present to a sufficient degree, supportively suggest that the client might be depressed and that help is available. Then encourage and help find appropriate professional counseling such as a pastoral counselor, family therapist, or physician. Be sure to see your care receiver through to an established relationship with an appropriate helping professional.

---

18. For more information on gender dysphoria symptoms, see Bressert, "Gender Dysphoria Symptoms."

> **SIGNS OF DEPRESSION TO WATCH FOR IN YOUR CARE RECEIVER**
>
> - Sad mood; irritability
> - Negative, distorted thinking
> - Feelings of worthlessness or hopelessness
> - Low self-esteem
> - Inappropriate feelings of guilt
> - Repeated thoughts of death or suicide
> - Loss of interest or pleasure in activities
> - Finding it difficult to concentrate
> - Agitation
> - Loss of energy, fatigue
> - Change in appetite, significant weight loss or gain
> - Change in sleeping patterns
> - Physical symptoms, including: headaches, muscle aches, stomach aches
>
> If several of these symptoms persist for more than two weeks, assist your care receiver in finding help. Especially with depression, getting help very often brings improvement.

Occasionally, queer folks are labeled depressed when they are actually frustrated, sad, mad, confused, afraid, grieving, and so on. It is often difficult to distinguish clinical depression from simply having too much on one's plate. And, after all, many of us get into a bit of a depressed mood from time to time. If in doubt, seek help. Counseling, and often drug therapy, can frequently help.

## Obsessive-Compulsive Disorder (OCD)[19]

OCD is in the category of anxiety disorders and seems to be the emotional challenge of our age. The obsessive part has to do with mental activity

19. Campbell, *Psychiatric Dictionary*, 493.

and consists of recurrent, intrusive, and unwanted thoughts, impulses, or images that cause significant anxiety. The compulsive part is the acting out and has to do with (often ritualized) behaviors that are intended to suppress the anxiety caused by obsessions. Common examples include constant hand-washing, repeatedly checking if an appliance is turned off, overly zealous and unnecessary cleaning, an endless repetition of religious rituals or prayers, harming one's self, and/or angry or revengeful thoughts that too strongly affect one's life. In some religious traditions, this condition has been referred to in the past as scrupulosity.

Just as many of us get a bit depressed from time to time, some too are sometimes a bit obsessive compulsive. They are the people who get a lot of things done. That's not the level of emotional challenge you need to be concerned about. It's when you notice that your care receiver's life is negatively influenced by extreme obsessions or compulsive behaviors, when they interrupt the normal functioning of life that professional help is in order.

## Bipolar Disorder[20]

Also known as manic depression, bipolar disorder is a cognitive disorder that causes unusual shifts in a person's mood, energy, and ability to function. It's different from the normal ups and downs that everyone goes through; the symptoms of bipolar disorder are more severe. The moods fluctuate between the two poles of high energy/excitement (manic) to low energy/depression (depressive). If you notice these symptoms in any of your care receivers, assist them in finding professional counseling.

## ADDICTIONS, DRUGS, AND SEX

LGBTQ people are as prone to addictions as any other segment of the population. Often the stress of heterosexism/homophobia and transphobia are the catalysts that propel them into the addiction. Addiction can be defined as an overpowering urge to use a substance or engage in a practice, regardless of its potential or actual harm. Almost anything can become an addiction, including religion. There is a large amount of

---

20. Campbell, *Psychiatric Dictionary*, 422.

literature on addictions, a condition we have come to understand much more thoroughly in the last twenty years or so.[21]

When you are dealing with people suffering addictions of any kind—alcohol, drugs, gambling, or whatever—the first priority of your pastoral care is normally to focus on the addiction itself and not, in most cases, the possibly unrelated issue that the care receiver may want to deal with. That can come later, unless it's an emergency. For example, it might mean getting them into a harm-reduction program that begins by encouraging the person to reduce—rather than immediately cease—using the drug and/or engaging in the addictive behavior in question.[22]

An example: an older woman in your congregation approaches you after the morning worship service to ask you about a theological issue that is confusing and upsetting to her, but you notice right away that she is intoxicated. The theological issue can wait. First, find a way to focus on the possible addiction and help her to find appropriate treatment. This can require a good deal of finesse as you are changing agendas on your care receiver and you are likely to encounter strong resistance.

## Drugs

The challenge here for the pastoral caregiver is to avoid naïveté, to learn to recognize signs of drug use, to know where to refer, and to have consistent follow-through with people who are often difficult to work with when misusing drugs.

Certainly a percentage of "recreational" drug users are LGBTQ. There is one category of drug use that still deserves special attention at this time in history and that is the use of crystal meth among gay men. Statistics attest to the ongoing crisis that the use of this recreational drug continues to be.[23] The scientific name of the drug is *methamphetamine hydrochloride* or what used to be called "speed." Other common street

---

21. Ringwald, *Soul of Recovery*; and Minor, *When Religion*.

22. According to the Harm Reduction Coalition, "Principles of Harm Reduction," some tenets of a harm-reduction approach to addiction include the following principles: that one "[a]ccepts, for better and or worse, that licit and illicit drug use is part of our world and chooses to work to minimize its harmful effects rather than simply ignore or condemn them" and "[u]nderstands drug use as a complex, multi-faceted phenomenon that encompasses a continuum of behaviors from severe abuse to total abstinence, and acknowledges that some ways of using drugs are clearly safer than others."

23. See Fawcett, *Lust, Men, and Meth*.

names are "ice," "crystal," "glass," "jibb," and "Tina." It is relatively cheap and easy to produce but extremely dangerous to use and highly addictive.

> **RECOMMENDATIONS FOR PASTORAL CAREGIVERS IN RESPONSE TO THE USE OF CRYSTAL METH**
>
> - Leave naïveté, squeamishness, and hesitancy behind and become proactive in the campaign to fight this severely damaging drug.
> - Learn about the drug, its use in your locality, and the damage that it does.
> - Associate yourself with local secular or religious organizations that have programs, or an interest in creating programs, designed to deal with crystal meth abuse and education of at-risk populations.
> - In your preaching and teaching refer to its use and provide accurate information about the damage that it causes.
> - Have an up-to-date listing of recovery meetings and programs that are culturally appropriate for LGBTQ people and that address crystal meth recovery.
> - Become known as a community resource who, at the least, is willing to add the influence of your faith community to fight the severe damage wrought by this drug.

In higher doses, methamphetamine, especially if it is smoked or injected (other methods are snorting, pills, mixed in liquid, and imbibed, etc.), causes the user to experience a "rush" of intense pleasure, which lasts about thirty minutes followed by an increase of energy for several hours. Users can become addicted quickly, needing ever higher doses as the addiction progresses.

Negative effects include memory loss, aggression, psychotic behavior, heart damage, malnutrition, severe dental problems, disturbed sleep patterns, hyperactivity, delusions of power, and increased aggressiveness and irritability. Long-term negative effects, in high doses, can include heart, liver, kidney, and lung damage; even drug related psychoses; in general, methamphetamine can ravage the entire body.[24]

---

24. See Patterson, "Effects of Crystal Meth"; and Phend, "Psychosis Common."

In recent years, crystal meth has become a drug of choice in some gay men's party scenes. Commentators on the current situation state the use of crystal meth has become more common among urban gay and bisexual men than in the general US population.[25] It increases energy and reduces sexual inhibition and the superhuman feeling that often comes with a crystal meth high means that the sex is often unprotected. Such lack of protection can lead to an increase in HIV infection, which, of course, the statistics are showing in some specific geographical areas.[26]

Here is an urgent challenge for the effective pastoral caregiver, especially if you work in an urban center where there is a concentration of gay men: be a voice for health, wholeness, and holiness; don't be naïve; don't be afraid.

Yet the urban gay community is by no means the only one that is being negatively affected by this damaging drug. According to mental health workers, police, and research scientists, the people who use crystal meth also include large numbers among the rural and small town poor across North America, some young people in the rave and dance scene (who also use "Ecstasy"), and some people who want to lose weight.

So, five recommendations:

1. Know where to get information about drug use.[27]

2. Train yourself to recognize symptoms.

3. If you think you recognize signs of drug use, don't hesitate to ask your LGBTQ care receiver if they are using drugs —if for no other reason (you might say to your care receiver) than to set your own mind at ease.

4. Try not to be fooled. This recommendation is one you might fail several times because addicts are masterful at hiding their addiction.

5. Try to see the origins of addiction, any addiction, as a spiritual challenge, a desire for God gone wrong, a wish for goodness without the necessary experience and wisdom, and not simply as someone's moral weakness and lack of will.[28]

---

25. See Rodriguez, "After Party."

26. Rodriguez, "After Party."

27. See Fawcett, *Lust, Men, and Meth*; Sloane, "Perfect Storm"; and Drescher et al., *Crystal Meth*.

28. See Moore, *Tweaked*. In "Clarity About Crystal," Moore writes: "I think addiction is a spiritual disease.... Our intention when we use drugs is to communicate

## Sex Education, Safer Sex, Addictive Sex

Every religious congregation, those with schools and those without schools, should have a program of sex education adapted to their specific congregational needs. The prevailing ignorance about sexuality at this stage of human history is scandalous. No one should be without the necessary information they need—when they need it—to mature on all levels of human development.

Sexual maturity and integration are essential parts of spiritual maturity. How urgently religious communities need to know this! How vital is the teaching of sexual information in today's society! (See "Faith-Based LGBTQ Advocacy Groups" in Resources.) And how courageous is the congregation and the pastoral caregiver who takes this on!

Since one could credibly argue that the cause of this historical hesitancy, this embarrassment, this shame, is religion, why not suggest that religion take a strong leadership stance in encouraging complete and free access to information about human sexuality? It is certainly appropriate subject matter for religious bodies to foster and disseminate. The spiritual and the sexual shine as different facets of the same gem. Sexuality is the gift of a loving God and considered by many religious traditions to be a sacred and holy gift. Churches and synagogues must stop shrinking in fear and shame from the goodness and beauty and joy of the human body and its sexual expression or become burdened with even more blame for its lack of historical wisdom.

Imagine for a moment that you are a twelve-year-old gay boy (yes, many young people know their sexual orientation at this age; see "LGBTQ Youth" section below) sitting in your congregation week after week and attending the religious school classes religiously. Probably sex is never mentioned in this context or mentioned only in very negative terms; maybe sex is mentioned carefully, at a safe distance, and only in a heterosexual context. What is this boy (as well as everyone else who hears) to conclude? How is he to grow? Exactly what does his faith community expect from him?

In regard to safer sex: you must know what is meant by safer sex, what is included in safer sex acts, and what is excluded.[29] Be aware that the categories of safer sex have changed somewhat over the years and

---

with God."

[29]. For information on safer sex, see WebMD, "Preventing HIV and Other STDs With Safe Sex."

may well continue to change as new medical information is learned. At the very least, you need to be able to refer people in your care to the places where they can get reliable and up-to-date information.

Be aware of potential challenges your care receivers may have in trying to reconcile their faith communities' teachings on the use of birth control and condoms with their own sexual practices. If someone comes to you with the problem of sexual addiction, or if you suspect it because the person reports Obsessive-Compulsive Disorder (OCD) behavior around sex, I believe it is best to refer the person to a trained professional with experience and expertise in this area. Sexual addiction is often difficult to define and diagnose accurately.

In the same vein, if a care receiver approaches you with a problem of sexual abuse in their childhood, make a referral to competent, professional help. Still, as pastoral caregiver, you can continue to relate to, encourage, and otherwise sustain and guide these care receivers.

Both of the last mentioned situations, sexual addiction and childhood abuse, can serve here as a reminder to keep your referral list handy and up-to-date.

## THE PHYSICALLY CHALLENGED LGBTQ PERSON

Being LGBTQ adds a significant element of challenge for the physically handicapped person. The goal in this section is to encourage you to notice the presence of LGBTQ handicapped people and also to give you several referrals to helpful resources as you minister to them.

In general, the most important task of the caregiver is to notice LGBTQ people, in this case handicapped LGBTQ people, to see them as they are and with the needs and gifts that they ask from and bring to the community; and to help them find one another. One useful source is *Queers on Wheels* by Eva Sweeney, which calls for the many identities of people to be seen and valued.[30]

For vision-impaired or blind LGBTQ people, their families and friends, Blind-LGBT Pride International offers useful resources as part of its mission to offer advocacy, education, programs, alliances, and support for persons who are either blind or vision impaired and who are gay, lesbian, bisexual or transgender."[31] For hearing-impaired or deaf LGBTQ

---

30. Sweeney, *Queers on Wheels*.
31. Blind-LGBT Pride International, www.blindlgbtpride.org.

people, check out the resources available at The Deaf Queer Resource Center (DQRC), "a national nonprofit resource and information center for, by and about the Deaf Lesbian, Gay, Bisexual, Transgender, Transsexual, Intersex and Questioning communities."[32]

Just as non-LGBTQ people who are learning to deal with LGBTQ people tend to be hesitant and lack confidence that they know what to do or to say, so it is with non-handicapped people dealing with the handicapped. In both cases, ask from your care receivers what you don't know; ask them for help in learning. What's worse than interacting awkwardly with an LGBTQ handicapped person? Not interacting with them at all.

## VIOLENCE

We queer folks are a peaceful lot in general. "One would be hard-pressed to name another male culture in America—one, that is, outside formal structures of religious orders or intentional communities—whose public realm is so notably free of assault and aggressive violence among peers." So writes David Nimmons, speaking of gay men, and he quotes police statistics to back up his statement.[33] (However, in the area of domestic violence this is not the case; see "Domestic Violence" below.) For the most part, LGBTQ people are on the receiving end with regards to violence. The FBI's statistics for 2015 include the following information showing that nearly 20 percent of hate crimes involve LGBTQ people:

> There were 5,818 single-bias incidents involving 7,121 victims. Of those victims, 59.2 percent were targeted because of a race/ethnicity/ancestry bias; 19.7 percent because of a religious bias; 17.7 percent because of a sexual orientation bias; 1.7 percent because of a gender identity bias; 1.2 percent because of a disability bias; and 0.4 percent because of a gender bias.[34]

I want to focus on the direct and causal connection between the teaching of some religious organizations about LGBTQ people and the violence done to LGBTQ people. The causal connection, although probably not empirically provable nor even measured as far as I know, seems to me both irrefutable and scandalous. May these religious voices soon understand the role that their teachings and pronouncements play in the

---

32. The Deaf Queer Resource Center (DQRC), www.deafqueer.org.
33. Nimmons, *Soul*, 14.
34. See FBI, "Latest Hate Crime Statistics."

violence that is visited upon LGBTQ people. Their language can be—and indeed often is—interpreted as tacit permission by some to do violence.

The language the Catholic Church uses in documents issued by the Vatican is indicative: "the [homosexual] inclination itself must be seen as an objective disorder," and "Although the particular inclination of the homosexual person is not a sin, it is a more or less strong tendency ordered toward an intrinsic moral evil; and thus the inclination itself must be seen as an objective disorder."[35] More recently, a Vatican document on the priesthood and homosexuality issued in late 2016 was roundly criticized by the Association of US Catholic priests, as "disrespectful," "ambiguous," and "insulting."[36]

Although there are hopeful signs that attitudes within the Roman Catholic Church might be changing under the leadership of Pope Francis, this denomination still has a long way to go to become more affirming and supportive of LGBTQ people and their families.

Informal surveys and experience indicate that the typical (although not the only) perpetrator of physical violence against LGBTQ people ("gay basher") is an adolescent male who is insecure about his own sexuality, which is not an uncommon trait of many people in adolescence. I suggest that the tacit but well publicized criticism, scolding, and at times simple ranting by some representatives of some religious bodies can be a partial, but significant, source of the energy that fuels a potential criminal to act. Speaking of Christians, Miguel De La Torre writes that "Some people encourage violence toward gays and lesbians when they reduce sexual orientation to a disease or sin. . . . Christians become complicit with the violence they breed due to their attitudes, words, and actions."[37]

The violence done to transgender persons is especially alarming. According to GLAAD statistics,

> 2016 overtook 2015 as the deadliest year on record for transgender people in the United States. In 2016, twenty-seven transgender people were killed in the United States and nearly all of the victims were transgender women of color. . . . This number does not include transgender people whose deaths were not reported due to misgendering in police reports, news stories, and sometimes by the victim's family.[38]

35. Congregation for the Doctrine of the Faith, "Letter to the Bishops."
36. Morris-Young, "US Priests' Group."
37. De La Torre, *Reading the Bible*, 131.
38. See Schmider, "2016 Was the Deadliest Year."

If you think that there are no members of your congregation who are dealing with their trans- (or bi-) identities, you may be mistaken. I encourage you to appropriately seek out such members and provide them with care and support.

## "Flaunting It"

Violence toward LGBTQ people brings up the subject of flaunting. People, often supportive people of good will, frequently say to LGBTQ people, "You talk about it too much" or "You're too obsessed, too impatient and pushy."

Expressing our sexuality as openly and as naturally as heterosexuals express theirs is not "flaunting it": holding hands in public, wearing a wedding band, talking about one's partner, spouse, or boyfriend/girlfriend, celebrating an anniversary, and making casual references to other LGBTQ people in our lives is vital to our self-respect and well-being. To some people these acts may seem to be flaunting because they contrast with the almost complete invisibility of LGBTQ people in our culture. Also, many of us are not comfortable talking or hearing (publicly or privately) about personal sex of any kind, even though—amazingly and incongruously—our media is full of it. Perhaps such LGBTQ visibility is new for many people, but being out of the closet and comfortable with one's sexual orientation and/or gender identity is not flaunting.

Certainly, LGBTQ people, like all people, are capable of flaunting their sexuality. The definition of "flaunt" includes: "to display or obtrude oneself to public notice; to wave or flutter showily; to display ostentatiously or impudently; to treat contemptuously."[39] LGBTQ people flaunt no more than non-LGBTQ people—even though queer flaunting often makes for "better" media entertainment in some people's minds.

Be that as it may, there is a tendency of the oppressed to obsess or overstate when in the fervor of overcoming the oppression. That has been and always will be true for any minority fighting for its rights; it's simply the nature of oppressed people. So a little patience and positive feedback can help.

---

39. Merriam-Webster Online Dictionary, www.merriam-webster.com/dictionary/flaunt.

## Domestic Violence

Unfortunately, gays and lesbians are as likely to be both victims and perpetrators of domestic violence as their straight counterparts. And, contrary to some stereotypes, men can be victims and women can be batterers.

A standard and basic skill of every pastoral caregiver must be training in recognizing the symptoms or indications of domestic violence. It is one of the most underreported, undertreated, and widespread forms of violence in our culture today.

Here are a few statistics: on average, nearly twenty people per minute are physically abused by an intimate partner in the United States. During one year, this equates to more than ten million women and men. One in three women and one in four men have been victims of some form of physical violence by an intimate partner within their lifetime. One in four women and one in seven men have been victims of severe physical violence by an intimate partner in their lifetime. One in seven women and one in eighteen men have been stalked by an intimate partner during their lifetime to the point in which they felt very fearful or believed that they or someone close to them would be harmed or killed. On a typical day, there are more than twenty thousand phone calls placed to domestic violence hotlines nationwide.[40]

Indeed, domestic violence, perhaps more than any other form of violence, gives the lie to the stereotypes. Several characteristics that many people would assume to be true about domestic violence simply are not, especially with regard to LGBTQ people.

---

40. For statistics on domestic violence, see The National Coalition Against Domestic Violence (NCADV), "National Statistics"; and Brown and Herman, "Intimate Partner Violence."

## MYTHS AND FACTS ABOUT SAME-GENDER DOMESTIC VIOLENCE

Myths:

- Only straight women get battered.
- Gay, bisexual, and transgender men are never victims of domestic violence.
- Lesbians, bisexual, and transgender women do not batter.
- Battering is less common in same-gender relationships.
- Domestic violence occurs primarily among LGBTQ people who hang out in bars, are poor, or are people of color.

Facts:

- Men can be victims, and women can batter. Numbers reflect this: an annual study of over two thousand gay men reflects that one in four gay men has experienced domestic violence. These numbers are consistent with research done regarding battering among opposite-sex couples, and lesbian couples.
- Stereotypes about gender and sexual orientation are repudiated by the fact that gay men and lesbians are both victims and perpetrators.
- Domestic violence is a non-discriminatory phenomenon; victims, as well as violent and abusive offenders, come from all walks of life, ethnic backgrounds, socioeconomic groups, religions, and educational levels.
- Racist and classist and inaccurate stereotypes about domestic violence are common not just in the LGBTQ community, but also in the dominant heterosexual culture.[A]

A. See the GLBTQ Domestic Violence Project website, www.glbtqdvp.org.

Training in recognizing the signs of domestic violence can be self-conducted. Here are a few more resources that can give you a good basic knowledge of the issues. Of course, you should know well your local support organizations and the support that they provide:

- *Domestic Violence: What Every Pastor Needs to Know* by Al Miles.
- *Violence in Families: What Every Christian Needs to Know* by Marie M. Fortune and Al Miles.
- *Sexual Violence: The Sin Revisited* by Marie M. Fortune
- The Futures Without Violence Project, a national organization that focuses on ending abuse against women and children.[41]

## BISEXUAL AND TRANSGENDER

General awareness of bisexual and transgender persons and their challenges is probably where awareness of gays and lesbians was about twenty-five years ago. Thus, although recently getting better, enlightened understanding for these groups is still hard to come by.

> ### SOME GENERAL COMMENTS ON BISEXUALITY[A]
>
> - Bisexuality is a sexual orientation in which an individual feels sexual attraction toward both men and women, although not necessarily to the same degree.
> - A bisexual individual may experience conflict living in a homophobic society; however, such conflict is not a symptom of dysfunction in the individual but of the society and the confusion of language.
> - All sexual orientations (homosexual, heterosexual, and bisexual) are normal and natural for at least a minority of the population. An adult's orientation is not consciously chosen. It is not changeable through prayer, therapy, surgical intervention, etc.

---

41. Futures Without Violence website, www.futureswithoutviolence.org.

- Some persons who are sexually attracted to both men and women feel more strongly attracted to one gender than the other. Further, they may identify themselves as homosexual, heterosexual, or bisexual depending upon their primary attraction. A bisexual who feels more attracted to members of the same sex might identify themselves as gay or lesbian rather than bisexual. Others, who are attracted to members of the opposite sex, might view themselves as heterosexual.

- A person can feel attractions to both men and women, decide to remain celibate, and still be considered a bisexual by themselves and others.

- Bisexuality describes how people feel, not necessarily how they act.

- A bisexual might make a conscious decision to confine their sexual activity to person(s) of one gender and still be considered a bisexual by themselves and others.

- Confusion of meaning and terms abounds in regard to sexuality in general, but especially in the area of bisexuality. Be sure that all participants in the conversation agree on the meanings of the terms they use.

A. For more information on bisexuality, see Ontario Consultants on Religious Tolerance, "Bisexuality."

The encouragement that I would give to the pastoral caregiver is to increase both your awareness and your understanding: awareness of the presence of bisexual and transgender people in your communities; and understanding of their very real and challenging issues. The following books are a good place to begin:

- *Bisexuality: Making the Invisible Visible in Faith Communities* by Marie Alford-Harkey and Rev. Debra W. Haffner.

- *Trans-Gendered: Theology, Ministry, and Communities of Faith* by Justin Tanis.

- *The Transgender Teen: A Handbook for Parents and Professionals Supporting Transgender and Non-Binary Teens* by Stephanie A. Brill and Lisa Kenney.[42]

---

**IMPORTANT TOPICS TO CONSIDER WHEN MINISTERING WITH TRANSGENDER PERSONS**[A]

- **Names and/or pronouns:** Use the names and/or pronouns appropriate to the person's chosen gender identity. Remember that it is everyone's essential dignity to be called by their chosen name, and it is everyone's right to be recognized as the persons they see themselves to be. Find out what names and pronouns the individual wants to use if you're not sure.

- **Access to restroom and locker room facilities:** Make sure that everyone understands that transgender people want to use the restrooms that conform to their gender identity. If possible, designate gender-neutral restrooms (toilet facilities that anyone may use, irrespective of gender identity or gender expression). At the time of this writing, this "bathroom" issue remains widely politicized.

- **Dress code:** Make sure that the dress codes, if there are any in your programs, respect people's rights to dress in conformity with their chosen gender identity.

- **Confidentiality:** Make sure that any program you oversee maintains confidentiality with regard to the gender identity, gender expression, sexual orientation, and sexual behavior of all the people in the program.

- **Role models and accurate information:** Educate others about gender identity. Make sure that everyone you deal with is aware that there is diversity regarding human gender; male and female of course, but also going beyond these. Search out transgender support groups and LGBTQ-serving organizations in your area. Make sure that these groups and organizations are included on your resource and referral lists.

---

42. Alford-Harkey and Haffner, *Bisexuality*; Tanis, *Trans-Gendered*; Brill and Kenney, *Transgender Teen*.

> - Avoid any language that puts transgender people into surgical categories—pre- or post-op—since this encourages inquiries about genitals, which is always inappropriate, unless the care receiver so wishes and expresses.

A. This list is adapted from Peterson, "Health and Rights."

## LGBTQ YOUTH

What is the most obvious characteristic of LGBTQ youth? The answer is easy: being young and LGBTQ is much more dangerous and risky—and often more painful—than being young and straight. Other than that, I believe that queer youth are pretty much like all youth. They, like all youth, need affirmation, understanding, and clear expectations, not reprimands and rejection. They need responsible, informed adults to love them, encourage them, educate them, teach them (about limits, self-discipline, and some ways to enjoy life), never abandon them, and include them in affirming communities.

For many LGBTQ youth, the only way that they can achieve these values is to keep their core identity hidden in denial, shame, and fear. If they do come out as LGBTQ—and more are doing so and at younger ages than before—most of them will encounter trouble.[43]

> "Eight out of ten LGBT students experience harassment, but school-based resources and supports are making a difference," reports GLSEN, a group that aims to "improve an education system that too frequently allows its lesbian, gay, bisexual, transgender, queer and questioning students to be bullied, discriminated against, or fall through the cracks."[44]

Here are a few questions and concerns that possibly go through the minds of young LGBTQ people:

- "So am I gay or bi?"
- "What does it mean to be lesbian?"

---

43. On Gay-Straight Alliances in Catholic schools, see Gadoua, "Are Catholic High Schools Supporting."

44. For more information on GLSEN, see the organization's website, www.glsen.org.

- "Some people say that it's just a phase."
- "But I just want to be normal!"
- "Was I born gay?"
- "Should I tell someone I might be trans? And, if so, who?"
- "Is it possible I did something wrong to make me this way?"
- "It seems to me that everyone in my world hates gay people."
- "I'm not like most of the gay people I see, so how can I be gay?"[45]

Now imagine telling a fourteen-year-old gay kid this: it is likely that no one will reach out to help you if you have any of these questions. You are on your own and cannot expect understanding, maybe least of all from your religious community. In fact, you must not even mention the possibility, because if you do, you well might be disbelieved or punished. So the only person you can talk to, if you're lucky and you have one, is your same-age friend who knows as much or less than you do.

Imagine! It's a wonder to me that LGBTQ people get through youth at all, much less get through it in one piece. What might be some helpful and healthy support that the pastoral caregiver could provide when dealing with LGBTQ youth? Consider these options:

### PASTORAL PERSPECTIVES

## Pastoral Care with LGBTQ Youth

- Make the topic of being LGBTQ available to the community you serve, especially to the young. Make it a topic of conversation that is acceptable and accepted.
- Ask yourself: Am I approachable by LGBTQ youth who seek someone to talk with, someone whom they can trust? What can I do to become so?
- Familiarize yourself with organizations in your area that serve homeless and other at-risk youth.

---

45. Based on questions found on the website of AVERT, www.avert.org.

- Teach parents that throwing their children out of the family home is not effective in changing a person's gender identity or sexual orientation; in fact, it worsens the situation. Advise parents to seek guidance.
- Create safe and affirming spaces, both physical and psychic, for youths who don't fit the mold.
- Associate yourself with and support Gay-Straight Alliances (or their equivalents) in your area schools. Volunteer to give presentations or lead activities with them.
- Support and consider becoming an active member of PFLAG.
- Support and enlist the services of GLSEN, the Gay, Lesbian & Straight Education Network, which works to make schools safe for all students.

## Coming Out Young

The age when persons typically come out of the closet is getting younger all the time. With LGBTQ issues prominently in the news and entertainment media, young LGBTQ people are finding more encouragement and permission to reveal themselves to family and friends than they did just ten years ago; some are as young as eleven and twelve. Young people have access to more accurate—and inaccurate—information about issues such as gender transition and sexual expression than ever before. But the path they choose can be challenging and fraught with dangers. They need all the help they can get, including your pastoral care.

Caitlin Ryan, a clinical social worker, spent four years researching LGBTQ youth. She found that the average age of teens coming out was just over age thirteen, slightly younger than the late eighties when they came out between fourteen and sixteen. In the seventies, most teens waited until they were adults to come out. And it continues to get younger.[46]

With children (anyone younger than eighteen, or the majority age, or age of consent in your jurisdiction) who come out of the closet and seek your care, or who are simply within the purview of your care, keep the following in mind:

46. Ryan and Futterman, *Lesbian and Gay Youth*. See Krieger, *Counseling Transgender and Non-Binary Youth*.

- Involve the family as soon and as completely as possible. Always acknowledge that the parents, no matter what their reactions or feared reactions, have authority over the child, not you. In this delicate situation it would at least appear that you are acting *in loco parentis* and your interventions need to be as transparent and responsible as possible. In reality, you are acting to supplement unprovided and urgently needed parental-like care. However, since the well-being and safety of the young person is of paramount concern, family involvement should be sought only if the young person is completely safe in their presence.

- Whether or not family involvement is possible, and especially if it is not, consult a knowledgeable and experienced colleague for support who might serve as a consultant with whom you discuss, in professional confidence, your pastoral relationship with a queer youth; this colleague might even serve as an openly involved co-caregiver, depending on circumstances. You are making yourself vulnerable in this situation so aim for transparency and trackability to protect yourself and improve the effectiveness of your care-giving.

- Help your care receiver keep all possibilities open without denying the reality of their sexual orientation and/or gender identity. In preteen and even early teen years, one might be mistaken about one's sexual orientation and/or gender identity, but this is unlikely. Many people report knowing their sexual orientation very early, from eight or nine years old, or even earlier on some level of awareness.[47] Some children are aware of their gender identity and openly speak of a transgender identity while they are in preschool.

- The primary challenge here will be to engage the family. The next challenge will be keeping a balance between setting clear and responsible limits around behavior (including sexual) on the one hand, and affirming the person on the other. In caring for your LGBTQ youth, please don't overlook the primary importance of the family. If all's well in the family, the young person is more likely to survive and even thrive as an out queer person. This is especially true of trans youth.[48]

---

47. While some LGBTQ people realize the nature of their sexual orientation very early, it is not uncommon for others to recognize it later, even well into adulthood. See Ryan and Futterman, *Lesbian and Gay Youth*.

48. Holpuch, "Trans Children."

Even with bullying and without family support, the resilience of some young LGBTQ people is remarkable. Take the typical case of Brian who is from a white, middle-class, divorced, suburban family. He came out to his mother at age eighteen as a freshman in college. He reports struggling for years with his sexual orientation and finally just got tired of the never-ending struggle and pretending he was straight. When he came out to his mother, the result was a yelling match and he was sent off to live with his aunt and uncle. Brian is understandably upset about his mother's denial of his gay identity: you learn that she either avoids the topic, denies the truth of it, or talks to him about its sinfulness. "At first it was really hard for me. I just wished she'd accept me the way I am." The pain behind those words is evident, but eventually Brian speaks for a growing number of young LGBTQ people when he adds, "But I can't just stop living, put everything on hold for her."

If Brian were in your congregation, how could you see yourself giving effective pastoral care? First of all, would you notice him? That is key, of course. Why might you not notice him—that is, not be aware of what is going on for him and his family? Can you take steps to improve the possibility of noticing such members of your congregation?

Then, how might you begin by talking with the mother and try to understand her vehement stance? And the father: is he in the picture and what is his role in Brian's life? Are there siblings who might be torn in their loyalties and who might also benefit from your care? Does Brian need a safe and accepting place to talk about his life? Could he benefit from referrals to LGBTQ-positive groups, agencies, or organizations that are connected to Brian's religious tradition, if he has one?

---

### LGBTQ YOUTH AND BULLYING[A]

While trying to deal with all the challenges of being a teenager, lesbian/gay/bisexual/transgender teens also have to deal with harassment, threats, and violence directed at them on a daily basis. LGBT youth are nearly twice as likely to be called names, verbally harassed, or physically assaulted at school compared to their non-LGBT peers. Their mental health and education, not to mention their physical well-being, are at risk.

### How Is Their Mental Health Being Affected?

- Substance Use: Gay, lesbian, bisexual and transgender youth are more than twice as likely to experiment with drugs and alcohol.
- Happiness: Only 37 percent of LGBT youth report being happy, while 67 percent of non-LGBT youth say they are happy. However, over 80 percent of LGBT youth believe they will be happy eventually, with nearly half believing that they will need to move away from their current town to find happiness.
- Self-Harm: With each instance of verbal or physical harassment, the risk of self-harm among LGBT youth is 2.5 times more likely.

### How Is Their Education Being Affected?

- Gay teens in US schools are often subjected to such intense bullying that they're unable to receive an adequate education. LGBT youth identified bullying as the second most important problem in their lives, after non-accepting families. Non-LGBT youth, by comparison, identified classes/exams/grades as the most important problems in their lives.
- LGBT youth who reported they were frequently harassed in school had lower grade point averages than students who were less often harassed.
- LGBT youth feel they have nowhere to turn. Sixty percent of LGBT students did not report incidents to school staff. One-third who reported an incident said the staff did nothing in response.

A. Statistical information for this section on "LGBTQ Youth and Bullying" is taken from Mental Health America, "Bullying and LGBT Youth."

## Bullying

The effective pastoral caregiver will be aware in general of the extreme pain that bullying causes, especially to LGBTQ youth. Here are some suggestions for you, as caregiver, to address effectively the issue of bullying:

- Be alert to any signs that might indicate bullying: physical wounds, fear of school, social isolation, and so on.

- Work with public and private schools to offer programs on respect for all, school safety, and anti-bullying.
- Ask school personnel to have a discussion at an assembly or an after-school activity about LGBTQ prejudice.
- Help start a Gay-Straight Alliance (GSA) chapter at your local high school. Youth whose schools have these chapters are less likely to report feeling unsafe in their schools.
- Arrange for a group like GLSEN to present bullying prevention activities and programs at your area schools.
- Encourage anyone who is being/has been bullied to tell a teacher, counselor, coach, nurse, and/or their parents or guardians. Even if the bullying has stopped, report it yourself.
- Offer space in your community for LGBTQ youth groups to meet.

### RECOMMENDED FILM RESOURCES FOR ELEMENTARY AND MIDDLE SCHOOL STUDENTS: "THE RESPECT FOR ALL PROJECT"[A]

- *It's Elementary—Talking About Gay Issues in School* explores how teachers can include discussion about gay people in their classrooms with elementary and middle school students.
- *It's Still Elementary* revisits the themes and ideas of the original one.
- *Let's Get Real* takes an honest look at the epidemic of name-calling and bullying among middle school youth, told entirely from a youth perspective.
- *That's a Family* breaks new ground in helping elementary-age children understand the many different shapes that families take today.
- *Straightlaced* features intimate interviews with teenagers about the pressure to conform to traditional gender roles. Students talk about the toll it takes to live up to gender role expectations.

[A]. For more information on these films, see The Respect for All Project at groundspark.org.

## Suicide

Peer pressure is a powerful influence among all adolescents. Being different at a stage of development in which conformity is the rule adds insult to injury. LGBTQ youth are different in a way that most young people would name as the biggest—and possibly worst—way possible: they're Queer. The tension that is built up in some young people becomes too much for them to cope with and they resort to suicide or its attempt. The Centers for Disease Control (CDC) reports: "Gay, lesbian, and bisexual youth are four times more likely to attempt suicide than their heterosexual counterparts."[49]

Again, the first challenge is to find LGBTQ youth. The best chance of finding them will be by becoming an open and welcoming congregation (see chapter 5), to be approachable by youth, and to have some realistic and meaningful ways of connecting with young people. And keep in mind that adolescents, in particular, rarely tell anyone, especially adults, about their experiences with depression and/or suicidal ideation.

Next, become aware of the possible signs of suicide:

- Talking about suicide
- Statements about hopelessness, helplessness, or worthlessness
- Preoccupation with death
- Suddenly appearing happier, and calmer
- Loss of interest in things one cared about
- Visiting or calling people one cared about
- Making arrangements; setting one's affairs in order
- Giving things away[50]

If you hear comments like any of the following, take action:

- Life isn't worth living.
- My family would be better off without me.
- Next time I'll take enough pills to do the job right.

---

49. Mental Health America, "Bullying and LGBT Youth."

50. Based on information provided by Suicide Awareness Voices of Education (SAVE), "Warning Signs of Suicide."

- Take my (prized collection, valuables, etc.)—I don't need this stuff anymore.
- I won't be around to deal with that.
- You'll be sorry when I'm gone.
- I just can't deal with everything—life's too hard.
- Nobody understands me—nobody feels the way I do.
- There's nothing I can do to make it better.
- I'd be better off dead.
- I feel like there is no way out.[51]

Ask the young person directly, in clear language, if their intention is to commit suicide, to otherwise hurt themselves, or if they have ever considered suicide. If they have considered or attempted suicide, elicit a promise from them never to attempt suicide again before talking to you or to a responsible, available adult who cares for them. Get in touch with the family if practical and advisable. Get the young person professional help as quickly as possible: a doctor (psychiatrist) or social worker/therapist who is competent in dealing with suicide risk, including, in extreme cases, an emergency room.[52] Follow up soon and often with the professional. Keep your relationship with the young person active and check in often.

## Mentors

An excellent goal of pastoral care for LGBTQ youth is to help find mentors for youth within the queer community. This is not as easy as it might sound. I have been part of two such efforts that ended unsuccessfully because of various complications in regard to insurance. There are, however, successful LGBTQ mentoring agencies.[53]

---

51. Based on information provided by Stop a Suicide Today, "Learn to Act."

52. See The Trevor Project (www.thetrevorproject.org), a particularly valuable resource for preventing suicides among LGBTQ youth. The Project's toll-free telephone number: 866–488-7386.

53. The Point Foundation (pointfoundation.org) provides mentoring and financial aid scholarships for LGBTQ students of merit. Many colleges and universities offer mentoring groups for their LGBTQ students.

For many, the mentoring process can be casual and local. The key tasks here are to choose mentors who are trustworthy and morally, ethically beyond reproach and totally committed to the process in the long-term, and to establish a very proactive system of supervision. The organization Big Brothers Big Sisters, a valuable resource for all youth in need of adult mentoring, arranges for gay and lesbian mentors of gay and lesbian youth.[54]

## Online Challenges

Lastly, with regard to LGBTQ youth, is there some way for the pastoral caregiver to have an effect on the use and abuse of the Internet and other social media? LGBTQ youth are especially vulnerable to the pitfalls of social media precisely because society denies them the normal outlets for peer social contact.

I believe that the most valuable pastoral service in this area is the education of parents about the use and abuse of social media. Hold information sessions for the congregation's parents and find a trained professional to show them the beauty and the beast that is social media today: how to cope with Facebook, Twitter, Snapchat, Instagram, Grindr, Scruff, and other similar sites; the effective use of parental controls; the easy accessibility to hardcore pornography, including depictions of violence and harmful sexual activities; and lastly, the real dangers of deception and entrapment that can happen to children through the unsupervised use of social media today.

Spend some time on sites that are likely to be visited by LGBTQ children and teenagers. By acknowledging that responsible adults are aware of all that can happen online, it might give young people courage to seek the healthy and helpful while avoiding the degrading and dangerous. Provide information about reputable and helpful sites designed for LGBTQ teens. Can you imagine "surfing the net" with members of your congregational youth group? (Always do so in the company of ministry colleagues or other adults.) It is an activity that could offer fertile ground for moral teaching, spiritual insights, great conversation, building trust, and an imaginative expression of pastoral care.

---

54. See Big Brothers Big Sisters of America, www.bbbs.org.

## OLDER AGE

### Loss

Loss is perhaps the most characteristic attribute of older age; it certainly is the most inevitable. The losses of older age, aside from the constant losses of bodily health and functioning, include the loss of friends and perhaps also one's place in the community. The astute pastoral caregiver will acknowledge this and find ways to connect their elderly LGBTQ people with others, near or far.

The loss of presence in the world, in the community, in the form of invisibility, often returns to haunt people when they enter their senior years. Older LGBTQ people can seem to fade into a generic category of "old" when, in fact, they remain just as "different" now as they ever were. Transgender people face not only physical difficulties shared by everyone who ages but they may face additional challenges in obtaining the medical care that they need and admittance to nursing facilities. Some facilities separate same sex couples or do not provide them with the same visiting rights as their heterosexual peers, causing distress among people who may have spent their entire lives together and are facing their first real separation.

For the LGBTQ elderly who live in a care facility or other retirement facility, consider the loss of privacy that such living conditions can involve. In some institutions I have visited, there is literally no privacy for residents. Privacy is not always, or even generally, about sex or sexual expression; rather, it is about being who you need to be, with room for your private conversations, to be with people you want to spend time with, and to create a home with your important possessions (such as family photographs and other memorabilia), and the other things that represent your life. Being queer manifests itself in all of life's aspects and is expressed in one's created environment, just as it is for everyone.

In older LGBTQ people who were never out—or never fully out—watch for signs of internalized homophobia. Watch too for what is expressed as regrets and find ways to encourage conversation about them.

"I don't know why I never really acknowledged who I was; it seems so many young people today do it so easily. Why didn't I do that?" That's a paraphrase of a frustrated comment I heard from an infirm eighty-three-year-old man in a nursing home. He was a very successful business man, married briefly, with no children. He was, I believe, coming out for the first time, to me, his pastoral caregiver, after four or five visits. In spite of his age and infirmities, he was the live wire of the whole place, but his words carried deep regret. He felt that his popularity would wane "if they knew." He needed to be reminded that coming out in the 1940s and 1950s was practically impossible in all but the most unusual circumstances, and he needed to have an ongoing conversation about all that implied, then *and* now, at this moment of his life. He needed to be affirmed and engaged and acknowledged. Who among us doesn't—especially in older age?

Retirement from the working world is a challenge for many LGBTQ people. As they go through the loss of their work or career, many of them feel a bit lost because they no longer fill a clear role and often feel that they have lost a meaningful purpose in life. Thus, many can easily slip into invisibility and isolation. Are there recent LGBTQ retirees in your congregation? A pastoral call might bring them—and you—great blessings.

## From Generativity to Integration

As your elderly LGBTQ people move from the developmental tasks that serve generativity and avoid stagnation into the final stage of achieving integration and steering clear of despair,[55] they will appreciate your help in remembering and discovering meaning from all the moments of their lives. They will be especially grateful to remember what is deeply meaningful and you may be able to help them find ways to continue or deepen that meaning.

The fifteen minutes you spend with an elderly LGBTQ person, simply providing them time and an interested listener for honest, unedited reminiscing is indeed a rich blessing and far more effective pastoral ministry than it may appear to be.

Recently my spouse and I were visiting a family member in an out-of-town care home for the infirm elderly. During our visit we both noticed a gentleman in the corner of the room who was quite obviously fixing us with a friendly stare and a smile. As we were leaving, I looked at him with a nod and a smile, which he returned. Then I winked at him, wanting to let him know we saw him and acknowledged him. His smile

---

55. The last two (of eight) stages of Erik Erikson's schema of human development are Generativity vs. Self-Absorption and Integrity vs. Despair. See McLeod, "Erik Erikson's Stages," and Erikson, *Life Stages Completed*.

grew into a broad grin and I felt grateful to be able to give a small recognition to someone who possibly received very little.

It is from the community of the elderly that you might well be able to find the LGBTQ mentors mentioned above ("LGBTQ Youth"). Can you see an expression of pastoral care in bringing together the generations, that is, in finding queer seniors to mentor queer youth?

## Dignity

The large majority of seniors, those who have fought the good fight and kept the faith, have achieved a high degree of dignity. I believe that a good general rule for the pastoral caregiver working with older care receivers is to always serve and enhance the care receiver's dignity. This will be especially true for those suffering from mental impairment, including people living with Alzheimer's disease or other age-related dementias.

You will find challenges to that dignity at every turn in the lives of the elderly. Ours is a culture that honors youth and not older age. Here are four challenges to dignity that you might encounter with your LGBTQ elderly: freedom of sexual expression; keeping partners together; physical and/or mental frailty; and, of course, the nearness of death.

- Sexual Expression. I have heard people in their eighties scoff at the idea of older people engaging in sex; I have heard people of the same age affirming that it is an important part of their lives. A percentage of elderly people have, want, and enjoy an active sexual life. Especially for people who live in care facilities, or have mobility challenges, how can you facilitate desired intimacy? First of all, be aware of the issue; exercise prudence; then never hesitate to delicately inquire.

- Keeping Partners Together. Recall Pastor Leonard (chapter 2) and his intervention that facilitated the coming together of long-time lesbian partners. It is an immense loss of dignity to have anyone—be it a health care professional, a politician, or even a sibling or other family member—decide that a person's long-term relationship/marriage will not be acknowledged, much less honored, by separating them from their partner/spouse in older age. Even though separation may be unavoidable at times, it still may feel to the person that they are being treated like a child. Anything you can do to facilitate elderly LGBTQ partners staying together will add stars to your crown.

- Frailty and Death. What is unique about frailty, death, and dying for LGBTQ people? Probably nothing, really. We all become very alike when faced with the last moments of life and the door to eternal life. The pastoral caregiver who accompanies the frail old and the dying will be effective simply by adding an LGBTQ sensitivity and awareness to the entire process. In addition to pastoral skills required in dealing with anyone who is frail or dying, one might need this sensitivity especially in the following situations:

    - *Memento mori.* Learn to talk comfortably about death all during life, but especially toward the end of life. Talking about one's death in a healthy, honest way and accepting its inevitability is a great gift from a pastoral caregiver.[56]

    - The healing of old relationships. Your care receiver may ask for your assistance in contacting people who were once friends in hopes of finding reconciliation with those former friends.

    - Arranging for a pastoral visit (if it is to be done by other than you), if desired.

    - Watch for faith issues, past and present; look for resentment against the person's church or synagogue as a block to inner peace; look for self-exclusion from salvation. Here is an incident from my pastoral care ministry: I was called by the family to visit a frail and dying gay man at a veteran's hospital. He said to me when I arrived, "I'm never going to be saved. The church has excluded me from the very beginning of my life so why concern yourself about me now?" He then threw a glass of water at me. It was a forceful reminder of the pain and anger he carried. Subsequent visits brought some little—but by no means full—reconciliation. It was too late.

    - Facilitating access by family, with "family" understood in an LGBTQ sense: life partners, lovers, chosen family members, and close friends.

    - Ensuring that transgender people are referred to by the name and gender that they use(d) in life.

---

56. See Flynn, *Caregiving Zone.*

## "EX-GAY" MINISTRIES AND THE "IS IT A CHOICE?" QUESTION

Especially for the pastoral caregiver who is new to this topic, here is some background information. "Ex-gay" ministries is an umbrella term that covers programs that attempt to change a person's sexual orientation, through a combination of therapy and religious teachings, from gay or lesbian or bisexual to heterosexual. Currently, the majority of these programs are instituted and supported by Christian organizations. This kind of ministry is also referred to as reparative therapy or sexual conversion therapy.[57]

These "ex-gay" ministries, a logical outcome of highly negative religious beliefs about homosexuality, have been active for the past several decades in the United States and, to a lesser extent, in Canada as well. Sponsors of these ministries are often referred to as belonging to "the religious right" or as "Christian fundamentalists," but they also include representatives from many religious bodies, including the Roman Catholic Church, Orthodox Judaism, and independent churches. What is common among these ministries is a belief that homosexuality is not only sinful but a particularly heinous abomination in God's eyes; that being queer is a free choice made by those who engage in this "sinful" "lifestyle"; and that it is the religionist's duty to vigorously defeat its acceptance by society.

### "Is It a Choice?"

That is a basic question in the ongoing arguments of many religionists on the topic of queer acceptability: do people freely at some point in their lives make a choice to be lesbian, gay, or bi, presumably over the option of being straight? The vast majority of scientific experts and an ever-increasing number of religious people are answering with a clear and emphatic "no." When the same question is posed to straight people, "When did you decide to become straight?" the truth then often hits home. Mounting evidence also confirms that there is a genetic and hormonal component involved in being homosexual. "Scientific studies of genetics, brain physiology, and hormones increasingly suggest that for many (if not most) gay and lesbian persons, sexual attraction is not a choice, but

---

57. For a general treatment of the topic, see Shidlo, *Sexual Conversion Therapy*.

an inborn trait."[58] Plus, of course, there is the overwhelming testimony of the lived experience of people: this is the way that we were born.

But old contentions die hard and there are several widely published religious writers who continue to cling to pre-scientific religious teachings. They do so, I surmise, because were they to acknowledge that being gay or lesbian (these are the two categories most targeted) is a normal minority variation that has long been identified in human sexuality (as well as in the animal kingdoms),[59] then they would have to admit that there is nothing to cure, no addiction to conquer. Thus, they contend that it is a sinful choice, a mental illness, and/or a moral failing; and thus is the way paved for "ex-gay" ministries.

I believe the urgency and emphasis that is placed on this ministry comes from the realization that it has far-reaching implications for the question of who holds the ultimate authority: religion or science? When the dust settles on this disagreement, the balance of power will likely have shifted a bit. Perhaps no current topic better exemplifies the historically ongoing religion/science disagreements than the legitimacy of queer persons. Who gets to define the question: "spiritual" religion or "secular" science? This question, of course, avoids the clear reality of a multitude of persons who combine a full acceptance of science along with a fulsome religious faith.

To this science-or-religion argument, add the basic disagreements about how the Scriptures are read and interpreted—literally or not—and you have the two bases of the broad and deep divisions among contemporary religions about LGBTQ people in general. The challenge is significant because the way many people read the Bible makes it virtually impossible for them to accept homosexuality as a normal variation of human sexuality; to do so for these people could easily render the whole of Scripture doubtful if not false, thus destroying their faith and often their entire worldview. Thus, for some, the real issue is their scriptural orientation.

However, the reality is that we have to live our lives now. Waiting for religion is not a realistic option. Are queer people to put their lives on hold? To grant authority to any polity to allow or disallow one's validity would be, I believe, deeply irresponsible, both for those who expect it and for those who might follow it.

---

58. Weaver et al., *Counseling*, 193.
59. Hopke, *Jung, Jungians*, 57.

If the religious organizations were to acknowledge, as some communities of faith clearly do, what the scientific world as well as human experience acknowledge—that being LGBTQ for the vast majority of people is an innate quality, not a freely made choice—then religion itself would have to be reborn, simply by the power of the beauty of truth. John J. Smid, a (former) representative of one of the largest "ex-gay" ministries said, "If we define homosexuality as an identity, and inborn characteristic . . . there is no answer. . . . If, however, we call it . . . a 'struggle with sinful desires and behavior' (quotation marks mine)—then throughout Scripture we're given ways to handle it."[60]

## Pastoral Care

Pastoral care in this area is both individual and systemic. Individually, the pastoral caregiver can inform the care seeker who inquires about the topic of reparative therapy, about the truth of the experience as it has been reported by those who have undergone such therapy. As Smid eventually came to acknowledge, however, reparative therapy is remarkably unsuccessful. Most programs admit that, at most, they change the individual's behavior—but only for a short while. In their 2009 report, The American Psychological Association "concludes that there is insufficient evidence to support the use of psychological interventions to change sexual orientation . . . and encourages mental health professionals to avoid misrepresenting the efficacy of sexual orientation change efforts."[61]

Please understand and help your care seekers to understand that there is "evidence to indicate that individuals experienced harm from sexual orientation change efforts (SOCE). Early studies documented iatrogenic [introduced inadvertently] effects of aversive forms of SOCE. These negative side effects included loss of sexual feeling, depression, suicidality, and anxiety."[62]

Add to these ill effects the frustration of spending time and money, frequently a great deal of both, on a goal that is all but unattainable. The American Academy of Pediatrics states that "[t]herapy directed specifically at changing sexual orientation is contraindicated, since it can

---

60. Smid, "Love in Action."
61. American Psychological Association, "Resolution."
62. American Psychological Association, "Report," 3.

provoke guilt and anxiety while having little or no potential for achieving changes in orientation."[63]

Ultimately, I believe it is important to do all in your power as pastoral caregiver to dissuade your care seekers from submitting themselves to "reparative" therapy or to become involved in any way with "ex-gay" ministries. I hope that these four fundamental reasons are clear: it is based on essentially flawed assumptions about being queer; it is immoral and insulting to deny a person's stated experience; its "successes" are nonexistent or, at best, temporary and partial; and it is capable of doing, and regularly does, a great deal of harm to people already subjected to too much.

Also, in the spring of 2017 the US Supreme Court upheld an existing 2012 California law, challenged by a Christian minister, that prohibits the use of reparative therapy—this is, indeed, a significant step forward.[64] Currently, nine states and the District of Columbia have laws in place banning conversion therapy for minors.[65]

Systemically, education is urgently important and our ministry here is to teach. I believe the role of the pastoral caregiver is to help all who work in opposition to the harmful attitude that it is wrong to be LGBTQ and wrong to live out that God-given identity in natural and moral ways.

At the same time, it is equally important to create welcoming and affirming congregations for LGBTQ people. To dissuade people from a welcoming and encouraging "ex-gay" program (often attractively packaged, subsidized, and slick) and to offer them nothing or very little in its place is poor pastoral care at best, and morally irresponsible at worst (see chapter 5).

Finally, as pastoral caregivers, I believe that we must understand and accept that people will do what they choose to do, and that we should not try to force them against their will, having done our best at affirming who they are, encouraging and welcoming them, and teaching wisdom. "People will inevitably make choices with which we deeply disagree and may even cause us great pain," says Joretta Marshall. She goes on, however, to speak of "finding a way to sit at the table with them in the midst

---

63. Human Rights Campaign, "Policy and Position Statements." This source also lists statements on conversion (or "reparative") therapy from several professional mental and physical health organizations.

64. See Chung, "U.S. Top Court."

65. Movement Advancement Project, "Conversion Therapy Laws."

of that pain and disagreement."⁶⁶ If a gay man, for example, clearly and for whatever reasons, does not want to *be* who he *is*—the very expression speaks of disintegration—I believe we may not try to force a change in that intention, no matter how self-damaging and ill-conceived we believe it to be. Such an action would be going against the basic rights I am insisting on. But we can stay at the table with them and keep the pastoral care relationship open and welcoming.

However, the urgent question here is: what is the primary and ultimate source of the desire to rid oneself of being lesbian, gay, or bisexual? It would be hard to answer anything but "religion." So, in a very real way, religion is providing an "answer" ("reparative" therapy) to a problem that religion itself has created. Religion is trying to repair something that religion has damaged, and continues to damage. Logic, charity, and justice demand that the damaging stop.⁶⁷

### It's Much More Than Sex . . .

In concluding this chapter on your ministry to LGBTQ people as they experience the "tough times" of life, I want to return to a fundamentally important idea. It's an idea that seems particularly difficult for non-LGBTQ people to understand: being LGBTQ involves much more than just the way we are as sexual beings. It genuinely involves all aspects of life: the way we relate to all people, the way we create our homes, the way we raise our children, the way we express our faith and pray, the way we work and recreate, the way we walk and dress, the way we do business, the way we understand God, the way we talk and express our ideas, and so on and so on. In a few words, it affects everything.

But this is true of everyone. One's sexuality, no matter what one's sexual orientation and/or gender identity, has an effect on all aspects of everyone's life. I believe this is challenging for non-LGBTQ people to understand *because* they are the majority. The influence of one's sexuality on all of life is, for the sexual *majority*, so innate, so intimate, so natural, so normal, and especially so generally accepted by everyone, that they really don't have to think about it. For them it's just doing what comes naturally.

---

66. Marshall, "Caring."

67. See National Center for Lesbian Rights, "Born Perfect Campaign," which works to end conversion therapy.

Of course, for LGBTQ people it's the same: it is also innate, intimate, normal, and doing what comes naturally.

I make this point here to encourage you, the pastoral caregiver, to contextualize all your dealings with your LGBTQ care receivers: in good times and in bad and to see them as people—with the ups and downs, foibles and graces, special needs and common traits that are shared by all of the children in God's wonderful human family.

# 4

# Coming Out

### Bernard Schlager

One day, several years ago now, as I walked with my youngest son to the post office in our small New England town, we were approached by two Mormon missionaries. During the course of our conversation it became clear that these young men had assumed that I was married to a woman. This caused my twelve-year-old son to grin broadly. At that moment I realized that I needed to come out as a gay man to the missionaries not only for my own sake, but also because I wanted my son to see me come out. "You know, I'm gay," I offered, "and I have to level with you: I don't agree with the position of your church on homosexuality and queer people." Caught off guard, the missionaries took a few moments to collect their thoughts before launching into an earnest denunciation of homosexuality. I told them that neither I nor my son was interested in listening to their views on homosexuality, and I politely said goodbye. As we walked away from the young men I could sense, in the squeeze of my son's hand, that he was proud that I had come out to these strangers.

As a fifty-seven-year-old gay man who first came out of the closet in my mid-twenties, I face the decision daily about whether and to whom I come out. Rarely do I choose not to come out to others, and I am fortunate that, in my work at The Center for LGBTQ and Gender Studies in

Religion (CLGS), being an out gay person is an asset. As a white, cisgender, middle-class, college-educated man who identifies as both Christian and Buddhist, I usually experience coming out as something positive. Although I could "pass" as straight, I rarely choose that option because I see coming out (and being out) as an important part of my queer identity and an important part of my religious and spiritual identity. In my own life experience and in the experience of many other LGBTQ people I have met, coming out is a powerful affirmation of oneself as a loving, sexual person. It is also a bold witness to others of the value of living with honesty and integrity.

We devote an entire chapter to coming out because it is a pivotal and ongoing experience for most LGBTQ people. If you are a pastoral caregiver interested in establishing and nurturing a caring relationship based on faith with LGBTQ individuals, then you will want to understand what coming out is so that you can provide them with competent pastoral care.

## WHAT IS COMING OUT? WHY DO PEOPLE COME OUT?

To come out of the closet is to identify oneself as lesbian, bisexual, transgender, gay, or queer. It is a two-step process that involves acknowledging this identity to oneself and then speaking it aloud to others.[1] For transgender persons, coming out entails embracing a gender identity that is other than one assigned at birth and/or at variance with prevailing cultural norms, and it is important to note that transgender persons may consider themselves to be lesbian, queer, bisexual, and/or gay, or not.[2] Significantly, coming out is used to refer to the first time that one comes out to self and others as well as to the many subsequent experiences of coming out to others.

---

1. The Human Rights Campaign provides excellent online resources on coming out as LGBTQ in a variety of settings. Included are materials on coming out in African American, Asian/Pacific Islander, and Latinx communities as well as in a variety of religious contexts.

2. Tanis, *Transgendered*, 18, defines transgender people as "those individuals who do not fit comfortably into society's traditional understandings of sex and gender." He also notes that "transgender is commonly used as a broad term to encompass a whole range of people who transgress the commonly understood definitions of gender all or part of the time." Transsexuals, transvestites, drag kings, drag queens, and "gender benders," therefore, can be seen as "subsets of the transgender" (19).

People come out of the closet because being honest with oneself and with others about one's sexual orientation and/or gender identity is necessary for a healthy emotional and spiritual life.

- *People come out to leave behind the closet and its many ills.* Rosita came out as queer at the age of fifteen because she didn't want to keep pretending that she was interested in dating boys. She knew that she liked girls and that she wanted to date girls. By coming out as queer, she was able to take a stand for herself and live more authentically.

- *People come out to reject the lie that an LGBTQ identity is either a mental illness or a sinful condition.*[3] After several years of intensive psychotherapy designed to make him straight, Sanjay began to doubt that the therapy was accomplishing its goal. He also began to question for the first time in his life whether being homosexual was, in fact, evil. Discontinuing therapy, he sought out books that treated homosexuality as something healthy and good. He also met and socialized with other queer people, and, in time, he made a decision to come out to family and friends. His own experiences proved the lie of what he had been taught since childhood, namely, that being gay was a psychological disorder.

- *People come out to express pride and confidence in themselves as loving and lovable sexual persons.* Trevor came out as transgender because he needed to embrace the person he had always been inside. He now looks forward to exploring romantic relationships with other people who will know him for who he is. Coming out has opened up the possibility of building a loving relationship with another person. He feels that he is discovering a whole new dimension of life.

---

3. Many people remain unaware that the American Psychiatric Association (APA) removed homosexuality as a mental disorder from its *Diagnostic and Statistical Manual of Mental Disorders* (DSM-II) forty-five years ago (in 1973). Religious denominations such as the United Church of Christ, Reform Judaism, and Unitarian Universalism consider queer people as morally equivalent to straight people. None of these religious traditions teach that queer sexuality is sinful or disordered. For a list of statements from some of the many professional organizations in the United States that have denounced conversion therapy, see: Human Rights Campaign, "Policy and Position Statements." See also the Movement Advancement Project, "Conversion Therapy Laws," for a listing of states that have passed "conversion therapy laws [that] prohibit licensed mental health practitioners from subjecting LGBT minors to harmful 'conversion therapy' practices that attempt to change their sexual orientation or gender identity."

## WHY IS LIFE IN THE CLOSET SO DESTRUCTIVE?

The closet is a place of secrecy, fear, and shame for queer people. As pastoral theologian Larry Kent Graham writes, "Closets deny vitality; they choke creativity."[4] I know this to be true from my own experience: living in the closet prevented me in many ways from leading a productive and satisfying life. Rather than devoting my energies to the life-giving pursuits of rewarding work, meaningful relationships, and an authentic spiritual practice, I was deeply distracted by the secret that I felt I had to keep at all costs. My work life suffered, as did my relationships with other people; my prayer life was hobbled by my inability to be myself before God. In the words of Graham, queer people pay a dear price by seeking safety in the closet and denying their sexuality:

> If we hide our unique sexuality, our capacity to know and name the world truthfully is impaired, and our capacity to reflect God's image is diminished. Creativity is negated and love curtailed. Alienation dominates, oppression prevails, and life withers.[5]

People who live in the closet can suffer the following:[6]

- Poor self-esteem
- Loneliness and isolation
- Eating disorders
- Alcohol and drug addictions
- Sexually compulsive behaviors
- Severe depression and thoughts of suicide
- An inability to build or maintain strong friendships and healthy romantic relationships

For some LGBTQ people of faith, a closeted life leads them to withdraw from their church or synagogue for fear of being discovered or because they feel that they have no place within a community of faith. Gina had been an active member of her parish youth group beginning in her freshman year of high school. Once she decided to come out of the closet as a lesbian, however, she began to withdraw from the group because she

---

4. Graham, *Discovering Images*, 174.
5. Graham, *Discovering Images*, 174.
6. See Drescher, "Closet."

knew that homosexual behavior was forbidden by the Catholic Church. Rather than risk coming out to her friends in the youth group, Gina reluctantly left the group during her senior year in high school without telling anyone why. She deeply missed the companionship of her youth group friends and soon stopped attending church altogether.

Sadly, the shame of the closet causes some people to believe that they have been abandoned not only by other people but also by God.[7] Walter, a twenty-eight-year-old Mormon, realized that he was gay while serving as a missionary in Europe. He understands clearly the choice that he has to make: either continue to hide his homosexuality, or come out and be excommunicated by his bishop and risk ostracization from his family. Up to now he has chosen a life in the closet, but he feels as if he is slowly but surely losing his battle against depression. He has begun to think that his life is not worth living.

## HOW DO PEOPLE COME OUT?

People come out as adults, young people, or senior citizens; they also come out in a variety of life situations. For some individuals, coming out is an experience of gradual understanding over a period of many years. Phyllis came out as a lesbian at the age of forty-five when, after many years of living with a man, she fell deeply in love with another woman. She wasn't surprised that she now identified as lesbian nor was she disappointed that she hadn't come out earlier: her long journey toward a lesbian identity felt completely natural to her.

---

7. For a pastoral discussion of the damage done by life in the closet for queer people, see Tigert, "Trouble," 8–9.

> **PEOPLE COME OUT**
>
> - At various ages
> - In a variety of life situations
> - Internally and externally
> - Sometimes with little or no sexual experience
> - Continuously throughout life
> - To family and friends
> - At work, at synagogue, at church
> - When they move to a new neighborhood
> - To one person or to more than one person
> - And experience acceptance
> - And experience rejection
> - By being "outed"

Other people come out after a moment of seemingly sudden recognition. Toby, a junior in college, reports, "It was during one of the many times that I spent with my best friend since high school that I realized how much I loved him. I mean, the love was so intense that right then and there I knew that I was gay."

Some people come out during or shortly after their first relationship with a person of the same gender, while others come out after many years of loving persons of the same gender. One man comes out as gay while married to a woman. A woman comes out as bisexual only after she has come to know other bisexuals. Someone comes out as transgender after being inspired by the story of another transgender person. And, despite the stereotype of queer people as oversexed individuals, some LGBTQ people come out with very little, if any, sexual experience.

Coming out does not necessarily entail revealing one's queer identity to everyone. An individual, for instance, might come out only to a parent, a pastor, a counselor, or a friend. Some people choose to come out to several relatives at once or to a group of friends. Others find that an online community provides them with a safe and comfortable place to come out. Enrolling in school, beginning a new job, joining a faith community, and moving into a new neighborhood are some of the many situations that require an LGBTQ person to decide whether or not to come out to others.

As mentioned in chapter 1, some individuals are forced out of the closet by being outed, that is, having their queer identity revealed without their permission. Actors, politicians, and religious leaders are some of the most common targets of outing. Initially used as a means of defaming a person's character, outing began to be used in the late 1980s by AIDS activists and others in an effort to call attention to closeted politicians who had supported anti-gay legislation or who were viewed as enemies of LGBTQ communities. Whatever the circumstances, outing is frequently a damaging experience that can force a person back into the closet for a period of months or even years; it can also precipitate a personal crisis filled with anxiety and depression.

## COMING OUT IS AN UNPREDICTABLE RITE OF PASSAGE

In contemporary North American societies, most LGBTQ people view coming out as an important rite of passage. For many, it is an event to be celebrated and shared with family and friends. In the 1980s hit song "I'm Coming Out," Diana Ross captures the spirit of such celebration when she sings "I'm coming out / I want the world to know / Got to let it show." Soon after its release this song rose to fifth place on the pop charts and was embraced by many queer people as a veritable anthem of gay liberation. A more recent musical example of empowerment and liberation for queer—and many other—people is Lady Gaga's hit song "Born This Way." Released in 2011, this anthem contains these powerful lyrics: "I'm beautiful in my way / 'Cause God makes no mistakes / I'm on the right track, baby I was born this way." No doubt these songs have become popular within queer communities because their lyrics proclaim what an ever-increasing number of women and men continue to do in North American societies: come out of the closet with pride and enthusiasm.

For most LGBTQ people, coming out can be an unpredictable rite of passage because many do not know what to expect from family, friends, and employers until they come out to them. Some people rejoice when they hear the news, while others disapprove of or even reject the person who has come out. Coming out is an experience that mixes joy with pain, certainty with uncertainty, and gain with loss. Consider the following coming-out stories:

- Dylan was sixteen years old when his parents kicked him out of the house because they discovered that he is gay. Finding no support at school, he dropped out and moved to another city where he is now homeless and struggling to survive. He has had no contact with his parents since he left home, and he is increasingly depressed. Dylan doubts that he can survive much longer on his own.

- When Corliss and her lesbian partner Anne came out to their minister and to the members of their small Unitarian Universalist congregation, they were met with affirmation and acceptance. Within a few months they were married by the minister in the church's sanctuary, and they are more involved than ever before in the life of their congregation.

- Max admitted to his wife that he is gay, and they divorced within the year. In the divorce proceedings he was denied custody of his two children. While he is relieved that he is finally out of the closet, he is distraught and angry that he no longer lives with his children. He fears losing contact with them.

- After Amanda underwent reassignment surgery and completed her transition from male to female, she was fired from her job as a teacher. Her friends convinced her to contact the Lambda Legal Defense and Education Fund, an LGBTQ civil rights organization, which filed suit on her behalf against the school district. While awaiting a court date she has found work teaching in a neighboring district.[8]

- Abby is a young professional who decided to come out as bisexual to her family. Her parents greet the news with anger while her brother says that a person can't really be bisexual. Hopeful that her family will come to accept her sexual orientation, Abby commits herself to fostering a loving and respectful dialogue with them.

These stories indicate the range of responses that queer people encounter when they come out. While some high-school queer youth are fortunate to have a Gay-Straight Alliance or other queer support group in their schools, many young people, like Dylan, have no such resources

---

8. See Lambda Legal website, www.lambdalegal.org.

on which to draw; some young people are even cast out of their homes. Many queer couples are refused welcome and inclusion in their synagogue or church community, but there are others, like Corliss and Anne, who find acceptance and support.

Increasingly, LGBTQ people who come out of the closet while in heterosexual marriages reach amicable solutions with their ex-spouses about child custody, but many judges still consider homosexuality, bisexuality, or a transgender identity to be sufficient grounds for denying custody. Like Amanda, many transgender people face employment discrimination when they come out because most states do not protect transgender people from being fired. The good news is that organizations like Lambda Legal help fight discrimination against LGBTQ people in the workplace.

Coming out for many bisexuals reveals deep-rooted prejudices (sometimes even within queer communities) about the legitimacy of a bisexual identity. As Abby discovered in her brother's comments, some people believe that bisexuals are individuals who have not made up their mind about whether they are queer or straight. Bisexuals can face not only rejection from others when they come out, but also denial that bisexuality is a genuine sexual identity.

## COMING OUT IS A GRACED OPPORTUNITY FOR PASTORAL CARE

Family, friends, work colleagues, and members of one's faith community can provide valuable support for a person who is coming out. In fact, loving and lasting support from others is the single most important ingredient in coming out successfully. LGBTQ friends who have come out themselves are an added blessing because they can demonstrate through personal experience that life outside of the closet is good.

For LGBTQ people of faith, a pastoral care relationship can provide an excellent context in which to explore coming out. This is because a pastoral care relationship offers a unique environment in which a person of faith can connect more deeply with self, form stronger relationships with others, and build a more honest relationship with God. In the remaining pages of this chapter we look at some specific ways in which you, the pastoral caregiver, can provide care to a person in the various stages of coming out.

## Pastoral Care and the Stages of Coming Out

Effective pastoral caregiving with an individual in the process of coming out as queer requires the following basic pastoral skills:

- Deep sensitivity
- Active listening skills
- An understanding of the most common aspects of the coming-out process
- Openness to learning about LGBTQ sexualities and queer identities
- The ability to speak comfortably and knowledgeably about issues relating to faith and sexuality
- An awareness of the deep alienation that many LGBTQ people feel from churches, synagogues, and other communities of faith
- A willingness to recommend appropriate resources and support systems

Coming out is certainly a life-changing experience for most LGBTQ people, and it can also be transforming for you, the caregiver, as you work with a person coming out. You may find, for instance, that some of your preconceptions or misperceptions about LGBTQ people and queer sexuality need to be modified or discarded altogether. Your faith might be challenged as you come to appreciate more fully the deep-seated homophobia, heterosexism, transphobia, and biphobia that exist in our culture and in many religious traditions. Your appreciation for the strength and resilience of the human spirit in the face of adversity may also grow as you journey with an LGBTQ person who comes out in the face of considerable odds.

### THE FIVE STAGES OF COMING OUT

Eli Coleman, professor and director of the Program in Human Sexuality at the University of Minnesota, offers a flexible "Five-Stage Model of Coming Out" that is particularly useful for pastoral caregivers working with LGBTQ people:[9]

9. Coleman, "Developmental Stages," 31–43. I make extensive use of Coleman's article in this chapter, and I apply his five-stage model to include bisexual, transgender, and queer people.

> ### THE FIVE STAGES OF COMING OUT
>
> 1. Pre-Coming Out
> 2. Coming Out
> 3. Exploration
> 4. First Relationships
> 5. Integration

Coleman's model helps caregivers understand that many LGBTQ people experience coming out in similar ways and that coming out is a lifelong process of healthy identity development. Based on the psychologist Erik Erikson's view that a person must meet the challenges of one developmental stage before moving on to the next, Coleman's model describes coming out as a process that begins in the closet and culminates, ideally, in an integrated way of living. In each of these five stages, therefore, an individual has important developmental tasks to undertake and significant issues to resolve before addressing the tasks and issues of the next stage.

These stages should not be used as an inflexible gauge for assessing the mental health or psychological maturity of a person because many people may not fit neatly into this five-stage model. Nor does everyone move through these stages in the given order since there is great variation in how people experience and express their queer identities. Some individuals move between these stages as the changing situations of life demand and then return at times to an earlier stage to work on particular issues. In addition, a person might live, at least for a period of time, in more than one stage at once. Finally, the model does not presume that everyone reaches the last stage of integration.

### 1. PRE-COMING OUT

The developmental task for an individual during this first stage is to face and resolve the internal crisis brought about by the realization that one is different from others because of one's sexual desires and/or gender identity. Resolution of this internal conflict, according to Coleman, can happen in one of three ways:

1. An individual may hide her sexual feelings or gender identity (that is, stay in the closet).
2. An individual may attempt suicide (and perhaps succeed).
3. An individual will achieve a healthy resolution to this crisis of difference by acknowledging their same-sex attractions or gender identity.

We live in a heterosexist world. Among other things, this statement means that all of us are taught from an early age that everyone is, or should be, heterosexual and that everyone must subscribe to the gender norms as currently constructed in our society. Growing up LGBTQ in a heterosexist and transphobic world can be not only hazardous to one's self-esteem, but also dangerous to one's psychological and spiritual health and well-being.

Psychologists tell us that sexual orientation and gender identity are fixed at very young ages for most people.[10] Once LGBTQ individuals realize, however unclearly or subconsciously, that their sexual orientation or gender identity is different from the norm, many spend considerable amounts of energy working to hide their differences from others. Trying to hide one's queerness in a straight world leads many LGBTQ children to suffer persistent low self-esteem and feelings of alienation and loneliness. In fact, long before children are able to identify themselves as LGBTQ, this sense of being different from others may lead to a wide range of negative coping mechanisms. Some people become intensely shy and withdrawn; others become unhealthy perfectionists in an attempt to compensate for the confusion and shame that they feel about being different; still others live with a hidden, but very real, despair that their place in their families, schools, and religious communities would be jeopardized if they acknowledged their queerness to others.

> Rachel is a twenty-year-old woman who has recently shared with her rabbi, David, a secret that she has told nobody else: she fantasizes about having sex with another woman. Over the course of several meetings with her, David learns that Rachel believes that homosexuals are "dirty and perverted" people who should learn how to suppress their sexual desires if they wish to live upright and holy lives. She tells the rabbi that she has come

---

10. Current estimates of the average age at which a person identifies as LGBTQ in our culture vary, but many individuals come to see themselves as queer sometime during their teenage years or in their early twenties. See Tamashiro, "Coming Out."

to him for help in getting rid of these fantasies because she is afraid that she might soon act on them.

Rachel is clearly dealing with internalized homophobia, which can be especially damaging for LGBTQ individuals because it often prevents them from accepting in a healthy way their sexual desires and/or gender identity. If Rachel is ever to embrace her lesbian identity and come out of the closet, she will need to decide whether or not she can accept her differences as something good and holy.

What should you do if, like Rachel's rabbi, you meet an individual who is unable to come out because she is dealing with internalized homophobia? Perhaps the most important thing to remember is that people need to claim for themselves and on their own timeline a queer identity if that is who they feel they are. It is never the job of a pastoral caregiver (or anyone else, for that matter) to drag a person out of the closet; people have the right to decide for themselves how they will live their lives, and whether, to whom, when, and how they will disclose personal information about themselves. If a care receiver is unable or unwilling to embrace an LGBTQ identity (either temporarily or for the long term), then you, as caregiver, must respect this choice. Some people, as mentioned, stay in the closet because they fear that coming out will mean rejection from family or friends, discrimination in employment or housing, or ostracization from their synagogue or church community.

Since Rabbi David believes that embracing one's homosexuality or transgender identity is a good and life-giving choice, and because he is well aware that psychological research has demonstrated that attempting to "cure" an individual of their sexual orientation or transgender identity is not only unsuccessful but also potentially damaging to the person, he lets Rachel know this, so that—if and when she is ready to come out—he can be an affirming resource and reliable support for her. In fact, he realizes that she has come to him because she is struggling with the decision of whether or not to embrace her lesbianism. In talking with him about her desires, she may be signaling a readiness to reevaluate her own internalized homophobia.

Many individuals on the threshold of coming out seek out a caregiver who seems supportive of LGBTQ people. Such individuals have often also begun, however tentatively, to dismantle their internalized homophobia and take their first steps in coming out.

After a few weeks of attending a new church, Damon heard the pastor, Rev. Linette, preach a rousing sermon of welcome for queer people. Knowing that she read the gospel as a text of liberation and affirmation for LGBTQ people, he felt that he had at last found someone with whom he could speak about coming out as a gay man. In their pastoral care meetings Damon was in good hands with this minister. Linette had worked before with queer people, and she understood how one's Christian faith can be a powerful tool in overcoming internalized homophobia and external oppression.

Like Pastor Linette, you can help a person to experience coming out as something positive and life-giving. Indeed, as a pastoral caregiver you may be an important authority figure whose assistance to a person coming out can be a valuable sign of God's caring love. Over time, a positive experience of pastoral care can contribute significantly to a process of healing for a person who has found hurt and alienation in the closet.

## 2. COMING OUT

Two developmental tasks need to be accomplished by a person at this stage of coming out:

1. Acknowledging one's homosexual feelings or transgender identity
2. Telling others that one is LGBTQ

Internal acknowledgment does not necessarily mean that a person has it all figured out with regard to being queer, because such understanding comes only with self-reflection and lived experience. It may take time, as well, for individuals to label themselves as LGBTQ after internally acknowledging same-sex desire or a transgender identity. Similarly, the move from internal acknowledgment to public disclosure of a queer identity is not always immediate; some people take months while others may take years.

As a pastoral caregiver you will want to convey to the care receiver your conviction that an LGBTQ identity is wholesome and good and that coming out of the closet is the best way for queer people to live with integrity. By affirming the care receiver's sexuality or gender identity you make clear that they have your support as they embrace more fully their queer identity. Such affirmation also demonstrates that you are a valuable and affirming ally in their coming-out process.

As with any pastoral care relationship, establishing a comfortable rapport with a care receiver is an important first step. By focusing early discussions on how the care receiver has come to an awareness of homosexual desire or LGBTQ identity and why they have sought out pastoral care, you can come to know the care receiver and understand their unique story. During the first or second meeting you will also want to decide if you feel competent and comfortable working with the person who has requested pastoral care. If not, you should refer the care receiver to another professional who might be a better fit.

Three skills are particularly useful for the caregiver working with a person at the second stage of coming out:

- Attentive listening
- A supportive presence
- A knowledge of effective and available support networks

Through attentive listening, you provide the care receiver with a much-needed sounding board to explore sexual desire and gender identity; skillful listening on your part can also provide a comfortable context for the care receiver to speak aloud the hopes and fears that they have about coming out.

You can demonstrate a supportive presence by celebrating with the care receiver when coming out to others is a positive experience and by offering support and reassurance when coming out proves to be negative. One important goal of pastoral care with an individual is to help them keep in mind the positive aspects of coming out, such as:

- The potential for experiencing a healthier psychological and spiritual life
- The promise of forming loving relationships with others
- The joys of living more honestly and openly with self, others, and God

> Frank has recently entered into a pastoral care relationship with his parish priest, Father Andrew. At forty-five years of age Frank has decided to come out as gay to his family, but he does not agree with his friends who say that, in order to be out of the closet, he must come out to his colleagues at work.

The priest in this pastoral situation wisely recommends to Frank that he not come out at work until he is ready to do so. He also suggests to Frank that a person can be out of the closet even if he chooses not to tell everyone, including those whom he considers to be good friends. Few people are either completely in or out of the closet. For a variety of good reasons, many individuals choose to come out to some people and not to others. As a caregiver you need to keep in mind that coming out is a personal decision that is shaped by the unique circumstances of an individual's life, and you always need to respect a person's decision not to come out to certain individuals or in certain contexts.

Sometimes a person is forced out of the closet (or "outed") by others. In such cases you will first want to explore with a care receiver their understandable feelings of shock, anger, and betrayal. In time they will need to decide how and if they will embrace a public identity as a queer person.

Coming out as transgender and/or LGBQ is easier for most people if they can avail themselves of support networks. Your obligation as a caregiver is to have handy current information on such networks. Local LGBTQ community centers, for example, frequently sponsor support groups for individuals of all ages who are coming out. High-school and college-aged youth should be encouraged to avail themselves of any school-based services available in the form of a Gay-Straight Alliance or other LGBTQ-supportive clubs on campus.

The Human Rights Campaign (HRC) and PFLAG (Parents, Families and Friends of Lesbians and Gays) have excellent online resources for coming out as LGBTQ; local PFLAG chapters have long provided support groups for LGBTQ people and their families; and the International Federation of Black Gay Prides (IFBGP) and the National Black Justice Coalition (NBJC) have teamed up on a program to encourage black LGBTQ people to come out. For Latinx people and their families, the Latinx Roundtable Project at The Center for LGBTQ and Gender Studies in Religion (CLGS) has produced high-quality resources on coming out in English, Spanish, and Portuguese. The Network on Religion and Justice for Asian and Pacific Islander Lesbian, Gay, Bisexual, Transgender, and Queer People (NRJ) offers resources for individuals who are coming out in a variety of API communities. Out & Equal Workplace Advocates offers support resources for individuals coming out at work, and for people of faith, LGBTQ denominational caucuses and local congregations that are welcoming and affirming of queer people can offer valuable support.[11]

---

**COMING OUT: INFORMATION AND SUPPORT NETWORKS**

- Local religious congregations that are welcoming and affirming of LGBTQ people
- Local LGBTQ community centers
- Denominational LGBTQ caucuses
- People of color LGBTQ organizations
- Gay-Straight Alliances
- Queer social clubs
- The Human Rights Campaign Coming Out Project
- PFLAG
- Out & Equal in the Workplace
- "Coming Out Stories" on these websites: HuffPost, It Gets Better Project, the LGBT Foundation, and "Transgender Lives: Your Stories" in *The New York Times*
- Online chat groups and e-mail discussion lists for LGBTQ people of faith

---

An individual's first experiences of coming out to others are particularly critical because LGBTQ people have much at stake when they disclose their queer identities. As Coleman points out, if a person's first experiences of coming out are positive, those experiences can provide an important confirmation of the decision to come out. They can also offer a valuable boost to one's self-confidence and become a solid foundation for coming out to others. Negative experiences, on the other hand, can shake a person's self-confidence and make them less certain—at least initially—about coming out to others in the future.[12]

---

11. For a list of additional resources on coming out, see the Resources list at the end of this book.

12. See Coleman, "Developmental Stages," 34–35.

While many people have a good idea about who will react positively or negatively to their coming out, nobody knows with certainty. The pastoral care relationship offers an excellent opportunity for you to talk with your care receiver about the potential risk factors involved in coming out to various individuals. For example, a person might realize that they are not yet ready to come out to others in their family because they are quite certain that family members will react negatively to the news that they are bisexual. This same individual, however, may decide to come out to their closest friends because they feel that they will react positively and support them.

Role-playing with the care receiver can allow them to practice coming out to others and, in the process, consider some important issues, such as:

- Has the care receiver thought about where and when to come out to their family?
- How would the care receiver handle rejection from their parents? What would they say or do? Where and to whom would they go for support?
- Does the care receiver feel shame about their queer identity, and, if so, how might such shame influence their experience of coming out to others?
- What are the pros and cons of coming out to one friend versus to a group of friends?
- Would it be a good idea for the care receiver to give their family and friends a book on transgenderism or on being gay or bi when they come out?
- Are there anti-discrimination policies in place where the individual works so that they cannot be fired for coming out?
- How might the care receiver come out in church or synagogue?

Coming out to family can be an especially challenging experience. The revelation that a child, sibling, spouse, or parent is queer can be met with everything from shock and disbelief to anger and guilt. "Why didn't you tell us this before now?" or "Did we do something wrong that made you gay?" are two common responses. Emma, a woman in her early fifties, describes coming out to her family in this way:

I was well into my thirties when I came out as a lesbian to my parents and sisters, and I was surprised by how badly they handled it. My mom was angry and said that I was just confused; my dad begged me not to tell any family friends. My older sister really freaked out and said that I would go to hell if I didn't change. She wanted to help me find an attractive guy who would turn me straight! It was my younger sister, thankfully, who helped all of us deal positively with my coming out. She said that she was not surprised by my news, and she said that she didn't want to lose contact with me. Over the next several months she and I worked hard to keep the lines of communication open among all of us and, in time, my parents and older sister joined my younger sister in accepting me as a lesbian.

While there are families that react positively when a relative comes out, there are others who respond, at least initially, in ways that Emma experienced from her family: with anger, denial, and even rejection. It is often said that when a person comes out to family, their family members go into a closet of shame and hiding in order to avoid admitting to themselves and to others that they have a child, parent, spouse, or sibling who is queer. For many people, these negative emotions are conquered in time by love and acceptance once they come to know and accept their relative as LGBTQ. Other individuals, however, face long-term opposition from family members who seem unable to accept their queer identities.

You can be especially helpful to care receivers by acquainting them with resources designed for families struggling to accept a relative who is LGBTQ Be sure to have on hand contact information for your local PFLAG chapter (which will have information on support groups for families of queer people) as well as a list of other resources.[13]

### 3. EXPLORATION

Once individuals have begun the lifelong process of coming out to others, they enter a stage of exploration in which they learn how to interact socially and sexually as a queer person with other queer people. For many individuals this stage is similar to adolescence because it gives them an opportunity to explore their sexuality and gender identity in ways that

---

13. You can find a local PFLAG chapter at the PFLAG website, www.pflag.org.

they were unable to do during their teenage years when they were either unaware of their queer identity or they lived in the closet.[14]

Coleman lists three developmental tasks for people at this stage of coming out: developing good interpersonal skills, developing a sense of personal attractiveness and sexual competence, and recognizing that one's self-esteem is not based upon sexual conquests. They are helpful guideposts for you in your work as a caregiver with individuals at this stage.

## Developing Good Interpersonal Skills

> A few months after coming out successfully to her family and to her (straight) friends, Donna couldn't understand why she was unable to connect with other lesbians. "What's wrong with me?" she wondered. It was awkward for her to hang out at a neighborhood bar frequented by other middle-aged lesbians because she didn't know how to strike up conversation. She felt as if she didn't fit in with the other lesbians there. Donna was beginning to think that her life out of the closet might be as lonely as her life in the closet.

If Donna decides to seek out pastoral care, her caregiver would do well to work with her on improving her interpersonal skills. For instance, it may be helpful for Donna to call to mind those unique qualities that she brings to a relationship and to list the qualities that she is looking for in a friend or a lover. Her caregiver might also urge her to consider a variety of venues for meeting other lesbians: frequenting a local LGBTQ community center or volunteering for a local queer organization might be more comfortable settings than a bar. Joining a group of other newly out queer people might be another way in which she can learn how to become more at ease in queer social situations. She might find that an online dating service is a good way to meet suitable women to date. If she is a person of faith, Donna might try attending a welcoming congregation that provides social events and other programming for LGBTQ people.

Since our society attempts to socialize everyone as a heterosexual person, some people, like Donna, may need to sharpen their interpersonal

---

14. According to Coleman, "Developmental Stages," 35, the specific developmental challenge of this stage is to "interact with others who are open and honest about their sexuality [which, in turn] furthers the development of a positive self-image."

skills in order to relate more authentically to others who are queer. The good news is that such skills can be learned and, typically, the more comfortable a person is with their own queer identity, the easier it is for them to develop these skills.

## Developing a Sense of Personal Attractiveness and Sexual Competence

> Noah, a thirty-year-old gay man who has been in pastoral care with Andrea for several weeks, has recently come out of the closet. He has not been able to find suitable dating partners, however, because he believes that he is not handsome enough. He also worries increasingly that his lack of sexual experience will be a hindrance when and if he does find someone to date. Maybe, he says, he is not meant to find a boyfriend.

Like many gay men, Noah did not date other boys as an adolescent; therefore, he never developed a strong sense of his own personal attractiveness as a gay person. Now that he is out of the closet, he is finding it difficult to enter the dating scene. His caregiver, Andrea, believes that Noah's doubts about his attractiveness, which have contributed to his overall low self-esteem, need to be dealt with if he is ever to have successful dating experiences and, eventually, form healthy romantic relationships. She and Noah talk about how he might improve his self-image, and he has begun to understand that a positive self-image is a necessary first step in finding suitable dating partners.

Growing up in a heterosexist culture teaches many LGBTQ people to feel shame for their sexual desires, their unconventional gender identity, and/or their physical appearance. For some transgender individuals, feelings of insecurity about their unique bodies may erode their self-confidence and they may wonder if others will find them attractive or "normal enough."[15] Most LGBTQ people devote considerable energy while young to hiding those aspects of themselves that might give them away as queer, and, even after they come out, they can still find it difficult to appreciate, much less enjoy, what makes them attractive to others. Like Noah, many individuals need to discover and appreciate their own personal attractiveness before they are able to form healthy romantic relationships with others.

15. I am indebted to Justin Sabia-Tanis for this observation.

Noah's lack of sexual experience highlights three important skills required of pastoral caregivers who work with people coming out: (1) the ability to speak with genuine ease about sexuality in general and queer sexuality in particular; (2) the ability to recommend good resources on queer sexuality; and (3) the ability to put a care receiver in touch with local LGBTQ support organizations. Since our schools and congregations rarely, if ever, treat homosexuality and transgender issues positively in their sex education programs, many LGBTQ people need positive and up-to-date information on queer sexuality. If you, as a caregiver, are able to speak comfortably and knowledgeably about sex, then you can be an especially valuable resource for a care receiver in the process of coming out.

## Recognizing that One's Self-Esteem Is Not Based upon Sexual Conquests

> Tory, a queer man in his early twenties, has been out of the closet for almost two years. During that time he has enjoyed an active sex life. Recently, however, he has begun to feel an inner emptiness in connection with some of his sexual relationships. Tory asks Stuart, a longtime confidant and youth minister at his church, if they can meet to talk.
>
> Tory and Stuart decide to enter into a formal pastoral care relationship and explore what it means to live and love responsibly as a sexually active adult. They begin by discussing how Tory might draw upon his religious beliefs to construct a sexual ethic that affirms his queer identity and helps him to live out his values in his sexual relationships. This values-clarification work proves to be invaluable for Tory, helping him to realize that he has sometimes engaged in sex with others primarily as a way to bolster his own ego.

Many queer people enter into intense and adolescent-like periods of sexual activity after they come out. This is not surprising since most closeted queer people were never afforded the opportunity during their teenage years to explore openly their sexuality. Making up for the lost years of adolescence, which is what Tory has attempted to do, can be a healthy and productive experience for queer people who may be able to repair much of the damage done by having suppressed their sexual desires and avoided healthy youthful sexual experimentation. Indeed, several psychological researchers have concluded that homosexuals (and I would add all queer people) "may benefit from permission to explore and experiment with their sexual identity."[16] However, some individuals, in their attempt to make up for lost time in the area of sexual exploration, may lose sight of ethical considerations with regard to sexual activity.

The pastoral care relationship can be an excellent context for an individual to explore the ethical dimensions of sexual exploration after coming out. As caregiver you can talk with your care receiver and help them to gain a clearer understanding of their personal values with regard to sex and respectful interpersonal relationships. Such discussions can also help an individual to integrate more maturely their sexual behavior with their moral convictions and religious beliefs. The following questions are some possible "discussion starters" for you and your care receiver:

- What defines ethical and meaningful sexual activity with another person?
- Is it OK to be in a sexual relationship with more than one person at a time?
- Are anonymous sexual encounters ethical?
- Is sexual activity within a relationship that is not loving morally acceptable?
- Is it personally fulfilling?
- Is sexual activity within a relationship that is not long-lasting ethically responsible? Is it personally fulfilling?
- How does a person ground their sexual activity in their values and beliefs?

You will certainly need to challenge a care receiver if you learn of sexual behaviors that are compulsive or health-threatening; abusive sexual behaviors should also be addressed immediately and named as serious obstacles to healthy psychosexual development and interpersonal relationships.

For some LGBTQ people, substance abuse (discussed more thoroughly in chapter 3) can interfere with a successful resolution to the development tasks of the exploration stage of coming out. This is because

---

16. Coleman, "Developmental Stages," 37.

some individuals misuse alcohol and other drugs in an attempt to anesthetize the emotional pain that can accompany the challenges of learning how to relate to other people as an out queer person or to cope with the discrimination they face. Every pastoral caregiver, of course, should be well versed in detecting signs of substance abuse; in addition, you will want to have up-to-date information on local support groups for LGBTQ individuals dealing with such abuse.[17]

## 4. FIRST RELATIONSHIPS

Coming out of the closet is an inherently relational process because it means that the out person is now free to interact with other people (queer and nonqueer alike) with greater honesty and integrity than before. Freed from the shame and fear that typify life in the closet, a person now faces the exciting challenge of building relationships that can enhance life in previously unimaginable ways.

For many people, romantic relationships are a wonderfully worthwhile and necessary aspect of life. Part of the insidious damage done to closeted LGBTQ people, however, is that it leaves many of them questioning their ability to sustain romantic relationships. In a culture that often hides, trivializes, or denigrates queer romantic relationships, a person who comes out of the closet can do so with little self-confidence about how to find and sustain a healthy relationship with another queer person.

> After a year of living with her partner Alice, Elena has sought advice from her minister because she worries that her relationship is floundering. "We don't seem to be as much in love as we once were," she reports. "Is this normal? Does is mean that we're not going to survive as a couple?"

The developmental task for the fourth stage of coming out is learning how to function maturely in one's first romantic relationship with another queer person in our heteronormative society. Whereas sexual and social experimentation was the development task of the third stage, the individual in this stage seeks to develop intimate relationships that are longer-term and demand more significant commitment. Of course, individuals at this fourth stage may have previously enjoyed enduring romantic relationships with other queer people, or they may be currently involved in a relationship that began in an earlier stage of the coming out

---

17. See chapter 3 for discussions of addiction and same-gender domestic violence.

process. The defining emphasis of a relationship at this stage of coming out, however, is on building and sustaining one's first romantic relationship as an out person.

The pastoral care setting can be an especially productive and supportive environment for the care receiver to reflect on a first relationship. Elena and her minister, for instance, have chosen to explore Elena's goals for her relationship with Alice and to help her normalize the strains that they are experiencing after their first year of living together. As a caregiver, you might consider some of the following questions when working with an LGBTQ person who is struggling with a first relationship:

- What expectations do you and your partner have for the relationship? Have you shared them with each other? Are these expectations realistic?
- Do you talk openly with each other about the challenges you face in your relationship?
- How do you resolve conflict in your relationship?
- Which aspects of your relationship are healthy, and which need to be improved?

By discussing some of the common pitfalls of first relationships you can help the care receiver to put into perspective the challenges of their own relationship. For example, Coleman lists "intensity, possessiveness, and [a] lack of trust" as typical strains in most first relationships.[18] In a culture that so often equates "first love" with "perfect love," you may need to remind a care receiver that such challenges are normal for any relationship, that they are opportunities for growth, and that they are not necessarily harbingers of the relationship's demise.

You should also be aware of the unique challenges that LGBTQ people face in their first relationships. Perhaps most significant of these is the pervasive lack of social, religious, legal, and familial supports for many queer people in relationships. LGBTQ youth, in particular, are rarely supported in their first relationships with one another, and many of them grow up with few, if any, role models of successful queer relationships.

> Tyrone and Jacob have been together for two years, and theirs is the first serious relationship for each of them. Jacob worries that their relationship is in trouble because Tyrone still seems

---

18. Coleman, "Developmental Stages," 38.

uncomfortable when they are out together in public and he has not yet introduced Jacob to his family or to his work colleagues. "Is he ashamed of our relationship?" Jacob wonders.

For some individuals, being in a first relationship with another queer person means adjusting to a higher level of public visibility and, therefore, embracing a greater degree of outness than when one was single. This may be uncomfortable for some and strain the relationship, as is the case with Tyrone and Jacob. Not coming out to family members and friends can pose a serious challenge for many LGBTQ people in their first relationships because it can lead to feelings of isolation, especially when times get difficult.

Queer individuals who have previously been in heterosexual relationships may be surprised by—and need time to adjust to—the different dynamics that may characterize a same-sex relationship, such as a more equitable sharing of tasks when living with a partner of the same gender. Transgender people may experience a certain amount of disorientation in adjusting to gender norms that are different from the norms they were socialized in as children: one example might be that boys and men are sometimes taught to hold doors open for girls and women.

You may find as a caregiver that individuals need to work through a variety of internalized negative stereotypes about queer relationships that can seriously undermine or even jeopardize their relationships. A few of the more common misperceptions and stereotypes include the following:

- The only genuine relationships are those that imitate straight relationships.
- Gay male relationships are inherently unstable and short-lived.
- A relationship between two people will end when one of them makes a gender transition.
- Bisexuals are incapable of making lasting commitments.
- Long-lasting lesbian relationships eventually become sexless.
- LGBTQ people are promiscuous.

Finally, be open to exploring other issues that may arise for individuals in their first relationships, especially those that involve the often unspoken expectations that all individuals bring into a relationship. For instance, you may be called on to discuss with a care receiver the normal ebb and flow of sexual desire and the challenge that this may pose to a romantic relationship. Issues relating to sexual monogamy; living together; disparity of income; age, class, racial, and/or ethnic differences; and deciding whether and when to meet the family members or friends of one's partner are other issues that many queer people deal with in their first relationships. Keep in mind that lessons learned in a first relationship can be valuable for an individual in any future relationships.

## 5. INTEGRATION

In this final stage individuals strive to "incorporate their public and private identities into one self."[19] Having acknowledged queer desire and shared with others the truth of their LGBTQ identity (stage 2), individuals have come to know themselves more deeply through sexual and social exploration (stage 3). They have also begun to learn how to love others in romantic relationship (stage 4). In this fifth stage of coming out, which usually takes several years to reach after an individual first becomes aware of same-sex desire or begins to question his or her gender identity, the LGBTQ person is able to draw upon a mature confidence born of life experience. This final stage of integration is obviously not static; rather, it encompasses the rest of a person's life with all of its challenges, especially those related to interpersonal relationships and loss. Coleman paraphrases social science researcher J. Grace to describe this final stage as

> open-ended, [and] an ongoing process of development that will last for the rest of the person's life. New feelings about self will continue to emerge, new labels and concepts will be discovered, new social networks will be identified and explored, and new relationships and intimacies will be enjoyed.[20]

As a caregiver working with persons engaged in the ongoing work of integration, you may be called upon to offer them support and encouragement as they deal with a wide variety of issues relating to family, interpersonal relationships, career, illness, aging, and the death of loved ones. You will need to continue to educate yourself, of course, about the circumstances of queer people's lives since they are different in many ways from the lives of non-queer individuals.

---

19. Coleman, "Developmental Stages," 39.
20. Coleman, "Developmental Stages," 39.

## COMING OUT AS A SPIRITUAL JOURNEY

Coming out of the closet is "deliverance from oppressive structures to liberating values, from self-hatred to communal love and support. It is a sacred journey because it involves courage and steadfast faith in God."[21] These words of Antonio Salas remind us that coming out can be a marvelous experience of liberation as well as a lifelong journey requiring stamina and fortitude. Coming out is similar in many ways to the journeys from oppression to freedom that countless women and men of faith have taken throughout history. It is also an ongoing experience filled with many ups and downs along the way. Clearly, coming out is not for the faint of heart.

If you are not queer, I invite you to take just a moment—right now—to imagine what it might be like to come out. Keep in mind that you have grown up in a culture that presumes you are straight. At some point in your life you come to identify queer desire, realize a longing to dress in clothing generally reserved for the other gender, or realize an LGBTQ identity within yourself, but you retreat, out of fear, to the safety of the closet. After much soul-searching, however, you come out to yourself and then to others.

By coming out you have arrived at a summit in the journey of self-acceptance. Hopefully you have arrived with a sense of relief and joy. If you are fortunate, you have had help in the climb to this summit—your faith has sustained you, and there have been other people who have supported you and will continue to support you on the lifelong journey of coming out. Nevertheless, as you look out from your perch and survey the landscape of your future, you see that there are many more mountains, some quite formidable, to climb: perhaps ostracization by family and friends, discrimination in housing, loss of employment, and, if you are a person of faith, possible rejection from a faith community that condemns LGBTQ people and their sexuality. By imagining yourself as queer, you, as a caregiver, can begin to understand some of the many unique challenges that face an LGBTQ person of faith who comes out.

The story of Exodus in the Hebrew Bible offers a wonderful biblical metaphor for understanding coming out as a sacred journey. Long a favorite of queer Jews and Christians who identify with this profound example of divine deliverance from human oppression, the Exodus story reminds us of the power of faithful risk-tasking in the face of overwhelming odds.

21. Salas, "My Journey of Deliverance."

After years of suffering at the hands of the pharaohs, the Hebrews courageously followed Moses out of the land of their bondage. Once they had fled into the desert they began the arduous and dangerous trek to a promised land that they had never seen. These desert years were filled with doubt and despair for the Hebrews, but God never abandoned them. Quite the contrary: God led this journeying people back home to the land of their ancestors.

LGBTQ people of faith understand what it is like to journey with God from an old life of oppression to a new life of freedom. As gay Episcopal Bishop Gene Robinson has written, the Exodus story can be seen as the "greatest coming-out story in the history of the world":

> Queer people know what it's like to be slaves in Egypt. We know what it's like to hear of the promise of freedom in the Promised Land; we know how scary it is to step out and leave Egypt [by] leaving the closet; and we know what it's like to wander in the wilderness for forty years and wonder why it's taking so long.[22]

The good news, of course, is that many LGBTQ people of faith also know that the promise of the Exodus was fulfilled by a God who led God's people from a barren wasteland into a land flowing with milk and honey. And we LGBTQ people know from personal experience that the Exodus promise is realized every time a person embraces their queer identity after years in the closet. We LGBTQ people of faith know, as well, that the experience of coming out is an experience of coming home: to oneself, to others, and to the God who has called us to be the beautiful queer people that God intended us to be.

---

22. Robinson as quoted in Duin, "Gay Bishop."

# 5

# Creating Communities of Care for LGBTQ People

BERNARD SCHLAGER

BAPTIST MINISTER JACKI BELILE recommends a three-fold task for congregations seeking to welcome LGBTQ people: (1) "take into account the depth of people's betrayal and pain at the hands of the institutional church in all the dimensions of fellowship, preaching, teaching, and pastoral care"; (2) offer "significant opportunities for LGBT people to have visibility, voice and leadership roles in the life of the community"; and (3) ask this question: "to what are we welcoming folks?" In addition, Belile believes that members of a welcoming congregation "must reckon with the realities that they may be called to go places which push the envelope of respectable Christian doctrine or moral teaching . . . that seeks to 'main-stream' LGBT folks."[1]

In this chapter I explore how congregations can become communities of care for LGBTQ people by welcoming and including them in all aspects of congregational life. This is no small task given the fact that queer people have long experienced significant alienation and outright discrimination from churches and synagogues. For centuries religious institutions of all kinds have persecuted queer people because of their

1. Belile, "Building Well-Coming Communities," 4–5.

sexual desires and sexual activity and, despite the fact that several Christian denominations now affirm LGBTQ people and their sexuality, most, in fact, still teach that homosexual activity is sinful and that transgenderism is somehow disordered.[2]

LGBTQ people have always been present and active in congregations of every religious tradition and denomination, however closeted many have been in order to survive in their local faith communities. To speak of straight people "welcoming" LGBTQ people into congregations, therefore, can cause us to ignore this long-time presence of queer members and attenders. Perhaps more accurate terms for congregations that seek to become communities of care for LGBTQ people would be "recognizing," "acknowledging," and "embracing" congregations. Whatever terms are used, however, it is important to recognize the fact that "welcoming" LGBTQ persons may mean beginning with those who are already present within the congregation.

A congregation that commits itself to becoming a community of care will necessarily be transformed by the queer people who are invited to live as out and full-fledged members of the congregation. In fact, I believe that a congregation whose members fear such transformation is not yet ready to become a community of care because it is unable to incorporate and celebrate LGBTQ people who bring unique gifts, talents, and needs to the religious community. The process of creating a welcoming community may challenge straight individuals in profound ways. For instance, open displays of affection between queer people, recognition of LGBTQ families, the preaching of sermons based on queer readings of Scripture, and calling LGBTQ individuals to positions of visible leadership—these may cause discomfort for some straight members of a congregation.

To welcome queer people into congregations of faith is risky precisely because it is an invitation that involves change on the part of those who have the power to do the welcoming. We know that people were deeply unsettled by demands from the Hebrew prophets and from Jesus to welcome and love the poor, the stranger, the immigrant, and other outcast persons. In similar fashion people today can become unsettled by calls to welcome queer people into congregational life. And yet, just as many people in the Hebrew and Christian Scriptures were blessed with

---

2. For a description of Christian positions on transgender people, see Tanis, *Trans-Gendered*, 85–114. See Meir, "Resources," for an excellent bibliography on transgender identity, history, and related topics in Judaism.

unexpected gifts when they heeded a call to embrace the marginalized and the outcast, so too can congregations today expect spiritual growth and a revitalization of community life when doors of welcome are opened to LGBTQ people.

> **THREE BASIC STEPS TO BUILDING A COMMUNITY OF CARE FOR LGBTQ PEOPLE**
>
> 1. Create a Genuine Welcome
> 2. Integrate LGBTQ People Into the Life of the Congregation
> 3. Build Alliances with LGBTQ Communities Outside of the Congregation

There are a variety of ways in which a congregation can realize these three steps and the recommendations below are not offered as fail-safe instructions for every religious congregation wishing to welcome and provide care for queer people. Rather, they reflect some of the most important ways in which congregations have successfully accomplished this.[3]

## 1. CREATE A GENUINE WELCOME

Everyone can distinguish a genuine welcome from one that is half-hearted and it is not difficult for LGBTQ people to realize whether they are welcomed or not in a particular congregation. Merely posting a welcome sign or publishing a statement of acceptance does not prove, of course, that a congregation is actually welcoming and inclusive. Signs and statements can certainly be important indications of welcome and inclusion but they must be backed up by reality, that is, by a congregational commitment to an ongoing process of learning how to become a community of care for LGBTQ people and their families.

A church or synagogue that cares for queer people is one that honors them as morally complete human persons, invites them into full membership, and celebrates their life experiences in all aspects of congregational life. Building a community of care requires reversing age-old prejudices and doing away with insidious practices of exclusion, however

3. See Schlager, *With Open Arms*.

unintended they may be. Building a community of care also calls upon the leaders and members of a congregation to expand their notions of community in ways that are counter-cultural because they violate the heterosexist norms of our society and call into serious question the anti-queer theologies and practices of many of our religious traditions.

A congregation that seeks to open doors of welcome to LGBTQ people may face disapproval from some members who believe that they do not have a legitimate claim to membership in the community. A congregation may also face censure from denominational officials who oppose any change in belief systems and policies that marginalize queer people. To become a community of care may, indeed, mean that some members will leave the congregation or that a congregation's institutional affiliations will be jeopardized or even terminated. For the congregation that feels called to welcome and include all people, however, these risks are worth taking because they are outweighed by the opportunity to grow as a community that welcomes, loves, and includes all of God's children.

---

**A GENUINE WELCOME IS**

- Educated
- Stated
- Transforming

---

## A Genuine Welcome Is an Educated Welcome

A congregation interested in becoming a community of care should begin with education and compassionate dialogue. The leaders and members of a church or synagogue will need to educate themselves about sexual orientation, gender identity, and the most genuine and effective ways to integrate LGBTQ people into the life of the congregation. Throughout this process a congregation needs to make and realize a commitment to engage in open and honest conversation with queer people about their lives.

## A SELECTION OF RESOURCES FOR BUILDING A WELCOMING CONGREGATION

Note: Full bibliographical details are available in the Resources list

- *Coming Out While Staying In: Struggles and Celebrations of Lesbians, Gays, and Bisexuals in the Church*, by Leanne Tigert.
- *Enfold: A Reconciling Congregation Explores What it Means to Welcome All People*, edited by Karen Oliveto.
- *Homosexuality and Judaism: A Reconstructionist Workshop Series*, edited by Robert Glück.
- *Inclusion: Making Room for Grace*, by Eric Law.
- *Kulanu: All of Us—A Program and Resources Guide for Gay, Lesbian, Bisexual, and Transgender Inclusion*, edited by Richard Address, Joel Kushner, and Geoffrey Mitelman.
- *Living the Welcoming Congregation*, by The UUA Office of Bisexual, Gay, Lesbian, and Transgender Concerns.
- *Made in God's Image: A Resource for Dialogue about the Church and Gender Differences*, by Ann Thompson Cook.
- *More Than Welcome: Learning to Embrace Gay, Lesbian, Bisexual and Transgendered Persons in the Church*, by Maurine Waun.
- *Rainbow Theology: Bridging Race, Sexuality, and Spirit*, by Patrick S. Cheng.
- *Talking About Homosexuality: A Congregational Resource*, by Karen Oliveto, Kelly Turney, and Traci West.
- *Their Own Received Them Not: African American Lesbians & Gays in Black Churches*, by Horace Griffin.
- *Transitioning to Inclusion: Embracing Lesbian, Gay, Bisexual, Transgender, and Questioning Youth in Faith Communities*, by Kelsey Pacha, The Center for LGBTQ and Gender Studies in Religion (CLGS).
- *Umoja: Unity in the Community Curriculum* [for African American Christian congregations], by Roland Stringfellow.

- *The Welcoming Congregation Handbook: Resources for Affirming Bisexual, Gay, Lesbian, and/or Transgender People*, by The UUA Office of Bisexual, Gay, Lesbian, and Transgender Concerns.
- *Where the Edge Gathers: Building a Community of Radical Inclusion*, by Yvette Flunder.
- *A Whosoever Church: Welcoming Lesbians and Gay Men into African American Congregations*, by Gary David Comstock.

Many congregations have found it helpful to form a welcoming taskforce to facilitate the process of deciding how to become welcoming and inclusive. Composed of laity and clergy, queer and non-queer people, congregational staff members and perhaps individuals from outside of the congregation, this taskforce should be commissioned at a Sabbath or Sunday worship service. The primary duties of the taskforce include exploring current denominational and congregational attitudes toward homosexuality and transgenderism and working to educate the congregation on how to build a community of care. The ultimate goal of this taskforce should be to draft a statement of welcome for the congregation's consideration.

The taskforce will also want to consult resources on building welcoming congregations, including curricula that have been developed within the congregation's own religious tradition. Soon after its formation the taskforce should engage the entire congregation in a process of learning and dialogue by means of weekly classes, panel presentations, reading materials, and/or discussion groups that explore the following important questions and issues:

- How do non-queer members feel about welcoming and including queer people in the life of the congregation?

    Take a survey of congregants to understand better their current attitudes on homosexuality, transgenderism, and bisexuality.

- In some congregations discussions about sexuality can be highly charged and potentially contentious.

    Be prepared for potentially heated discussions and work to create a safe environment for individuals to disagree with each other. State clearly that differing points of view are welcome and

## Creating Communities of Care for LGBTQ People 159

emphasize that all opinions expressed in a spirit of love and respect will be heard.

- What does the congregation's faith tradition have to say about human sexuality in general and homosexuality, bisexuality, and transgenderism in particular? How have queer and non-queer individual theologians, clergy, and laity (from inside and outside the congregation's particular tradition) dealt with issues relating to sexuality and LGBTQ people in the past thirty years?

    Offer education nights and/or weekend classes on homosexuality and LGBTQ issues for your congregation. Have your minister or rabbi preach on homosexuality and queer people. Mention frequently the congregation's journey toward welcome in congregational worship.

- What do psychologists and other medical professionals have to say about sexual orientation, gender identity, bisexuality, and homosexuality?

    Provide accessible reading materials on homosexuality, bisexuality, and transgenderism that have been written by respected doctors and psychologists.

- Listen to the experiences of queer people of faith.

    Host a panel discussion with queer people, recommend books and articles by queer theologians and spiritual writers, and include writings by queer people of faith in your congregational newsletter. Invite any LGBTQ individuals, couples, or supportive relatives or friends of queer people who are already in your congregation to speak about their life experiences.

- What can the congregation learn from congregations that are known to provide excellent pastoral care for queer people?

    Invite lay members and clergy from nearby welcoming congregations as well as representatives from denominational LGBTQ groups to share their knowledge of how to build communities of care. Visit welcoming congregations to see firsthand how their members welcome and include their queer members.

## A Genuine Welcome Is a Stated Welcome

LGBTQ people understand from years of experience that they are unwelcome in most congregations. Since our culture is saturated with the anti-queer rhetoric of religious leaders who claim to represent the only authentic Jewish and Christian positions on homosexuality, a congregation that seeks to become welcoming needs to state clearly and publicly its welcome in order to be heard. A public statement of welcome, therefore, is the best way for queer people in search of a religious community to know that a congregation is welcoming. It also reassures those LGBTQ people already present in a congregation that they are not excluded or relegated to second-class membership.

When the members of the welcoming taskforce, in concert with congregational leadership, believe that their congregation is ready to decide if it will become officially welcoming, they should draw up a statement of welcome and present it to the membership at large for its consideration and approval. In many congregations the governing board may need to approve such a statement before the congregation as a whole votes on the matter. Some congregations may decide to vote after several months of education and discussion while others may need more time. Many congregations celebrate the passage of their welcoming statement in a worship service that ritualizes the decision and confirms the congregation's ongoing commitment to build a community of care. Print your statement frequently in your congregational newsletter, in your weekly Order of Service, on your congregational website, and in your local news media. Many queer people today go first to a congregation's website to assess its climate of welcome for LGBTQ folks: if a statement of welcome and inclusion is not easily found on the site, then most people will not risk a visit to a faith community that might be unwelcoming or even hostile.

A well-crafted statement of welcome is brief but clear in its message. It is also one that makes specific mention of LGBTQ people. While some congregations choose to model their statements on those written by denominational advocacy groups, others write their own. Keep in mind that your statement serves not only as a welcome to queer people but also as an ongoing reminder for your entire congregation of its ideals and as a gauge to assess its growth over the years. Below are four examples of welcoming statements from a variety of religious traditions:

> Sha'ar Zahav is a Jewish community that affirms the sacred in each and every one of us. Rooted in our history as San

Francisco's gay and lesbian synagogue, we offer the warmth and comfort of chosen family. To that end, we embrace a diversity of individuals of all sexualities, genders, races and abilities. We welcome a diversity of families, including single members, interfaith, single-parent, and multicultural families.[4]

*Congregation Sha'ar Zahav, San Francisco*

First United Methodist Church is an inclusive, Christ-centered community of faith. Our mission statement is to welcome all people, to be guided by the teaching and unconditional love of Jesus, and to inspire people to live as faithful disciples of Jesus Christ. We are a Reconciling Congregation, and all persons—without regard to race, sexual orientation, economic condition, or prior religious background—are invited to participate in our ministries and programs, and may become members of our congregation. We want to meet people where they are in their spiritual journey. We seek to link Christian spirituality with concern for justice and the well-being of our community and all creation. We hope to help people cultivate a passionate, compassionate, and thoughtful Christian faith.[5]

*First United Methodist Church, Duluth, Minnesota*

We are a Welcoming Congregation, recognized by the Unitarian Universalist Association. This means we affirm and include people who are lesbian, gay, bisexual, transgender, and queer at every level of congregational life—in worship, in program, and in social occasions—welcoming them as whole people. As a Welcoming Congregation we have pledged to:

- Honor the lives of all people and equally affirm displays of caring and affection without regard for sexual orientation.
- Celebrate diversity by using inclusive language and content in worship.
- Incorporate an understanding of the experience of lesbian, gay, bisexual, transgender, and queer persons throughout all of our programs, including religious education.
- Affirm and celebrate lesbian, gay, bisexual, transgender, and queer issues and history.
- Affirm marriage equality and conduct same-sex weddings.

4. Congregation Sha'ar Zahav (www.shaarzahav.org).
5. First United Methodist of Duluth (www.fumcduluth.com).

- Advocate for lesbian, gay, bisexual, transgender, and queer people, promoting justice, freedom, and equality in the larger society. We speak out when the rights and dignity of lesbian, gay, bisexual, transgender, and queer people are at stake.[6]

> *The Auburn Unitarian Universalist Fellowship,*
> *Auburn, Alabama*

Third Church is committed to the full participation of all persons in our church community without regard for sexual orientation, personal background, or human condition. Our More Light Committee works on ways to make all of us more aware of the contributions Presbyterian lesbian, gay, bisexual and transgender persons are making and could make to further God's Commonwealth.[7]

> *Third Presbyterian Church, Rochester, New York*

Of course, a welcoming statement does not mean that a congregation has completed its work of becoming a community of care for LGBTQ people because such work is continual. However, a statement does send an important and bold message that a congregation has begun to educate itself about queer people and is eager to welcome (more) queer people into all areas of its life.

## A Genuine Welcome Is a Transforming Welcome

By genuinely welcoming and integrating LGBTQ people into a congregation all members can experience transformation. When individuals who once were unwelcome and perhaps even unnamed are brought into a community of faith, new perspectives are gained on what it means to live as people of faith. When individuals who have been marginalized for so long enter more fully into congregational life they also are transformed because they have been freed, perhaps for the first time ever, to live as out queer people of faith.

Following are some ways in which a congregation can be transformed by welcoming out queer people into its midst:

---

6. The Auburn Unitarian Universalist Fellowship (www.auuf.org).

7. Third Presbyterian Church, Rochester (www.thirdpresbyterian.org/service/serve_morelight.shtml).

- *Visibility*: As word of a congregation's welcome and inclusivity spreads there will be an increase in the number of LGBTQ people who attend worship services and other congregational programming. Some individuals in your congregation may begin to recognize for the first time the presence of queer people in their midst, some of whom, of course, may have been present for a long time. If a church or synagogue feels genuinely welcoming, some queer people with children may begin to attend events designed for families, queer couples may be present at programs designed for married couples and feel comfortable expressing their affection for one another by holding hands during a service. Some long-time members and visitors may come out as transgender and new transgender individuals may come to check out the congregation and eventually become members. Some straight congregants may reveal for the first time that they have queer children, parents, or other relatives.

- *The Emergence of New Perspectives on Faith*: The inclusion of out LGBTQ individuals as board members, ushers, worship leaders, and religious education teachers will contribute to the richness of a congregation's faith life. The learning experiences of children in a congregation's religious education program, for instance, will be enriched by the age-appropriate life stories offered by their out lesbian teacher; participants in a Bible study group may hear for the first time how a transgender or bisexual person interprets a particular biblical story; and the wedding ceremony of two gay men may expand some congregants' notion of love and family.

- *A Growing Diversity*: Welcoming LGBTQ people is a progressive act of faith that often attracts other individuals who have felt alienated from faith communities for a variety of reasons. People who disagree with the beliefs and practices of the congregation in which they were raised, couples and families in search of a diverse faith community, and young people eager to experience a congregation that encourages questioning and exploration will be attracted to check out a synagogue or church known for its welcome of queer people.

- *An Expanded Consciousness of Social Justice Issues*: Building a community of care for LGBTQ people may spur the members and leaders of a congregation to address other social justice issues such as fair housing, immigrant assistance, anti-racism work, environmental protection, and world peace. Many of the skills and processes that the congregation has employed in creating a community of care for queer people can be useful in welcoming and including other marginalized people, including those who are separated, divorced, other-abled, unemployed, those living with mental illness, and/or recovering from substance abuse or domestic violence.

- *An Ethos of Welcome*: Hospitality is wonderfully contagious. Welcoming a diversity of people into congregational life expands a congregation's sense of itself. As previously marginalized people are welcomed into full membership the members and leaders of a congregation begin to realize that the best way to ensure vitality and growth is to continually broaden their hospitality. Building a community of care is an ongoing project that includes welcoming everyone, especially the outcast in our society.

## 2. INTEGRATE LGBTQ PEOPLE INTO THE LIFE OF THE CONGREGATION

Once a congregation has publicly declared its welcome, it needs to work toward including and integrating queer people more fully in all aspects of congregational life. Since a community of care assumes, accepts, and celebrates the presence of queer people within its midst, the day-to-day life of the congregation should reflect this. Renovating congregational life so that it speaks its welcome and inclusion loudly and clearly is a process of trial and error. It is also a process that requires effort, time, and patience since most congregations naturally and often unconsciously reflect the larger heterosexist biases of our culture that have been in place for decades and that can take years to change.

Relatively simple changes in three important areas of congregational life can help begin the process of making a congregation more welcoming: by using inclusive language, creating inclusive space, and celebrating inclusive rituals a congregation can become a more effective community of care for queer people.

## Use Inclusive Language

With the rise of feminist consciousness and the Women's Movement in the 1960s and 1970s many congregations began to understand that the language of worship (that is, biblical translations, liturgical prayers, and hymnody) reflected deep sexist biases. In similar ways, the rise of a queer presence in local communities of faith has raised the awareness that LGBTQ people are often rendered invisible by language with a heterosexist bias. There are several simple, but important, ways in which congregations can address the issue of making language inclusive:

- *Formulate an inclusive language policy* that reflects the congregation's commitment to welcome all people. Since language both mirrors and reinforces our view of the world, making a conscious decision to include LGBTQ people in a congregation's vocabulary can help to remind everyone that the words they use can be an important means of welcome and inclusion.

- Undertake *a thorough review of the language* used in all congregational publications—including worship texts, educational curricula, and other program materials—so that those texts that presume a straight audience are expanded to include queer people. For example, after his church developed an inclusive language policy, Robert, a religious education director, became aware that every example of a family in the congregation's religious education textbook series included a mother and a father. He began to encourage his teachers to add examples of families with two moms, two dads, a single parent, or children raised by their grandparents in an effort to reflect the congregation's commitment to inclusion.

- *Be aware of transgender language issues.* By keeping in mind that the use of highly gendered language can exclude those who do not think of themselves as belonging to one gender, a congregation can speak its welcome to transgender and gender-fluid individuals. Seek the advice of transgender persons in your congregation or local community on how to speak in ways that welcome transgender and gender-fluid people. In terms of addressing individual gender-variant people in the congregation, a good rule of thumb is to ask people how they would like to be addressed rather than make assumptions and risk offending an individual by using the wrong name or pronoun.[8] Consider alternatives to the commonplace binary phrase "brothers and sisters" and use, instead, words like "siblings" and "friends."

- *Transform language* that excludes into language that includes. Language, of course, can include the visual as well as the aural. For example, when Melinda, a leader of her church's youth group, pointed out to other members that a recent poster advertising their upcoming dance had photographs of only straight couples they decided to issue a new version of the poster that included images of same-gender couples.

## Create Inclusive Space

Congregational space can be exclusive space especially with regard to transgender individuals. For instance, most congregations still do not provide all-gender restroom facilities and this omission can be a considerable barrier for transgender persons who belong, attend, or visit your congregation. Providing at least one accessible all-gender restroom is an important sign of welcome because many transgender individuals encounter hostility from others when they attempt to use a single-gender restroom. (Such restrooms, incidentally, are also particularly useful for a parent with an opposite gender child and for people with caregivers.)

Your congregation will also want to consider how educational and social programs restricted by gender can create exclusive space. This does not mean, of course, that women's groups or men's groups no longer have a home in the congregation but that such groups should be encouraged to consider the fact that the congregation is striving to become a community of welcome and care for transgender people. Each group should be asked to discuss and explore how they can include transgender individuals who may want to take part in the group's activities.

---

8. Tanis, *Trans-Gendered*, 119, writes that "calling transgendered persons by pronouns and names that do not represent their current gender presentation or identity" can be a devastating experience. It is better to ask someone how they want to be addressed rather than to assume that you already know.

## Celebrate Inclusive Rituals

A congregation that is a community of care not only includes LGBTQ people as leaders and participants in its rituals and liturgies but it also celebrates their lives, their relationships, and their families through worship.[9] Most important, worship in a congregation that welcomes and includes queer people takes account of their presence and recognizes their needs. For instance, the vocabulary of worship should be sensitive to the fact that there are families in your midst with two mothers or two fathers. When planning a memorial service with the survivors of a single gay man, ask them who should be invited to play special roles in the service and, in particular, who should be asked to offer words of eulogy. Forms of prayer that divide a congregation into women and men may alienate some transgender people who don't identify as either one gender or the other. Developing sensitivity to the presence and needs of queer people in worship can be a positive learning experience for the entire congregation and one way to facilitate such learning is to include LGBTQ individuals as members of the congregation's worship committee or as ad hoc members of a group planning a particular service.

In addition to making all worship inclusive, congregations can celebrate those events that are unique to queer people. Below are a few examples of the ways in which a congregation can do this through *worship* and ritual:

- *Coming Out Services*: Since coming out is a pivotal event in the lives of many queer people, your congregation might consider devoting one worship service a year to celebrate people in your congregation who have recently come out as LGBTQ. Recognition of individuals who have recently come out can also be celebrated as one part of a larger Sabbath or Sunday worship service.

- *Rituals Marking Gender Transitions*: There are several events in the lives of transgender people that can be recognized and celebrated within the context of congregational worship, including the decision of an individual to embrace their true gender, the choice of a new name, and the preparation for and completion of surgical procedures for a person who is transitioning. Of course, planning for a

---

9. Turney, *Shaping Sanctuary*, is an excellent resource for planning Christian worship services. For Jewish rituals and liturgies that celebrate queer people, see Ritualwell, www.ritualwell.org.

worship service or ritual moment within a larger service should be done with the transgender person(s) involved; there are now several resources available that provide creative models for ritualizing important moments in the lives of transgender persons.[10]

- *LGBTQ Pride Services*: Celebrate gay pride and honor the LGBTQ civil rights movement sometime during June, which is recognized the world over as Gay Pride Month. Special prayers, sermons, and songs can be especially effective ways of celebrating LGBTQ pride and raising awareness within the congregation about queer history and culture. Decorating the interior worship space with rainbow colors, the traditional colors of queer pride, or hanging a rainbow flag outside the church or synagogue are other ways to highlight your congregation's pride celebrations; they will also be especially meaningful to many queer people.

- *International Transgender Day of Remembrance*: First marked in 1999, this day remembers and honors annually the many transgender people who have been murdered during the past year. Your congregation can join in solidarity with countless other people around the world who mark this day through vigils held in November. "The Transgender Day of Remembrance serves several purposes. It raises public awareness of hate crimes against transgender people, an action that current media doesn't perform . . . [it] publicly mourns and honors the lives of our brothers and sisters who might otherwise be forgotten. Through the vigil, we express love and respect for our people in the face of national indifference and hatred. Day of Remembrance reminds non-transgender people that we are their sons, daughters, parents, friends and lovers . . . and [it] gives our allies a chance to step forward with us and stand in vigil, memorializing those of us who've died by anti-transgender violence."[11]

- *Marriages/Holy Unions, Separation, and Divorce*: Make your congregation a place of welcome for LGBTQ couples who want to marry or enter into covenants of commitment or holy unions. Congregations of many religious traditions have been celebrating the marriages and unions of LGBTQ couples for many years now, of course, and

---

10. For resources on Jewish liturgy and rituals for transgender persons, consult Transtorah (www.transtorah.org/resources.html). See "A Liturgy of Re-Naming for Transgender Persons," and "Liturgical Resources," in Tanis, *Trans-Gendered*, 187–93.

11. International Transgender Day of Remembrance (tdor.info/about-2).

they remain uniquely powerful opportunities for the recognition of the love and commitment of queer people within the context of a faith community. For LGBTQ individuals and/or couples who want to ritualize their separation or divorce, extend your welcome by providing liturgical opportunities to mark these losses.

- *Celebrations to Honor Queer Families*: Your congregation can honor the lives of LGBTQ people and their families in many ways. The adoption of a child by a queer individual or couple, the reconciliation between parents and their queer child, and the celebration of wedding/holy union anniversaries provide opportunities for celebrating LGBTQ lives, loves, and families.

- *AIDS Liturgies*: While AIDS is a disease that does not discriminate on the basis of sexual orientation, living with HIV/AIDS is a continuing reality for many queer people, especially queer people of color. The annual recognition of World AIDS Day in December provides an excellent opportunity for your congregation to pray for everyone throughout the world who is living with the disease and to remember those who have died from it. Consider hanging AIDS quilts in your sanctuary as a way of reminding congregants of the ongoing reality of HIV/AIDS in our local, national, and international human community.

- *Recognition of LGBTQ Religious Leaders*: Your congregation can celebrate in worship an LGBTQ person whom it has supported, sponsored, or called to the ordained ministry. Supporting an LGBTQ member who has entered the seminary or calling an out queer person to ordained ministry are some especially appropriate events to celebrate in spoken prayer and ritual.

## A SELECTION OF PRAYERS AND LITURGIES FOR WELCOME AND INCLUSION

- *All Whom God Has Joined: Resources for Clergy and Same-Gender Loving Couples*, by Leanne McCall Tigert and Maren C. Tirabassi.

- *Blessing Ceremonies: Resources for Same-Gender Services of Commitment*, by United Church of Christ Coalition for LGBT Concerns.

- *Ceremonies of the Heart: Celebrating Lesbian Unions*, by Becky Butler.

- *Courage to Love: Liturgies for the Lesbian, Gay, Bisexual, and Transgender Community*, edited by Geoffrey Duncan.
- *Daring to Speak Love's Name: A Gay and Lesbian Prayer Book*, by Elizabeth Stuart.
- *Equal Rites: Lesbian and Gay Worship, Ceremonies, and Celebrations*, edited by Cherry Kittredge and Zalmon Sherwood.
- *The Essential Guide to Lesbian and Gay Weddings*, by Tess Ayers and Paul Brown.
- *For Another Flock: Daily Advent and Christmas Meditations for Gay and Lesbian Christians*, by Jeffrey Lea.
- *I Am This One Walking Beside Me: Reflections and Prayers on Being a Gay HIV-Positive Man*, by Daniel Gebhardt.
- *Kulanu: All of Us—A Program and Resources Guide for Gay, Lesbian, Bisexual, and Transgender Inclusion*, edited by Richard Address, Joel Kushner, and Geoffrey Mitelman.
- *Passionate Holiness: Marginalized Christian Devotions for Distinctive People*, by Dennis O'Neill.
- *Race and Prayer: Collected Voices, Many Dreams*, by Malcolm Boyd and Chester L. Talton.
- *Recognizing Ourselves: Ceremonies of Lesbian & Gay Commitment*, by Ellen Lewin.
- *Ritualwell.org*: Ceremonies for Jewish Living. Reconstructionist Rabbinical College.
- *Shaping Sanctuary: Proclaiming God's Grace in an Inclusive Church*, edited by Kelly Turney.
- *A Time to Every Purpose: The Language of Sexual Morality, Justice, and Healing*, by Debra Haffner.
- *To the Tune of a Welcoming God: Lyrical Reflections on Sexuality, Spirituality, and the Wideness of God's Welcome*, by David Weiss.
- *TransTorah*, by Rabbi Reuben Zellman et al.

In addition to renovating language, space, and rituals to reflect a commitment to welcome and include LGBTQ people, a congregation that strives to become a community of care needs to devote itself to increasing queer membership and queer leadership in every area of congregational life. Being explicit in welcoming and accepting queer people into all facets of a congregation's life can help individuals realize that being a community of care entails the full integration of queer people. Advertise in the local (queer and straight) press that your congregation is welcoming of LGBTQ people and keep in mind that, increasingly, queer people get their news from "straight" news sources. Programming that includes queer people will prove to be an especially effective way to let the world outside your congregation know that you are serious in your efforts to build a community of care for all people.

The best way to increase the presence and involvement of LGBTQ people in congregational life is to continue the process of education and dialogue begun in the early stages of building a welcoming community of faith. Many congregations find that a standing committee on LGBTQ persons and their concerns can help advance the process of building welcome by offering educational programs and fostering continued dialogue between queer and non-queer people. By serving as a catalyst for learning and conversation this committee can help to model and foster increasing trust between LGBTQ persons and non-LGBTQ persons.

- Specifically mention in your congregational brochures that LGBTQ persons are welcome not only to become members of the congregation but also to join the various groups and committees that make up the congregation; do not limit your invitation to groups and committees that deal only with queer issues.

- Invite the LGBTQ people in your congregation to form a social or support group that might include as one of its works the welcoming of new queer members into the congregation.

- Review your congregational policies on membership, hiring of staff, and recruitment of clergy to be sure that these are aligned with your congregational statement of welcome.

- Support and join a denominational LGBTQ advocacy group.

- Offer education nights with queer instructors and panelists. Topics might include explorations of heterosexism, transgenderism, racism within white queer communities, queer immigrants and refugees, the Bible, LGBTQ parenting, and the history of LGBTQ people within your denomination.

- Create opportunities for continued dialogue between queer and non-queer members of your congregation.
- Explore how all programs within your congregation might be transformed by your welcoming and inclusive stance. Keep in mind that the goal is to weave queer people and issues into all aspects of congregational life.
- Encourage your clergy to preach occasionally on issues related to the welcome and inclusion of queer people; invite a local queer clergy person to preach.
- Celebrate June as LGBTQ Pride Month in your congregation with educational events and a special Pride worship service. Observe other important dates such as World AIDS Day and the International Transgender Day of Remembrance by offering educational programming and special liturgies.
- Provide educational opportunities for your clergy to develop skills in the pastoral care of queer people and their families.

---

**LGBTQ RELIGIOUS/DENOMINATIONAL ADVOCACY GROUPS**

Note: Web addresses for these groups are available in the Resources list

- Affirm: LGBT members of the United Church of Canada.
- Affirmation: LGBT Mormons.
- Affirmation: United Methodists for Lesbian, Gay, Bisexual and Transgender Concerns.
- The Association of Welcoming and Affirming Baptists: For LGBT persons and their allies in the Baptists traditions.
- AXIOS: Eastern and Orthodox Gay and Lesbian Christians.
- Beyond Ex-Gay. An online community for those who have survived ex-gay experiences.
- Brethren Mennonite Council for LGBT Interests.
- Dignity USA: LGBT Catholics.

- Emergence International: LGBT Christian Scientists, their families, and friends.
- Extraordinary Lutheran Ministries: LGBTQ Lutheran leaders.
- Evangelicals Concerned: LGBT Evangelical Christians and friends.
- Fortunate Families. Catholics families with LGBT children.
- Friends for Lesbian and Gay Concerns: An association of LGBT and allies in the Religious Society of Friends (Quakers).
- GALA (Community of Christ): LGBT persons, friends, and allies in the Community of Christ.
- GALVA-108 (The Gay & Lesbian Vaishnava Association): LGBT Vaishnavas and Hindus.
- Gay Christian Network: For LGBT Christians and those who care about them.
- Integrity: LGBT Episcopalians and allies.
- Interweave: Unitarian Universalists for LGBT Concerns.
- Jewish Mosaic: The National Center for Sexual and Gender Diversity.
- Keshet Rabbis: Gay-Friendly Conservative/Masorti Rabbis and Cantors.
- Lutherans Freed in Christ: For LGBT Lutherans in the Missouri Synod and Wisconsin Evangelical Lutheran Synod.
- More Light Presbyterians.
- Muslim Alliance for Sexual and Gender Diversity (MASGD).
- National Gay Pentecostal Alliance.
- Nazarene Ally: To make the Church of the Nazarene a safe place for LGBT members.
- Network on Religion and Justice for Asian American and Pacific Islander LGBT People.
- New Ways Ministry: "A gay-positive ministry of advocacy and justice for lesbian and gay Catholics and reconciliation within the larger Christian and civil communities."

- Open and Affirming Ministries: LGBT members and allies in The Christian Church (Disciples of Christ).
- Open and Affirming (ONA) Program: The United Church of Christ.
- Queer Dharma: Buddhist.
- Rainbow Baptists: LGBTQ Baptists, their families, and friends.
- Reconciling in Christ Program: The Lutheran Church: For LGBT Lutherans.
- Reconciling Ministries Network: The United Methodist Church: For LGBT Methodists.
- Room for All: The Reformed Church in America.
- Sanctuary: For LGBT Moravians.
- Seventh-Day Adventist Kinship International: For LGBT Seventh-Day Adventists.
- United Methodists of Color for a Fully Inclusive Church (UMOC): Engaging racism, heterosexism, and homophobia in Christianity and the United Methodist Church.
- Unitarian Universalist Association (UUA) Office of LTBTQ Ministries: For LGBTQ people and families in the UUA.
- Universal Fellowship of Metropolitan Community Churches (MCC): the world's first and only predominantly LGBT Christian denomination.
- Voices for an Open Spirit: Supporting dialogue on LGBT issues in the Church of the Brethren.
- Welcoming Community Network (WCN): The Community of Christ.

## 3. BUILD ALLIANCES WITH LGBTQ COMMUNITIES OUTSIDE OF THE CONGREGATION

Once your congregation has made the decision to welcome and include LGBTQ people, don't keep the news of your welcome within the walls of the congregation—spread the word! There are many effective ways of doing this, including regular congregational advertisements in the gay and straight press (both online and print); postings on the main page of your church or synagogue website; listings in the local telephone book and wherever your congregation is mentioned in online and print local community calendars or denominational publications. Find as many ways as possible to proclaim your welcoming and inclusive stance and make visible your commitment to queer people. Most congregations also post a sign of welcome, a pink triangle, a rainbow, or a denominational symbol of welcome on their buildings. Stories abound of individuals who have chosen to visit a local faith community because they saw a sign of welcome in front of a synagogue or church.

Perhaps the most important external work of a welcoming congregation is finding opportunities to become an ally to the larger LGBTQ community. Through outreach to individual LGBTQ people and by building alliances with a variety of queer groups and social justice organizations a congregation can "walk its talk" of living as a genuine community of care. People of faith can be valuable allies not just inside congregations but also out in the community where there is often discrimination against queer people and their families in employment, housing, and educational opportunities. Your congregation might consider some of the following ways to become an ally:

- Find opportunities to educate your local community about religion and queer people. By speaking from a progressive faith perspective you can demonstrate that not all people of faith consider homosexuality a sin or seek to restrict the rights of LGBTQ people and their families.

- Find ways to work with PFLAG (Parents, Families & Friends of Lesbians & Gays), GLSEN (the Gay, Lesbian & Straight Education Network), your local LGBTQ community center and other organizations whose missions are to advance the rights and well-being of queer people.

- Host a weekend workshop or retreat at your church or synagogue for LGBTQ people of faith and their allies. Organizations such as The Center for LGBTQ and Gender Studies in Religion (CLGS), the Institute of Welcoming Resources, and other national LGBTQ religious organizations offer a variety of resources for educating and energizing local faith communities about issues relating to queer sexuality and religion.

- Pay attention to local, state, national, and international legislation that affects queer people and educate your congregants about ways they can become agents of political change. Learn from organizations such as The National LGBTQ Task Force (NGLTF), the Human Rights Campaign (HRC), and your own state's equality organizations that serve as valuable civil rights watchdog organizations for queer people; they also work with progressive people of faith who are eager to take part in public debates and undertake political activity in support of LGBTQ people.[12] In addition, the Gender, Sexuality, and Identity Project of Amnesty International and the LGBT Rights Project of the American Civil Liberties Union (ACLU) provide important resources and support for protecting the rights of LGBTQ persons and their families.

- When the civil rights of queer people are being threatened, speak up! The leadership and membership of congregations can offer vital support when a municipality is debating whether or not to include LGBTQ people in non-discrimination policies, enact trans-inclusive legislation, write laws to prevent hate-motivated violence against queer people, and/or remove queer-affirming materials from local libraries. Remember that the voices of progressive people of faith were instrumental in moving many state legislatures to extend marriage rights to all persons.

- Offer space in your building (at low or no cost) for local queer and queer-friendly organizations. Organizations (especially those with small budgets) greatly appreciate free or inexpensive space for their meetings.

- Celebrate/mark LGBTQ cultural events such as Queer Pride Days, Coming Out Day in October, International Transgender Day of Remembrance, and World AIDS Day. Your congregation might also consider marching in the local gay pride parade or hosting interreligious worship services that are open to members of the local community.

---

12. See Equality Federation (www.equalityfederation.org/members) for a listing of state organizations allied with the Federation.

Creating Communities of Care for LGBTQ People

## A SELECTION OF STORIES OF CONGREGATIONAL WELCOME AND INCLUSION

- *Balancing on the Mechitza: Transgender in Jewish Community*, edited by Noach Dzmura.
- *Coming In: Gays & Lesbians Reclaiming the Spiritual Journey*, by Urs Mattmann.
- *Face to Face: Gay And Lesbian Clergy on Holiness And Life Together*, by Jeffrey Heskins.
- *Queer Jews*, by David Shneer and Caryn Aviv.
- These Roundtable Projects of The Center for LGBTQ and Gender Studies in Religion (CLGS): The African American Roundtable; The Asian and Pacific Islander Roundtable; The Jewish Roundtable; The Latinx Roundtable; and The Transgender Religious Roundtable.
- *Theology of Gay and Lesbian Inclusion: Love Letters to the Church*, by D. G. Hanway.
- *We Were Baptized Too: Claiming God's Grace for Lesbians and Gays*, by Marilyn Alexander and James Preston.

## EMBRACING THE CHALLENGE OF CARE

Building a community of care for queer persons is an exciting, challenging, and rewarding experience for congregations that choose to welcome and integrate LGBTQ individuals into all aspects of their congregational life. Most people of faith need supportive and dynamic religious communities within which to explore and express their faith. Queer people, like other marginalized people, often feel a deep desire to connect spiritually with others in a community of faith given the fact that congregations have excluded them for so long. I dream that someday every faith community will welcome, include, and care for LGBTQ people as full and equal members. The only way to make that dream a reality is by rolling up our sleeves and building those communities of care, one congregation at a time.

# 6

# Caring for LGBTQ People in Their Interpersonal and Family Relationships

BERNARD SCHLAGER

AM I PREPARED TO offer care?

Engaging in pastoral care with LGBTQ people means that you will be invited to work with them as they explore, wrestle with, and take joy in their interpersonal and family relationships. Like all persons, queer people experience life-giving satisfaction as well as significant challenges in their relationships with friends, loved ones, and family members. The ministry of providing effective pastoral care to LGBTQ people, however, is unique in many ways and it requires that caregivers be honest about their willingness and their abilities to offer high-quality and effective care.

First and foremost, the pastoral caregiver needs to deal with any inner conflicts that they may have regarding queer people. Joretta Marshall writes that "pastoral care specialists who want to offer the most appropriate and genuine care to women in lesbian partnerships must work conscientiously to discover the biases, prejudices, or internal fears that they carry into their praxis."[1] This advice is equally valuable for caregivers who work with gay men, transgender persons, and bisexuals because the

---

1. Marshall, *Counseling*, 131.

best pastoral care for LGBTQ persons is that which affirms their sexuality as a gift from God.

As one way to assess your readiness to offer care, you might ask yourself the following questions:

- Do I respect and value LGBTQ persons and believe that they should be full and equal members of our civic and faith communities?

- To what degree do homophobia and heterosexism enter into my view of LGBTQ persons? Am I willing to rid myself of these destructive fears and attitudes?

- Am I prepared to listen with an open mind and open heart to the personal and relationship experiences of the LGBTQ person(s) in this pastoral care situation without rushing to moral judgment?

- Am I open to models of relationship and family that may be markedly different from the marriage-nuclear family model that many religious traditions and societal structures support as the preferred (and frequently the only legitimate) model of relationship and family?

- How will I deal with the internal tensions that may arise if/when I offer advice to an LGBTQ care receiver that is at odds with the current moral teachings and ethical traditions of my own particular religious tradition? If my reputation for offering such advice becomes known publicly, am I able to withstand the pressures and possible condemnations and censure that I might receive from religious and denominational authorities?

- Am I willing to be a voice of public support for LGBTQ people?

- Can I commit myself to ongoing reading, study, and conversation with others about innovative psychological, biblical, theological, and pastoral paradigms that support positive and life-giving care models for LGBTQ people in relationships?

The above list is not meant to be exhaustive; rather, it is a starting point for self-assessment as you consider whether or not you are prepared to provide positive and affirming care for queer people in relationships. If you find that you are presently unable to engage in such pastoral care, consider assembling and keeping current a list of competent pastoral caregivers whom you can recommend to those who approach you for pastoral care.

If you are ready and able to take on the exciting and rewarding challenges of caring for queer people in their relationships, I encourage you to continue reading this chapter in a spirit of openness and humility because, to be frank, many LGBTQ people within our Jewish and Christian faith communities bring questions, concerns, and life situations to pastoral caregiving that often require a bold rethinking and reevaluation of current Jewish and Christian models of relationship and family. Such rethinking and reevaluation does not mean, of course, that a pastoral caregiver need set aside their beliefs or moral principles when working with LGBTQ people. However, it does mean that you, as caregiver, should be prepared to weave together the relational and familial experiences of queer people with the moral teachings of your own religious traditions in ways that truly honor the people in your care and also maintain fidelity to the best and most life-giving aspects of your own traditions.

## SOME WAYS OF UNDERSTANDING LGBTQ RELATIONSHIPS

Over the past forty years or so several Christian and Jewish theologians have written creatively on lesbian and gay understandings of relationships and, in an effort to offer constructive theological grounding here for this chapter's discussion of pastoral care and LGBTQ relationships, I would like to include a few ideas from some of this work. My goals are to provide an introduction to some ethical dimensions of queer relationships and to pique your interest in how the experiences of some LGBTQ people have been understood in theological terms.

Given the long Jewish and Christian theological traditions of denigrating homosexuality and condemning queer people and their relationships as sinful, it is no surprise that many pastoral caregivers know little, if anything, about the varied ways in which LGBTQ people build and sustain their relationships. For instance, a caregiver may be unaware that while some couples desire to enter into monogamous unions or partnerships that closely resemble the ideal of heterosexual marriage, not all do. Many queer people have extended networks of friendship that include former lovers; some couples may view sexual involvement outside of their main relationship not as a violation of the relationship but rather as an agreed-upon and life-giving aspect of their primary relationship. A queer person who is single may find deep meaning in their singleness and have no desire for a live-in companion with whom to share their life. Assuming that every LGBTQ person desires to marry or condemning every person who does not restrict their sexual involvement to one other person are mistakes for the caregiver who is interested in working effectively, ethically, and productively with LGBTQ people.

Even though many religious leaders and theologians continue to teach that lifelong celibacy is the only morally permissible option for LGBTQ people, most queer people of faith have learned from experience that they, like most non-queer people, are not called to a life of permanent celibacy. Moreover, many North Americans, including those who are people of faith, have come to see that the varied ways in which many queer persons structure and negotiate their relationships are worthy of appreciation and even emulation. In many congregations and seminaries LGBTQ people of faith are speaking out as morally responsible individuals whose relationships, while often significantly different from the model offered by heterosexual marriage, are valid expressions of love. Queer theologians have taken the lead in reflecting theologically and ethically on the nature of LGBTQ relationships and it is upon their work that I principally draw in my discussion below. Not only is such a consideration of queer (and feminist) theological reflection on relationships necessary for effective pastoral care but it also can expand Jewish and Christian understandings of the goodness and beauty of all human relationships.

### FIVE CHARACTERISTICS OF QUEER RELATIONSHIPS

1. The Foundation of Friendship
2. Hospitality and Community-Building
3. A Celebration of Embodiment
4. Liberation as a Shared Experience
5. Queer Love as Generative

The above five interrelated characteristics of LGBTQ relationships are worthwhile for you, the pastoral caregiver, to consider as you prepare to work with queer people in relationships. These five items represent ideals, of course, but they are ideals that are rooted in the real-life experiences of many queer people.

## 1. THE FOUNDATION OF FRIENDSHIP

Friendship is the most important characteristic of queer relationships. As gay theologian Robert Goss has stated, "Friendship serves as the primary paradigm for understanding [queer] individual, coupled, and extended relationships."[2] In my own experience I have found this to be true: friendship best describes the broad variety of relationships that I, a gay man, enjoy with other queer people, from my thirty-five-year relationship with my partner to my relationships with a variety of other LGBTQ people in my life. It was to queer friends, significantly, that I first turned when I began to acknowledge my gay identity and it was among queer friends that I celebrated when I came out of the closet. Since then I have continued to delight in the friendships that I share with other LGBTQ people and I know that life without these friendships would be arid and colorless. It is they who have made it possible for me not only to feel so at home in queer culture but also to thrive as a well-adjusted gay man in the larger straight world.

Lesbian Roman Catholic theologian Mary Hunt argues convincingly that friendships constitute "the central relational experience for women" and I would argue that the same is true for many gay, transgender, and bisexual people as well.[3] With a common experience of loneliness and isolation that comes from living in the closet and as people who have suffered discrimination from family, civic institutions, employers, and our faith communities, LGBTQ people have long turned to each other in friendship as a way to endure and bring meaning to their suffering.

Hunt's theology of friendship also stresses that healthy and well-functioning friendships rest on the important foundations of equality and mutuality and that these two elements give rise to genuine empowerment for each person in the friendship. To be empowered means that persons make their own choices about how to live their lives and they decide what is best for themselves and for those in their care. To be empowered also means that friends work to shed those harmful relational dynamics that grant power to one friend at the expense of the other(s). In the ideal,

---

2. Goss, "Queering Procreative Privilege," 17.

3. Hunt, *Fierce Tenderness*, 91. In this same work Hunt, 87–106, also posits that traditional western philosophies of friendship, with their exclusive focus on male relationships, are simply inadequate in helping us understand friendships between women. Her own model of friendship consists of four key elements: love, power, embodiment, and spirituality.

queer individuals are sensitive to the widespread damage done to friendships because of poisonous patriarchal notions of male dominance and female subservience that still infect so much of our culture. Having been marginalized by others because of their queerness, LGBTQ people have the opportunity and obligation to fashion their friendships along more egalitarian lines. And indeed, queer people throughout history have a long-standing tradition of building such relationships.

By valuing friendship rather than heterosexual marriage as the most important of human relationships, the pastoral caregiver can begin to understand and appreciate the variety of ways in which LGBTQ people form their relationships with one another. A deep and ongoing relationship with a current or former partner or lover (which may surprise those who assume that such relationships must be characterized by anger or tension), the camaraderie of a few close intimates, and a supportive network of a large circle of friends—each of these counts as genuine friendship for queer people. Viewing friendship as the key relational experience in life dethrones marriage (whether straight or same-sex) from its problematic place in our culture as the best kind of human relationship for each and every person. Friendship is something, as Hunt stresses, that every person can enjoy; it is also something that takes many innovative and life-giving forms as we see in the friendships that queer people create and sustain with one another.

You may find it helpful to call to mind and share with your LGBTQ care receivers the high regard with which same-sex friendship is held in the Hebrew and Christian Scriptures. Ruth and Naomi share an intimate friendship as do David and Jonathan; Jesus and the Apostle John are portrayed as particularly close friends. The gospels stress time and again Jesus' message that the greatest love of all is that which friends have for one another. In fact, Elizabeth Stuart reminds us that "[t]he only model of relating that we can definitely see operating in the life of Jesus, as presented to us by the Gospels, is friendship. One could say that the essence of Jesus' ministry was simply befriending—the forming of mutual, equal, loving, accepting, and transforming relationships."[4]

The scriptural emphasis on friendship should offer hope to LGBTQ people of faith who may find themselves under siege from—and sometimes overwhelmed by—those religious and political leaders of our day who insist that marriage between a woman and a man is the highest form

---

4. Stuart, "Just a Perfect Blendship," 171.

of a loving relationship, that a wife and husband are the only suitable parents for children, and that our society should retain its preferential option for married straight people. The Christian biblical record certainly reminds us that marriage (understood, as it is today, as the romantic partnership between two people of different genders) was not held up as the highest form of life for Jesus' followers, and the great value it places on friendship can encourage LGBTQ people of faith to treasure more dearly the delightful variety of friendships that they create and sustain.[5]

## 2. HOSPITALITY AND COMMUNITY-BUILDING

Hospitality is another biblical value that imbues the relationships of many queer people who have a keen personal understanding of what it means and how it feels to be an outsider. At an early age, many LGBTQ individuals come to realize that their differences make them unwelcome in families, communities of faith, and society at large and, therefore, they understand how important and life-saving it can be to welcome the outcast and the stranger. Perhaps this sense of being an unwelcome minority hints at why so many queer people throughout history have been particularly drawn to work in education, religious ministry, medicine, the arts, entertainment, the travel industry, and social work—endeavors that require a high level of skill in hospitality and building community.

Rev. Nancy Wilson, the former moderator of the Universal Fellowship of Metropolitan Community Churches (MCC), recalls the value of hospitality in the desert cultures of the Hebrew Bible when she proposes a queer theology of sexuality that joins this biblical value of hospitality with the experience of LGBTQ people who have such a strong desire to welcome others. "Perhaps our neediness or loneliness," she writes, "has made us almost 'promiscuous' in our desire to provide hospitality. Being shut out has made us want to *include* with a vengeance."[6] Wilson suggests that the biblical notion of hospitality, which calls everyone to welcome the stranger into one's home, is key to any queer sexual theology because queer people understand how sex can be a way to extend welcome to others—not in the sense of relating sexually with strangers but rather in the sense of viewing our sexual relationships as unique opportunities for welcoming our lovers into our lives and into our very selves: "To share

---

5. See Tolbert, "Marriage," 41–51.
6. Wilson, *Our Tribe*, 233. Her emphasis.

sexually with someone is literally to *make room* for them in our body and in the space surrounding our bodies."[7]

Community-building is another talent of many LGBTQ people and one that informs the ways in which they relate to one another. For many years now queer people have formed and maintained vital communities of support (be they neighborhoods, social service agencies, synagogues, churches, clubs, and other organizations) that continue to provide safe spaces in which they can socialize, find mutual care, and gain political power in democratic societies. One could say that the art of forming community is the making of friends writ large and queer people are indeed true masters of this art.

In a fascinating analysis of contemporary gay male culture in the United States, David Nimmons writes of the remarkable communal sensibilities of gay men that are evident in high rates of volunteerism, altruistic practices of care-taking for the sick and infirmed, and unique bonds of deep friendship with straight women. Nimmons urges his reader to consider the lessons that such community-mindedness offers for American society as a whole and he likens these "gay enclave cultures" to intentional communities of service that have appeared in various guises throughout history:

> Gay experiments in affection, the norms and rituals of our intimacies, echo ethics taught by a wide variety of religious traditions. These values are strikingly consonant with Judeo-Christian ethics of communalism and social liberation. They sound a lot like what Jesus preached. The innovations in love and community we are crafting today have previously been seen primarily in religious orders, secular communes, utopian settlements, intentional communities, and fraternal brotherhoods. Our habits of diffuse bonding and support, voluntary caretaking, and service recall practices of the first Christian apostles. They recall values espoused by spiritually constituted brotherhoods from early Christian practice, to medieval monasteries, to modern-day religious orders.[8]

Pastoral caregivers who work with LGBTQ people in relationships should keep in mind the gifts that many queer people possess in the areas of hospitality and community-building because such networks of care and support, both formal and informal, can be of immense help

7. Wilson, *Our Tribe*, 249. Her emphasis.
8. Nimmons, *Soul*, 139.

for LGBTQ care receivers. Queer support groups of various kinds are an excellent example of a community resource that can provide individuals with a quality of care that is comfortable, safe, and rooted in authentically queer experience. By encouraging your care receivers to take advantage of these existing networks of care, you, as pastoral caregiver, can help them benefit from the hospitality and community of other queer people.

### 3. A CELEBRATION OF EMBODIMENT

Embodiment means being at home both in the macrocosm of nature and in the microcosm of one's own body. Embodied persons feel connected to and genuinely comfortable with their physicality because they understand that the human body is a great good and not, as some schools of Jewish and Christian theology have taught, a dangerous beast that must be tamed if one is to live a holy life. To be embodied means that one does not see the desire for or enjoyment of sensual or sexual pleasure as necessarily evil or inherently sinful; rather, it means that one delights in one's body and revels in bodily pleasures because they are an integral and healthy aspect of human existence. Many LGBTQ people are "embodied knowers," Carter Heyward suggests; they feel at home in creation and in their bodies in such a way that they value what they experience through their senses and their emotions, and they enjoy the physical pleasure mediated by their bodies.[9] Such an embodied understanding of human nature has no use for dualistic philosophies, theologies, or ethical systems that equate the body with fallen human nature, chaos, and evil while glorifying the soul as the uniquely spiritual, dispassionate, and redeemable part of the person.

Judith Plaskow, a feminist theologian in the Jewish tradition, has proposed a sexual theology that is based on an embodied understanding of human existence. Rejecting traditional patriarchal theologies that view women's sexuality as something that must be brought under control by men via the institution of marriage, she constructs a theology that posits sexuality as crucial to our capacity for feeling and as an essential means through which we communicate with God and other persons. In this view, sexuality is not some evil force that needs taming but is rather a good and essential aspect of who we are as embodied persons.[10]

---

9. Heyward, *Touching*, 7.
10. Plaskow, "Toward," 141–51.

Many LGBTQ people treasure and celebrate the gift of their sexuality and gender identity because they have risked much in naming and claiming their gender identity and sexual desires as an integral part of who they are. Put another way, many queer people bring a hard-won and keen appreciation of their incarnated state and a celebration of their embodiedness to the sexual relationships that they have with other persons. Elizabeth Stuart suggests that "[p]erhaps because we are defined by our sexuality, lesbian and gay people are more acutely aware of the part sexuality plays in all our relationships—that it is our embodied passion that incarnates itself in every friendship, although the level of intimacy and its expression will vary."[11]

As a pastoral caregiver, you can help your LGBTQ care receivers appreciate their embodiedness and begin to recover from years of living in social and religious environments that bombard queer people with toxic messages about their bodies and their gendered and sexual desires. You may find, in fact, that many LGBTQ people in relationships have internalized highly negative views of their own bodies and absorbed understandings of their erotic desires as displeasing to God. More broadly, your pastoral care of LGBTQ persons may also teach you and your care receivers that embodiment is a Jewish and Christian virtue that all humans are called to practice.

## 4. LIBERATION AS A SHARED EXPERIENCE

In chapter 4 we explored some of the ways in which coming out of the closet is an experience of profound liberation for most LGBTQ people. Acknowledging one's true gender identity to self and others, embracing a queer identity, and proudly naming oneself as bisexual, transgender, lesbian, and/or gay is like crossing a threshold into a new world filled with the promise of living more authentically. For LGBTQ people of faith the experience of coming out calls to mind stories of liberation from the Bible in which the people of Israel are set free from the bondage of slavery and the followers of Jesus are liberated by his healing words and actions.

This shared experience of liberation shapes queer relationships in many ways. Knowing what it is like to live in oppression and then taste the sweet freedom that comes from accepting one's queer identity, many LGBTQ people feel a common bond with others who yearn to be

11. Stuart, "Just," 173.

liberated from oppressive systems and structures of all kinds. There are many queer people who are able to draw upon their own experience of liberation from the closet as they do the life-long work of building and tending relationships with others, queer and non-queer alike. To live as a liberated person entails being in right relationship with others in ways that honor and respect the freedom and integrity of every person.

Pastoral care with queer people in relationship involves understanding, validating, and honoring this profound experience of liberation which requires that one act ethically and justly in one's relationships with others. Given their own experiences of oppression and liberation, LGBTQ people can be especially effective agents of justice-making and peace-building in their own lives and relationships—and in ways that help to heal the whole human family.

## 5. QUEER LOVE AS GENERATIVE

All human relationships (including those of queer people) are potentially generative, meaning they can be life-giving both for those who take part in the relationship and for those outside of the relationship. For example, the fruits of an equitable and well-functioning friendship are often enjoyed by the many individuals who come into contact with the persons who make up the friendship. The love and generosity found in any healthy human relationship often overflow the relationship and contribute positively, frequently in unrealized ways, to the lives of countless others in our families, our faith communities, our workplaces, and, in fact, in our entire world. LGBTQ relationships, of course, are no different in this regard, despite the fact that they are often portrayed as selfish, hedonistic, and of little or no use to others or to society at large.

Generativity is often narrowly understood as the ability to procreate. Some traditional Jewish and Christian systems of morality continue to condemn queer sexual relationships precisely because they cannot lead to biological reproduction. And yet, the experience of many people—queer as well as non-queer—testifies to the wonderfully creative nature of many forms of sexual activity that are not linked to reproduction. Despite the insistence of those who demand that all sexual activity must be open to the possibility of conceiving children or that heterosexual sex alone is good because it is tied to procreation, LGBTQ people in relationships that are sexual *do*, in fact, experience their sexual activity as healing, uniting, expressive, loving, and creative. This understanding that sex between same-sex couples can be as procreative as sex between opposite-sex couples is expressed well by Robert Goss: "*Procreativity* may refer to the literal renewal of the earth through human reproduction or reproductive strategies, or it may also refer to the contributions made for renewal and transformation of society. Both opposite-sex and same-sex couples have an equal opportunity to express literally and metaphorically the procreativity of the Creator God."[12] Blessed by God with bodies that are good and holy, queer people share with all other human beings the ability and, indeed the responsibility, to enjoy sex as one of the many goods of creation.

Effective pastoral care of LGBTQ people in relationships helps them to understand that their relationships can be as procreative and generative as any other form of human relationship. Well-functioning friendships, partnerships, civil unions, and marriages between queer people provide positive testimony to this conviction. LGBTQ people in healthy relationships do indeed partake in the work of a creative and creating deity and one important goal of pastoral care with queer people is to help them understand that their relationships are needed to spread love and justice throughout the world.

## PASTORAL CARE FOR LGBTQ PERSONS IN RELATIONSHIPS

As a pastoral caregiver who is committed to providing the best possible care to LGBTQ people in relationships, you need, first and foremost, a genuine willingness and the proven ability to listen with an open mind and an understanding heart to the life stories and faith journeys of those who come to you for care. Since an individual's past and current relationships are an important part of what shapes them, you should familiarize yourself with and become comfortable discussing the various kinds of relationships that queer people form with one another. Educate yourself and keep current on issues in the field of LGBTQ theology and pastoral care and commit yourself to exploring new ways of applying Jewish and Christian ethics in your work with LGBTQ persons in relationship. Like everyone else who comes to you for care, an LGBTQ person in

---

12. Goss, "Queering Procreative Privilege," 12. Emphasis original.

relationship needs you to be a knowledgeable, empathetic, and affirming caregiver.

What you offer your care receivers is the wisdom you have gained from your own life experience, your education and pastoral training, and the faith tradition(s) that have shaped you. The teachings of your own spiritual tradition(s) may, in fact, support the condemnation of LGBTQ people and their sexual relationships while your pastoral care with queer people demands that you find affirming ways to care for them. Your ongoing relationships with these care receivers may also lead you to interrogate with renewed intensity established theological positions that pathologize LGBTQ people so that you can provide them with a constructive and true-to-life ministry of care and ethical assistance that they will expect (and deserve) from you.

Since the Hebrew and Christian Scriptures—and many Jewish and Christian ethical systems that draw upon these sacred writings—have been used for centuries to denounce and demonize LGBTQ people and their relationships, you may be the first pastoral caregiver that a particular queer person has ever approached for care. You may also be a person's last hope for receiving pastoral care that affirms queer sexuality as a gift from God and values LGBTQ relationships as holy and healthy forms of love. You carry a heavy responsibility here: you are called to bring a message of hope and healing to those who have long been marginalized by faith communities because of how and whom they love. Certainly Jewish and Christian religious and ethical traditions can be of help to LGBTQ people of faith in terms of their relationships but it requires a serious rethinking on your part of some important aspects of those traditions as they have developed over time. Perhaps most importantly, you will need to take seriously the lives and loves of queer people themselves despite the fact that these lives and loves have often been dismissed as immoral and therefore not worthy of even a hearing by many religious leaders and theologians. An exciting pastoral challenge? Without a doubt.

> ### A BRIEF SELECTION OF RESOURCES ON LGBTQ RELATIONSHIPS
>
> Note: Full bibliographical details are available in the List of Resources
>
> - *From This Day Forward: Commitment, Marriage, and Family in Lesbian and Gay Relationships*, by Gretchen Stiers.
> - *Just Good Friends: Towards a Lesbian and Gay Theology of Relationships*, by Elizabeth Stuart.
> - *Our Families, Our Values: Snapshots of Queer Kinship*, edited by Robert Goss and Amy Strongheart.
> - *Queer Jews*, by David Shneer and Caryn Aviv.
> - *The Soul Beneath the Skin: The Unseen Hearts and Habits of Gay Men*, by David Nimmons.
> - *Touching Our Strength: The Erotic as Power and the Love of God*, by Carter Heyward.
> - *Twice Blessed: On Being Lesbian or Gay and Jewish*, edited by Christie Balka and Andy Rose.

Grounded in the conviction that pastoral caregivers learn best by listening intently to and sincerely honoring the experiences of their care receivers, the exploration of caregiving that follows is based on the real-life experience of LGBTQ individuals and couples of faith who have freely chosen to enter into pastoral care in order to help them build and maintain loving and supportive relationships with other queer people. I share the conviction of lesbian minister Sally Boyle that "pastoral care has as its ultimate goal the empowerment of people to live in just and loving relationships";[13] therefore, the focus in this section is on pastoral care with LGBTQ people who seek to build just and loving—as well as healthy and mature—relationships with one other.

The seven vignettes that follow are composites of real-life situations and they will be used as case studies according to the following schema:

- I present a succinct case study of LGBTQ persons in relationship who are seeking pastoral care.

13. Boyle, *Embracing*, 15.

- Next, I briefly consider some theological and ethical considerations relating to each case.

- Finally, I discuss some courses of action, based on sound pastoral care practices that are informed by faith considerations, for helping the care receiver(s) and caregiver address the issue(s).

These case studies are necessarily brief and the theological viewpoints offered are intended as touchstones for your further reflection. The theological considerations following each case study are rooted, of course, in the conviction that lesbian, transgender, bisexual, and gay persons, their identities, and their desires are God-given and, therefore, good. A second conviction is that the yearnings of LGBTQ people for intimate relationships are healthy, life-giving, and necessary components of a life well lived.

Remember that your first task when entering into a pastoral care relationship with LGBTQ people is to assure them that you offer them a safe environment in which to talk about themselves. Once this has been established, you, as caregiver, have three main goals to accomplish, as Larry Kent Graham has written:

- Discern their need in clear terms.
- Validate it pastorally and communally.
- Help evaluate theologically and ethically the quality of life it makes possible in relation to self, God, and neighbor.[14]

Let's see what that looks like when applied to particular individuals in relationship. As you read these case studies, put yourself in the position of the caregiver and consider how you might best serve your own care receivers with sensitivity, understanding, and an open heart.

## LENORE AND DIXIE: SAME-SEX MARRIAGE

Lenore, thirty-five years old, and Dixie, thirty-nine years old, have come to you for pastoral care because they are trying to decide if they should marry each other. Having lived together in a monogamous relationship

---

14. Graham, *Discovering*, 185: "To provide strategic care, then, is to help lesbians and gays—as well as straight persons—discern their sexual orientation in clear terms, validate it pastorally and communally, and help evaluate theologically and ethically the quality of life it makes possible in relation to self, God, and neighbor."

for almost four years, they feel ready to commit themselves in marriage to each other in the presence of their family and friends who have, over time, come to support their relationship. Raised as conservative Christians, they have never attended church together as a couple but you learn that they have an interest in finding a congregation where they might not only get married but also become active members. They are uncertain about how to go about planning a Christian wedding ceremony for two women.

As you get to know Lenore and Dixie, you learn that they are a couple who undoubtedly have a deep and mature love for one another. They also are two people who approach the question of marriage with appropriate gravity and typical nervousness as they move toward a lifelong commitment with each other. After only a few pastoral care sessions with them you come to realize that what they are seeking from you is assistance in determining whether or not they are ready to make a marriage commitment. Before referring them to a minister who can offer them marriage preparation classes and perhaps preside at their marriage in the context of a welcoming congregation, you agree to work with them for several sessions so that you might come to know them more fully and offer them your pastoral counsel on their readiness to marry.

Given their four-year relationship of living together as a couple, Lenore and Dixie have grown in love and navigated successfully a few crises, including Dixie's extra-relational affair. They tell you that they received counseling two years ago from a marriage and family therapist to help them work through issues relating to Dixie's affair and it appears that they have come to a healthy resolution of the problems that the affair caused. Lenore says that she feels their relationship emerged from the therapy stronger than before and Dixie agrees with her.

You find that much of Dixie's and Lenore's uncertainty over entering into a Christian marriage has to do with their similar experiences of having been ostracized by their parents when they first came out in their early twenties and leaving behind congregations whose ministers strongly disapproved of homosexuality. Understandably, Lenore and Dixie want to be sure that they are respected as lesbians and that their relationship is honored in the congregation where they marry and become members.

> **A BRIEF SELECTION OF RESOURCES FOR LESBIAN COUPLES**
>
> - *Counseling Lesbian Partners*, by Joretta Marshall.
> - *Lesbian Couples: A Guide to Creating Healthy Relationships*, by D. Merilee Clunis and G. Dorsey Green.
> - *Lesbians in Committed Relationships: Extraordinary Couples, Ordinary Lives*, by Lynn Haley-Banez.
> - *Midlife Lesbian Relationships: Friends, Lovers, Children, and Parents*, edited by Marcy Adelman.
> - *Permanent Partners: Building Gay and Lesbian Relationships That Last*, by Betty Berzon.

Your relationship with this couple spurs you on to further reading in the area of pastoral care with lesbian couples and you discover Joretta Marshall's insightful writing on the covenantal models that many lesbians use in their relationships. Upon your suggestion, Dixie and Lenore read Marshall's book on lesbian partnerships and the three of you decide to use it as a study text for your remaining pastoral care sessions. Despite Marshall's preference for the terms "lesbian relationships, covenants, or partnerships" instead of marriage (due to the patriarchal history of the institution and the many heterosexist notions associated with it), Dixie and Lenore articulate clearly their own reasons for preferring the term "marriage" for their relationship. They do identify deeply, however, with Marshall's discussion of love, justice, and mutuality as the key components in many lesbian partnerships and, given their experience of Dixie's affair, they ask to discuss with you in further detail Marshall's description of what fidelity means in covenantal lesbian partnerships, which reads as follows:

> In the lesbian and gay community, the meaning of monogamy and fidelity is questioned intensely. Monogamy and fidelity have traditionally been defined by the heterosexual community as sexual faithfulness to one's primary relationship. However, in the lesbian and gay communities it is seen as important not to simply employ the heterosexist definition of fidelity in relation to lesbian covenantal partnerships. Instead, fidelity in lesbian relationships centers on how women covenant mutually about

the boundaries of their external friendships, accepting responsibility and accountability for maintaining clarity about the agreed-upon emotional and sexual perimeters for relationships with others.[15]

Your ongoing discussions with Dixie and Lenore about the meaning of fidelity help them to clarify what a monogamous commitment means to them as a couple. They tell you that their understanding of monogamy is based on an agreement to be open and honest with each other and to strive to respect the boundaries that they mutually set for their relationship. They thank you for bringing Marshall's views into your discussions with them because they value an understanding of women's committed relationships from the perspective of a lesbian expert on pastoral care.

You encourage Lenore and Dixie to get in touch with several denominational LGBTQ advocacy groups to learn which churches in the area welcome queer people. With their permission you offer to contact a minister at one of these churches and learn that she offers marriage preparation classes for same sex couples; she has also married several lesbian couples in the past two years. Lenore and Dixie begin to meet with this minister and eagerly sign up for her next marriage preparation course. In your final meeting with this couple you offer them a bibliography of Christian worship resources for LGBTQ couples who are considering marriage.

### QUEER AND SAME-GENDER MARRIAGE: A FEW RESOURCES

- *Blessing Ceremonies: Resources for Same-Gender Services of Commitment*, by The United Church of Christ Coalition for LGBT Concerns.
- *The Essential Guide to Lesbian and Gay Weddings*, by Tess Ayers and P. Brown.
- *Recognizing Ourselves: Ceremonies of Lesbian and Gay Commitment*, by Ellen Lewin.

---

15. Marshall, *Counseling*, 60–61.

## JARED: CLAIMING A TRANSGENDER IDENTITY

Jared makes an appointment to see you. In your first meeting he tells you some of his story: now nineteen-years old, he changed his name from Rebecca when he was fifteen and refused to wear women's clothes any longer. Since then Jared has had a very stormy relationship with his parents who don't understand his transgender identity but have recently come to accept grudgingly his decision to identify as male. For the past year or so he has been attending a dynamic Reform synagogue as an out transman and the rabbi there has been, in Jared's words, "supportive but really clueless when it comes to trans people." Jared wants to find other trans youth for support and friendship. He says that he is especially eager to date another trans person.

After this first meeting with Jared you return to some of the books on transgender identity and transgender spirituality that you have in your library in order to refamiliarize yourself with the stories and experiences of transgender people. You also decide to search on the web for more information and discover a list of resources recommended by several organizations, including Transfaith, TransTorah, the National Center for Transgender Equality, and The World Congress of Gay, Lesbian, Bisexual, and Transgender Jews. Keenly aware that nearly all queer youth are in desperate need of peer support when they are newly out, you also contact an area parent from the local PFLAG chapter who tells you of monthly meetings for trans teenagers in the area, including one support group sponsored by a local hospital. During your second pastoral care session with Jared, you share these resources with him—he is clearly happy to have this information.

After a few meetings, you and Jared establish a relationship of trust and mutual learning and he discusses with you what he is looking for in a person to date. You learn that is he open to dating either an FTM ("Female-to-Male") or an MTF ("Male-to-Female") individual and he begins to talk about the possibility of someday undergoing gender reassignment surgery. Once again, you recommend several resources on the topic, including those available from The World Professional Association for Transgender Health, Inc., which maintains a searchable database of physicians, lawyers, psychologists, and other professionals who work with transgender individuals.[16]

---

16. The World Professional Association for Transgender Health, Inc. The association publishes (in many languages) the "Standards of Care (SOC) for the Health of

In your last pastoral care session with Jared you are happy to hear that he has taken the lead in organizing some educational events on queer issues at his synagogue. Although he was initially reluctant to suggest such an event to his rabbi, Jared was pleasantly surprised when the rabbi introduced him to several lesbian, gay, and queer members of the congregation, including another teenager, who are eager to work with him on developing a series of educational nights on queer people and the Jewish faith.

---

**A BRIEF SELECTION OF RESOURCES FOR TRANSGENDER PEOPLE OF FAITH**

- *Balancing on the Mechitza: Transgender in Jewish Community*, edited by Noach Dzmura.
- *Call Me Malcolm: One Man's Struggle with Faith, Love and Gender Identity*, film, 2004, United Church of Christ and Filmworks, Inc.
- *Crossing Over: Liberating the Transgendered Christian*, by Vanessa Sheridan.
- *Omnigender: A Trans-Religious Approach*, by Virginia Ramey Mollenkott.
- *Transgender Good News*, by Pat Conover.
- *Trans-Gendered: Theology, Ministry, and Communities of Faith*, by Justin Tanis.
- "Welcoming Transgendered Jews," by Charlie Anders in *Tikkun* magazine.

---

### YOLANDA: POLYAMORY

A local minister whom you know asks if she might refer to you for pastoral care a middle-aged lesbian in her congregation who revealed to her a month ago that she is living in a long-term polyamorous relationship with two other women. This minister tells you that she disapproves of

---

Transsexual, Transgender, and Gender Nonconforming People" and offers a searchable database of providers at its website, www.wpath.org/.

polyamorous relationships. Her congregant, an "out" lesbian, is a beloved member of the church community who currently serves on the church's board of trustees. You accept the referral.

Yolanda, a fifty-six-year-old lawyer, appears ill at ease when you meet her in your office for the first time. She asks you if you have ever met a person in a polyamorous relationship and you respond that, to the best of your knowledge, you haven't. You tell her that you are a person with an open mind who would be happy to work with her as a pastoral caregiver if you both decide that is a good idea. Upon hearing this, she breathes a sigh of relief and smiles. You ask Yolanda what she hopes to gain from pastoral care. She says that she needs to talk with someone about the turmoil she is experiencing since coming out to her pastor as a person in a polyamorous relationship. Yolanda is considering leaving this church where she has belonged for almost ten years and "taking a break" from Christianity altogether because of her minister's disapproval of polyamory, which, she understands, reflects the long-standing teachings of the Christian faith.

Are polyamorous relationships moral? This is a question you find yourself asking as you reflect upon your first meeting with Yolanda. You realize that in order to offer her good pastoral care you need to understand polyamory in greater depth and explore how some progressive theologians are approaching it as a moral issue. Your reading to date has made you aware that both straight and queer individuals enter into polyamorous relationships but that there is little reliable statistical data in the psychological or pastoral literature on how common such relationships are today. Nevertheless, the opportunity to care pastorally for Yolanda leads you to read about polyamory and to consider those frameworks of pastoral care that might be helpful to Yolanda.

> ### A BRIEF SELECTION OF RESOURCES ON POLYAMORY
>
> - *Polyamory: The New Love Without limits: Secrets of Sustainable Intimate Relationships*, by Deborah Anapol.
> - Unitarian Universalists for Polyamory Awareness (www.uupa.org).

In your second meeting with Yolanda you both agree to meet regularly and work through her dilemma about whether or not she will stay in her congregation. After mentioning that she has not gone to church since her pastor told her that she did not approve of her polyamorous relationship, Yolanda tells you about her deep love for her partners Therese and Abigail. Together for fifteen years, the three of them met while working together in the same law office one summer. Now all in their late fifties, these women own a house together and see themselves as a loving family made up of adults whose love for another is life-giving; they have chosen not to be sexually active with anyone outside their relationship. Neither of Yolanda's partners belongs to or attends a faith community but she is a lifelong Presbyterian who finds great joy and meaning in Sunday worship and in the service she provides the congregation as a board member.

Following your second meeting with Yolanda you decide to talk with a few trusted pastoral care colleagues about polyamory and you learn to your surprise that one of them has had considerable experience working with individuals in polyamorous relationships. This colleague shares with you his own "conversion" to an understanding that polyamorous relationships can be healthy and ethical. He has come to know well three gay men who live together in a polyamorous union and he believes that theirs is an example of a relationship that blends love, equality, and mutuality.

This same colleague also lets you know of the existence of Unitarian Universalists for Polyamory Awareness (UUPA), a group that is working to create greater understanding and acceptance of polyamory. You find this organization's definition of polyamory particularly helpful as you prepare to work further with Yolanda:

> [P]olyamory [is] the philosophy and practice of loving or relating intimately to more than one other person at a time with honesty and integrity. We advocate for any form of relationship or family structure—whether monogamous or multi-partner—which is characterized by free and responsible choice, mutual consent of all involved, and sincere adherence to personal philosophical values.[17]

---

17. Note: Unitarian Universalists for Polyamory Awareness is an independent organization with no official connection with the Unitarian Universalist Association. The UUPA mission statement is "to serve the Unitarian Universalist Association and the community of polyamorous people within and outside the UUA by providing support, promoting education, and encouraging spiritual wholeness regarding polyamory"(www.uupa.org).

You share this document with Yolanda and she states that it mirrors her own position on polyamory. She also says that she finds the traditional Christian prohibition of polyamory wrong because of her own experience with her two partners. "Our relationship is ethical," she tells you, "because it is between consenting adults and is based on mutual love, real equality, and genuine respect."

In your subsequent meetings with Yolanda the two of you continue to talk about whether or not she will retain membership in her current congregation. You encourage her to consider meeting with her pastor again but she decides against this course of action because she feels that this minister has "slammed the door shut" on any further discussion. As Yolanda reflects on why she has hidden her polyamorous relationship over the years from everyone in her congregation she realizes that she needs to find other polyamorous people of faith for support. She locates and joins an online support group, relieved to know that there are others who share her experience and understand her values.

Yolanda thanks you often for the opportunity to meet with you in a safe environment to talk about her relationship. During your fifth and final pastoral care session with Yolanda she says that she has decided not to return to her congregation. Rather, she has chosen to "take a break" from church for a while and begin the search for a different faith community. "My hope is to find a community," she says, "in which I can be open and proud about who I am and whom I love."

## CECIL: CONSTRUCTING A MEANINGFUL SEXUAL ETHIC

A bisexual man in his mid-twenties, Cecil possesses enormous energy and a winning personality. Since graduation from college a few years ago he has become active in a local Christian congregation with a reputation for progressive theology and a diverse membership. Cecil e-mails you and asks if he might meet with you sometime. He says that a friend recommended you as a caregiver who has a reputation within the queer community as an empathetic and easy-to-talk-with caregiver. You arrange to meet with him the following week.

Bounding into your office just a few minutes late, Cecil says hello, shakes your hand, and sits down ready to talk. Within a short amount of time he tells you some of his story: he has identified himself as bisexual ever since he was fifteen and he has enjoyed several sexual relationships with both women and men. He is not yet ready to settle down with one other person and he says that a "healthy sex life" is one that offers him the richest and most rewarding way to live. Having left the conservative Christian denomination in which he was raised, he searched during his college years for a church that preached a progressive gospel of justice, equality, and peace. He eventually found such a congregation that did not demand he live a celibate life until marriage.

"Thanks for telling me a bit about yourself, Cecil," you respond with sincerity. "So, tell me: what brings you here today?"

"Well," he answers, "I want to talk with another person of faith about my sexual relationships. Sometimes I feel empty inside about them . . . and I guess I wonder why."

As your first meeting with Cecil comes to a close you suggest that he and you explore, over the course of several sessions, sexual morality within a Christian context. You ask him to think about his own value system in the coming weeks and consider how he decides which sexual relationships are good and which are not. He leaves the session full of energy, ready to carry out his "assignment."

Over time the two of you establish a comfortable and productive relationship of care. You listen intently to what he has to say and, in return, he is eager to hear your comments. After a few sessions he says that he has come to realize more clearly that those sexual relationships not rooted in a genuine concern for the other person often leave him feeling empty inside and that most of those one night stands with someone he had just met turn out to be disappointing in the end. What he had yet to figure out was *why* this was so since, in his words, "I never accepted those rules about sex that I had been taught as a kid in Sunday School." He simply couldn't agree that the only morally permissible sexual relationships were between a man and woman who had committed themselves to each other in marriage. You suggest to Cecil that he read a couple of articles by the Christian ethicist Kathy Rudy on sex outside of monogamous heterosexual marriage.

Rudy writes that the non-monogamous sexual mores of gay male culture offer Christians valid and valuable ethical standards for evaluating their sexual relationships. Although the non-monogamous sexual practices of some gay men have long been viewed by religious authorities as promiscuous and non-relational, Rudy believes that they can be highly ethical and, in fact, authentically Christian because of their communal nature.[18] Noting that everyone has a deep yearning for connection with others, she suggests that the morality of sexual activity is best judged by whether it unites persons in meaningful ways:

> We are all, I believe, trying to escape meaninglessness in our lives. . . . We want to escape the hurt that accompanies not belonging anywhere. Some of us do this with people of the same sex, others with people of the opposite sex. Some of us do this by having long-term, monogamous relationships, others by living in communities where love and support and belonging exist in different patterns. In any case, the pertinent question is not which kind of partner or pattern is the only ethical one, but rather which kinds of sexual interventions change our lives and make us part of one another, which acts unite us into one body, which contexts fight meaninglessness.[19]

The "progressive sexual ethic" that Rudy calls for is one that has people evaluate their sexual relationships not in terms of monogamy but according to the standards of "unitivity" and hospitality. That is, those relationships that bring us into communion with others and with God and that also help us to care for one another are good relationships.[20]

In your remaining discussions with Cecil he says that Rudy's theology of sexuality is helping him to formulate a sexual morality that aligns his Christian faith with his own experience of sexual relationships. Cecil shares with you his growing conviction that sex with other persons is indeed good when it helps him make and sustain meaningful connections with other people. He says that he is coming to understand that sex which is devoid of such connections, on the other hand, is much less rewarding because it risks treating other people as objects and not as persons. Cecil also shares with you his growing appreciation that good sex for him is much more than the search for mutual pleasure with another person. Following Rudy, he agrees that good sex is that which contributes positively to relationships of genuine care. As the two of you bring your pastoral care sessions to a close you feel confident that Cecil has made real progress in living more reflectively and more ethically in the world.

---

18. Rudy, *Sex and the Church*, 77.
19. Rudy, *Sex and the Church*, 83.
20. Rudy, *Sex and the Church*, 127.

> **A BRIEF SELECTION OF RESOURCES FOR BISEXUAL PEOPLE OF FAITH**
>
> - *Blessed Bi Spirit: Bisexual People of Faith*, by Debra Kolodny.
> - *Swinging on the Garden Gate: A Spiritual Memoir*, by Elizabeth Andrew.

## DEREK AND LIONEL: THE CHALLENGE OF AN OPEN RELATIONSHIP

Ten years into a monogamous relationship and three years after civil and church marriage ceremonies, Derek and Lionel are in crisis: Lionel wants "to open up their marriage" so that they are free to have outside sexual relationships. Derek, however, is opposed to this because he believes that monogamy is required of all married Christian couples. He also believes that non-monogamous marriages eventually lead to divorce. Their minister has recommended that Derek and Lionel consider entering into a pastoral care relationship with you.

In your first session with Derek and Lionel it is clear to you that their relationship is at a crossroads. Derek is angry and resentful because "Lionel is unfairly changing the rules of our relationship after ten years." In response, Lionel says that he still loves Derek as his lifelong partner but that he has come to realize, over the past few years, that a monogamous relationship is not what he wants in life. He says that he isn't interested in anonymous sex but rather in keeping open the possibility of sexual relationships with good friends. When you ask them what it is they hope to get from working with a pastoral caregiver they respond in unison, "Help!"

After learning more about the history of their relationship you understand that these two men care deeply for one another and that they seem to have weathered well many of the challenges that come with a ten-year relationship, including the death of parents, job losses, and a recent move across the country. You also discover that Derek and Lionel have recently joined a local Metropolitan Community Church where they feel very much at home. It is, in Lionel's words, "the first congregation where we can be Christian and gay—with no hiding who we are from others."

Your challenge in this pastoral situation is to help Derek and Lionel work through their current impasse and, by encouraging them to reflect upon and talk about their values, come to an agreement about how to move forward in their relationship. At the end of your first session the three of you decide to meet weekly for the next couple of months. Derek and Lionel express gratefulness that they share a Christian identity with you, their caregiver, and, as they leave your office, you realize that you will be exploring with them in considerable depth issues of fidelity and monogamy. After they have left your office you continue to think about the place of monogamy in the lives of Christian married couples, many of whom find deep meaning in a marriage that is grounded in an exclusive sexual commitment to each other. You realize that it will be important in future sessions with this couple to explore with Lionel why he wants a non-monogamous relationship: is he feeling that something is missing in his relationship with Derek and, if so, might there be a way for this couple to meet each other's needs more fully? It might also be helpful to provide space for Derek as well to say more about his reasons for valuing monogamy in this relationship.

There are LGBTQ couples who value non-monogamy as a vital dimension of their relationships, including Christian couples who have married or entered into civil unions or other forms of partnership. These couples permit sexual activity outside of their primary relationship, albeit usually within certain limits and according to agreed-upon rules. Whereas a pastoral caregiver can easily draw upon traditional Christian teachings on marital monogamy when working with LGBTQ care receivers, are there any sound theological principles for supporting non-monogamy in queer marriages or partnerships?

Carter Heyward, a lesbian Episcopal priest, has written on the connections between Christian spirituality and lesbian sexuality and she argues that non-monogamy is not necessarily synonymous with promiscuity. Indeed, in her "ethic of erotic friendship" for adults, which stresses the goodness of human sexual pleasure, the importance of mutuality, and the requirement that we not harm others in our sexual relating, Heyward speaks of non-monogamy as a legitimate way of relating sexually to others in friendship:

> To be nonmonogamous is not necessarily to be, in the pejorative sense, "promiscuous"—wanton and nondiscriminatory—in our sexual practices and choices of sexual partners. It may be rather a way of participating in the embodied fullness of different

special friendships. Gay men, more than either lesbians or heterosexual persons in our society, seem to have developed ways of being honest and open in relation to two or more lovers over a single period of time. Often, in these cases, a primary commitment to a particular lover is sustained.[21]

Your reading of Heyward has given you some theological context for understanding that Lionel's desire for an open relationship may reflect a desire for experiencing friendship more deeply. However, as you come to know this couple better, you realize that Derek's attachment to a monogamous relationship is firmly rooted in his beliefs.

In subsequent sessions with this couple you work on facilitating conversations in which each of them can state clearly his own views and work toward understanding more deeply the other's views. The goal, of course, is a mutually-agreed-upon resolution to their dilemma, but in the meantime it is important that each of them clearly articulate for himself and then for the other his own point of view. You share with them the views of Hunt and others that the best relationships are those that embody equality, mutuality, and individual empowerment, and you compliment them often on their willingness to be honest with one another about their disagreements. You acknowledge that this is hard work for any couple and, quoting Carter Heyward, tell them that the "vital work of 'taking care of the relationship' requires negotiating the conflicting feelings, needs, desires, and expectations that are present, to some extent, in all relationships."[22]

During one of your sessions with Lionel and Derek you bring up the issue of fidelity in relationships and this proves to open an especially fruitful discussion that enables them to explore more deeply a value that each of them says is vital to their relationship. While Derek says that he understands sexual monogamy as the deepest sign of fidelity within any marital relationship, Lionel sees a commitment "to be there for the other person through everything" as the core meaning of fidelity.

After several weekly meetings with Derek and Lionel you agree to their request to continue meeting with them. Clearly, this couple is committed to deepening their dialogue and finding a way to come to an agreement about their sexual relationship and, in the process, save their marriage. You look forward to continuing pastoral care with them.

21. Heyward, *Touching*, 136–37.
22. Heyward, *Touching*, 130.

> **A BRIEF SELECTION OF RESOURCES FOR GAY MALE COUPLES**
>
> - *Doing the Work of Love: Men and Commitment in Same-Sex Couples*, by J. Michael Clark.
> - *Gay Male Christian Couples: Life Stories*, by Andrew Yip.
> - *Intimacy Between Men: How to Find and Keep Gay Love Relationships*, by John Driggs and Stephen Finn.
> - *Love in the Time of HIV: The Gay Man's Guide to Sex, Dating, and Relationships*, by Michael Mancilla and Lisa Troshinsky.
> - *Permanent Partners: Building Gay & Lesbian Relationships That Last*, by Betty Berzon.

## VIVIAN: END-OF-LIFE PLANNING

For several years now you have served as an on-call chaplain at a local hospital. Typically, this means that you receive a phone call once or twice every month to visit with a patient late at night who has requested a chaplain's visit. Recently, you were called to the hospital after midnight to visit with Vivian, a seventy-three-year old lesbian who is in the final stages of living with a terminal cancer. During your visit with her you learn that she identifies as Buddhist and Christian; that she has a long-time partner who lives in another state; and that she has been estranged from her two surviving brothers for many years now. Although she says that "she is not afraid to die," she is deeply worried that her two brothers might contest her will after her death because she has decided to leave her entire estate to her partner.

When you arrive at Vivian's hospital bed you meet an individual who seems to have remarkable energy, given her struggle with terminal cancer. During your hour-long conversation you also discover that she is a person with a deep spiritual life that is rooted in her Buddhist and Christian beliefs. Raised in a traditional Japanese American family, she attended a Buddhist Church of America as a child and then chose to be baptized a Christian when she attended graduate school. Later in life she found, in her own words, "a good balance between my Buddhist and

Christian spiritualties" and she and Amy, her long-time partner, regularly attend Zen centers and churches when they are together on the weekends.

The reason that Vivian has called you to the hospital is her concern that her brothers might contest her will after she dies. Neither of her brothers has been supportive of her relationship with Amy and one of her brothers has stated many times that he thinks that homosexuality is both a mental illness and a sin. "What if they drag Amy into court after my death and try to prevent her from receiving my estate?" Vivian asks you.

Your discussion with Vivian reminds you that unmarried queer people still face many unknowns regarding their relationships, including the fear that their immediate family members might attempt to prevent a lover or partner from hospital visitations and/or decision-making in a time of medical emergency. In Vivian's case, her fear is that her brothers might attempt to dispute her will and prevent her partner from receiving what Vivian has chosen to give her.

Given your solid training as a certified hospital chaplain and your growing experience in working with LGBTQ persons and their families, you are able to recommend to Vivian that she contact her lawyer as soon as possible to make sure that her legal documents are in order and to find out how she can best ensure that her will is honored after her death. You ask her if you can visit her again the day after tomorrow to check in with her and she says that she would be deeply grateful to visit with you again. She thanks you for your sound advice and you conclude your pastoral visit with Vivian by praying with her.

> **A BRIEF SELECTION OF RESOURCES ON ADVANCED PLANNING FOR LGBTQ PEOPLE**
>
> - "5 Estate Planning Tips LGBT Families Need To Follow In 2016," by Melissa Chapman.
> - "End-of-Life and Advance Care Planning Considerations for Lesbian, Gay, Bisexual, and Transgender Patients," by Andrew Lawton, MD; Jocelyn White, MD; and Erik Fromme, MD. Palliative Care Network of Wisconsin.
> - *Estate Planning for Same-Sex Couples*, 2nd ed., by Joan M. Burda.
> - "Protect Yourself and Those You Love: A Step-By-Step Guide to Life & Estate Planning for LGBT Americans and Their Families," by Human Rights Campaign (HRC).

## MARY MARGARET: CELIBACY AND AN LGBTQ IDENTITY

For forty of her sixty years Mary Margaret has been a member of a Roman Catholic religious order. Entering the convent right out of high school, she tells you that she had wanted to be a nun since she was a little girl. She says that she has lived her life with a high degree of satisfaction and, in particular, that she has found college teaching to be a ministry that has sustained her throughout her many years as a religious. What brings her to pastoral care at this moment in her life, however, are some nagging questions about her own sexual desires. Lately, she finds herself yearning deeply for the company of other lesbians.

Sister Mary Margaret tells you in your first meeting with her that she loves being a nun and that she has never regretted her decision at the age of eighteen to enter the novitiate and begin her training for the religious life. She enjoys communal living, daily prayer, a shared apostolate with other women, and the lifelong opportunity to work as a minister of the Gospel. You are genuinely impressed with how satisfied Mary Margaret appears to be with her life but when you ask her about her desire to seek companionship with other lesbians her facial expression changes to one of weariness and she speaks with less assurance in her voice.

"When I was in my mid-thirties," she tells you, "I fell in love with another nun in the convent and it was an earth-shaking experience because I'd never felt that way about another person before." You learn that, after much struggle, the two nuns decided that they could not live in the same house and remain true to their vows of chastity. Mary Margaret tells you that, although this relationship never became sexual, it was genuinely loving. Following their move to separate convents, she worked hard to sublimate her sexual feelings and she decided to devote herself ever more diligently to her teaching and community responsibilities. Of particular help in this difficult time was another sister in her community who served as Mary Margaret's spiritual director; together they read *The Sexual Celibate* by Donald Goergen.

Over the course of several sessions you and Mary Margaret explore her current desire to be with other lesbians. She emphasizes repeatedly her deep and ongoing commitment to her religious vow of chastity and says that she is afraid that becoming emotionally involved with other lesbians might lead her to break this vow. "I need to spend time with other lesbians but I'm afraid that I might fall in love again with a woman. And then what might happen?" she asks.

Mary Margaret's mention of *The Sexual Celibate* leads you to suggest that the two of you reread this book and see what, if anything, might still be of value to her as she works on understanding more deeply the nature of her call to a committed life of celibacy as a religious sister.[23] It turns out that this book provides a helpful framework for your pastoral care sessions with Mary Margaret because of its frank and theologically based discussions of vowed celibacy. She calls to mind how much she appreciated, in her earlier reading of the book, the author's claim that celibate religious women and men are sexual beings who, like everyone else, need to love others if they are to be well-integrated and fulfilled.

After four months of pastoral care, Mary Margaret comes to the point of realizing that she needs the friendship of other lesbians to be happy. Shedding many of her earlier fears that socializing with lesbian women will lead her into a sexual relationship, she says that she now understands that living in fear of intimacy is an unhealthy way to live. She looks forward to learning how to enjoy the friendship and support of other lesbians as she continues to value and deepen her vocation as a religious sister.

---

23. Goergen, *Sexual Celibate*.

> ### A BRIEF SELECTION OF RESOURCES FOR LGBTQ SEXUAL CELIBATES
>
> - *The Power of Erotic Celibacy: Queering Heteropatriarchy*, by Lisa Isherwood.
> - *Selling All: Commitment, Consecrated Celibacy, and Community in Catholic Religious Life*, by Sandra Schneiders.
> - *The Sexual Celibate*, by Donald Goergen.

## PASTORAL CARE AND QUEER FAMILIES

LGBTQ persons typically belong to two types of families: families of origin and families of choice. A family of origin refers to the biological family into which one was born and raised or the family into which one was adopted and raised. Families of choice, on the other hand, describe those families that a person creates on the basis of love and friendship. A family of choice may or may not entail a sexual relationship between the adults in the relationship and it may or may not include children.[24] For the many LGBTQ people who have experienced alienation and rejection from their families of origin, their families of choice have been a saving grace, providing them with the love and acceptance that has sometimes been tragically withheld by members of families formed on the basis of blood or legal ties. Many queer people, of course, eventually reconcile with and find support from their families of origin around issues relating to their gender identity and sexual preference but for most LGBTQ people their families of choice continue to hold an essential place in their lives and their hearts.

Some queer families of choice may resemble the conventional modern nuclear family with two parents and their children. Most, however, take decidedly different forms. Whatever their makeup, these families come in many and varied configurations that reflect the wonderful creativity with which LGBTQ people create family. Here are some examples:

- Five lesbian women who live together as friends

---

24. See Weston, *Families*, 38–41, 118.

- A group of men living with HIV who form an extended, non-residential network of mutual care and support
- A long-time queer support group at a local synagogue
- A transgender couple raising their adopted children
- A group of LGBTQ college students who live on the same floor in a university dormitory
- A lesbian couple co-parenting their son with a gay male couple
- Three men who live together in a polyamorous relationship
- A straight married couple who are parents of a gay teenager

Given the discussions above on queer relationships without children, I focus here on four issues that frequently arise in connection with queer families that include children: the choice to bear or to adopt children; seeking support as a queer parent; issues of isolation for children in families with queer parents; and creating a supportive religious community for queer youth.[25]

## MARISSA: CHOOSING BIOLOGICAL OR ADOPTIVE PARENTHOOD

Marissa is a thirty-year-old lesbian and grade school teacher who has decided to become a single parent. She has lived in a large house with two other lesbians and a gay man for six years now. They consider themselves a family and everyone in the household is happy about and supportive of Marissa's decision to have a child. A committed Christian who is active in her congregation's religious education program, Marissa is having difficulty deciding whether to have a child biologically or to adopt an infant from a local social services agency.

During your first pastoral care session with Marissa you learn a good deal about the love, care, and support present in her household, which she describes as both a "co-housing community" and "a real, honest-to-goodness family." As co-owners of the house in which they live, she and her three adult friends share a close common life that includes meals and frequent socializing together. Although nobody is romantically or sexually involved with another household member, they are a family that

---

25. On issues relating to LGBTQ people and their families of origin, see chapter 4, "Coming Out."

hopes to remain together indefinitely. You learn from Marissa that her decision to have a child has come after many years of personal reflection and discussion with her family members. In fact, she would like to share some of the parenting responsibilities with her housemates whom she hopes will be "like aunts and an uncle" to her child.

In your subsequent pastoral care meetings you explore more deeply with Marissa the issue of whether she should have a child through alternative insemination or adoption. On the one hand she would love to have the experience of pregnancy and childbirth; she also likes the idea of having a biological connection to a child. On the other hand she knows that there are thousands of children awaiting adoptive families through public and private foster care and adoption agencies. "How am I going to decide which is the best thing for me to do?" she wonders.

You encourage Marissa to pray about her questions and to talk with queer parents; you also recommend that she meet with a lawyer to understand all of the legal issues involved in single parenting, including whom to identify as a person to make decisions on her behalf and on behalf of her child should she ever become incapacitated. Marissa soon joins a local support group for LGBTQ parents-to-be that you've recommended to her and she begins to talk regularly with a lesbian couple in her congregation who have adopted children. In time she discovers that she wants to adopt a child.

## A BRIEF SELECTION OF RESOURCES FOR QUEER PEOPLE CONSIDERING PARENTING

- *The Essential Guide to Lesbian Conception, Pregnancy and Birth*, by Kim Toevs and Stephanie Brill.
- Friends In Adoption, www.friendsinadoption.org.
- *Gay and Lesbian Parenting*, edited by Deborah Glazer and Jack Drescher.
- *Gay Parent* magazine, Forest Hills, NY.
- *The Lesbian and Gay Parenting Handbook: Creating and Raising Our Families*, by April Martin.

## JOSÉ, MICHAEL, AND APRIL: A QUEER FAMILY IN SEARCH OF COMMUNITY

José and Michael, each in their late forties, have been together for fifteen years. They have one daughter, April, who is now four years old, and a year ago they moved from their urban neighborhood with few children to a suburban neighborhood with many children. José and Michael have begun to feel isolated in this new setting, however, because they are the only gay couple with children.

This couple has been referred to you by their rabbi who has no experience working with gay couples with children. Her congregation has a few lesbian and gay couples who are members but none of them are parents. After speaking briefly with Michael on the phone you agree to meet with him and José the following week.

In your first meeting with this couple you understand how deeply isolated they feel as gay parents. Their move to a neighborhood with no other gay or lesbian couples has proven uncomfortable for them because, as they report, they are a shy and rather introverted couple with little experience making friends with straight couples. They worry in particular that their daughter April will grow up with few friends because they are so disconnected from the families who live around them.

As you get to know this couple you realize that their isolation is causing significant problems within their relationship. With little understanding of the challenges of gay parenting, their family and friends seem unable to provide them with much support. Clearly, this couple is showing signs of stress and they are feeling increasingly inadequate and ill-equipped as parents. Realizing that they need to find networks of support for themselves as a couple and as gay parents, you point them in the direction of local resources, including a queer parenting group at the LGBTQ community center and a nearby PFLAG chapter. In addition, you suggest that José and Michael consider some ways in which they might get to know their neighbors in order to discover which of them might be supportive of them as a family and help them feel more at home in the neighborhood.

After several sessions with this couple you learn that they are disappointed with the lack of support they feel from other members of their current congregation. Lately they have begun to wonder if the unwelcome they feel reflects a disapproval from some synagogue members about gay people raising children, even though responsible social science research dispels the myth that children do not fare well with parents who are LGBTQ.[26] Since synagogue involvement has always been an important part of their life together, they say that they are coming to realize that they need to find a faith community with at least a few other gay or lesbian parents. They also realize they need to become more involved in their daughter's preschool by serving on a school committee (in order to meet other parents) and by helping out in the classroom. You applaud this realization and suggest that their occasional presence in April's classroom can be an important way of normalizing for her and her peers the fact that she has two fathers. Finally, they decide to hold an open house so that they can begin the process of making friends in their neighborhood.

By encouraging José and Michael to make connections with other gay and lesbian parents in their area and to take the lead in meeting their neighbors, you have helped them to understand that *they* need to be more proactive in creating the kind of community in which they want live. After a few weeks of visiting other local congregations they find a temple with an active LGBTQ social and advocacy group that includes queer parents; they realize that it will offer them a vital supportive spiritual home for their family. You wish José and Michael luck as they get to know their neighbors and prepare to join a new faith community. Based on the newfound enthusiasm with which they are approaching this task, you expect that they will meet with success.

---

26. See Columbia Law School, "What Does the Scholarly Research Say?" for an extensive bibliography on children being raised by gay and lesbian parents.

## SOME RESOURCES FOR LGBTQ PARENTS

- *For Lesbian Parents: Your Guide to Helping Your Family Grow Up Happy, Healthy, and Proud*, by Suzanne Johnson and Elizabeth O'Connor.
- *Gay and Lesbian Rights: A Guide for GLBT Singles, Couples and Families*, by Brette Sember.
- *Gay Dads: A Celebration of Fatherhood*, by David Strah and Susanna Margolis.
- *The Lesbian Parenting Book: A Guide to Creating Families and Raising Children*, by D. Merilee Clunis and G. Dorsey Green.
- *Women in Love: Portraits of Lesbian Mothers and Their Families*, by Barbara Seyda.

## DAMON, CLARE, AND ABBY: BUILDING SUPPORT FOR A QUEER FAMILY IN A COMMUNITY OF FAITH

Damon is the only son of Clare and Abby. Now nine years old and in the fourth grade, he recently came home upset from Sunday School because two children had called his moms "dykes." After working successfully with their son's Sunday School teacher on ways to address the issue of bullying, Clare and Abby decided to begin a conversation with the pastor at their church about making the congregation more welcoming of children with LGBTQ parents. The pastor says that he is eager to help educate the entire congregation about ways to welcome families with gay and lesbian parents.

In your first meeting with Clare and Abby you talk with them about some ways in which they might work with their church leadership to build a congregation that welcomes and affirms all children, including those with LGBTQ parents. Clare and Abby have been active for a few years in a local chapter of COLAGE (Children of Lesbians and Gays Everywhere) and they believe that their experience as effective advocates for children of queer parents in the local school system has prepared them to help foster a productive conversation at their church about LGBTQ people and their families.

> **LGBTQ FAMILIES: A BRIEF SELECTION OF RESOURCES**
>
> - *Families of Value: Personal Profiles of Pioneering Lesbian and Gay Parents*, by Robert Bernstein.
> - *Families We Choose: Lesbians, Gays, Kinship*, by Kath Weston.
> - *Gay Marriage, Real Life: Ten Stories of Love and Family*, by Michael Deakin.
> - *Lesbian and Gay Families Speak Out*, by Jane Drucker.
> - *Same-Sex Marriage?: A Christian Ethical Analysis*, by Marvin Ellison.

You suggest to this couple that one of the most effective ways for a church to become welcoming to and inclusive of all families is through its educational programs. Given the increasing number of LGBTQ-welcoming resources designed and produced by individuals and groups representing various Christian denominations, you recommend that Abby and Clare explore The Institute of Welcoming Resources website.[27] You also encourage them to contact the UCC Coalition for LGBT Concerns, a national organization for LGBTQ members and their allies in the United Church of Christ, the denomination to which their church belongs. The Coalition has a particularly valuable resource in its Open and Affirming Program, which assists local congregations working to welcome and include LGBTQ people.[28]

Since lifelong religious education opportunities can be a particularly effective way to build acceptance and inclusion of queer individuals and families in a congregation, you suggest that Abby and Clare also check out the "Our Whole Lives" program, a comprehensive sexuality education program intended for church members at various stages of life from kindergarten through adulthood.[29] Produced by the United Church of Christ and the Unitarian Universalist Association, this curriculum is based upon the conviction that young people and adults alike make good decisions about sexual activity when they are well-informed

---

27. See Institute of Welcoming Resources, "Christian/Denominationally-Based LGBT Organizations."

28. See The Open and Affirming Coalition of the United Church of Christ.

29. See Unitarian Universalist Association, "Planning Guide."

about human sexuality in a holistic manner and when they engage in values-clarification processes that are appropriate to their age level. Homosexuality is included in the curriculum as a natural variation of human sexuality and LGBTQ people are rendered visible in the lessons that make up this program. By normalizing queer people and their sexuality, this curriculum teaches children, from an early age, the value of accepting all people. Use of the "Our Whole Lives" curriculum can also help communities of faith in their work to welcome and affirm LGBTQ people and their families as full-fledged members of a faith community.

Abby and Clare are excited to learn about this curriculum and, the more they come to understand it, the more they believe that it contains good ideas on how to explore the values of diversity with both children and adults. Soon these women are on the road to becoming certified teachers of the curriculum. They discuss with their minister and religious education director how they might incorporate aspects of the "Our Whole Lives" curriculum into their church's Sunday School program. "I think that we will spark a worthwhile discussion at our church about how to welcome queer parents and their children. We also hope to explore with other members of our congregation how we might include information on homosexuality in our religious education program," Clare says during your last meeting with this couple. "The good news is that folks at our church are open in exploring how we might do this. Who knows? Maybe we can begin to figure out a way to include issues about LGBTQ people and their families at *all* levels of our congregation's educational programming."

> ### A BRIEF SELECTION OF RESOURCES TO SUPPORT CHILDREN OF LGBTQ PARENTS
>
> - *Daddy's Roommate*, by Michael Wilhoite.
> - *Families Like Mine: Children of Gay Parents Tell It Like It Is*, by Abigail Garner.
> - *Heather Has Two Mommies*, by Leslea Newman.
> - *Out of the Ordinary: Essays on Growing Up with Gay, Lesbian, and Transgendered Parents*, edited by Noelle Howey and Ellen Samuels.
> - *Zack's Story: Growing Up with Same-Sex Parents*, by Keith Greenberg.

## LUKE AND ALICE: ACCEPTING A TRANSGENDER CHILD

Luke and Alice, parents of a twenty-one-year-old child, email you and ask if they might meet to discuss their child. They describe themselves as "devout Christians" who have not seen their child in more than a year because they have not been able to accept their child's transgender identity. "How can we, as good Christians, embrace a trans child?" they ask. You agree to meet with them the following week.

Alice and Luke are clearly upset as they greet you for the first time in your office. You shake their hands, invite them to sit down and make themselves comfortable, and then ask them to tell you more about their child. Alice begins eagerly:

"Our child Ella used to be Robert," she says, "but for the past year or so he, I mean *she*, has insisted on being called Ella. I don't know what we did wrong in raising our son to want to be a woman. We've always been a solid and faithful Christian family but I don't know how to accept my son who is now becoming a woman."

Luke continues, "I *do* want to love and accept my son but I don't know where and how to begin. He is lucky to be in a liberal college environment where evidently he is accepted as a she. To be honest, I'm relieved that our child no longer comes home to visit or attends church with us. I mean, what would we say to other people? How could we explain to the minister that our son is now our daughter?"

As you assess Luke and Alice's situation during your first pastoral care visit with them you see clearly that this couple not only feels isolated in their struggle to accept their child's transgender identity but that they have not availed themselves of any positive educational information on transgender people. Nor have they found a way to understand and accept their transgender daughter from a faith perspective. You suggest that they join you in learning about transgender people and that they consider joining a support group for parents of transgender children.

In your second pastoral care session with this couple you learn that they desperately do want to accept their child and her transgender identity but that they don't see how they can reconcile this acceptance with their Christian faith. "Doesn't God decide before we are born whether we are male or female?" Alice asks at one point. Luke adds, "I've always been taught that God doesn't make mistakes in making us who He wants us to be."

You invite Luke and Alice to read and pray about three passages in the Christian New Testament during the coming week: Matt 19:11–12; Acts 8:25–39; and Gal 3:28. These biblical references provide important messages of affirmation for transgender persons because they call upon us to reevaluate our understandings of "gender variance" in the light of faith. Drawing upon Justin Tanis's exegesis of these three passages, you explore with Luke and Alice the reference to "eunuchs for the kingdom" in Matthew's Gospel as a call for us today to accept transgender individuals as children of God; the message of radical inclusion for gender-variant people contained in the story of the Ethiopian eunuch in Acts; and Paul's profound description of a Christian unity that overcomes all sorts of divisions, including those relating to gender.[30] Luke and Alice are deeply moved to read Scripture passages that speak positively to them about transgender people.

The medical, psychological, and legal information on transgender issues that you recommend to Alice and Luke proves to be valuable in their journey toward understanding their daughter Ella and her transgender identity. Some of the most helpful resources come from The PFLAG Transgender Network (TNET), the National Center for Transgender Equality (NCTE), The National LGBTQ Task Force (NGLTF), and the

---

30. Tanis, *Trans-Gendered*, 72–83.

CLGS Transgender Religious Roundtable.[31] In addition, a local support group of parents of transgender children puts Alice and Luke in touch with other people struggling to understand and accept their children; it is this network of support that moves them to start a process of rebuilding their relationship with Ella. They take the first steps toward this goal by welcoming their daughter back into their home.

As your pastoral care relationship with this couple comes to a close, they thank you for your help in bringing them "out of the closet" as parents of a transgender child. In their last session with you Alice and Luke speak of the great distance they have come in embracing their daughter as their beloved child and they share with you their dream of someday becoming advocates for all transgender people.

### TRANSGENDER IDENTITY FOR COMMUNITIES OF FAITH: A BRIEF SELECTION OF RESOURCES

- *Made in God's Image: A Resource for Dialogue about the Church and Gender Differences,* by Ann Thompson Cook.
- *Omnigender: A Trans-Religious Approach,* by Virginia Ramey Mollenkott.
- *TransForming Families: Real Stories about Transgender Loved Ones,* edited by Mary Boenke.
- *Transgender Journeys,* by Virginia Ramey Mollenkott and Vanessa Sheridan.
- *Transgendering Faith: Identity, Sexuality, and Spirituality,* edited by Leanne Tigert and Maren Tirabassi.
- *Transgender Pocket* ("Personal stories, articles, resources, etc. about transgender identities, experiences, and Christian life"), UCC Open and Affirming Program.

---

31. See the Resources list for contact information for these organizations.

## WHAT QUEER RELATIONSHIPS AND QUEER FAMILIES CAN TEACH OUR FAITH COMMUNITIES

One need only peruse the Hebrew and Christian Scriptures to realize that they reveal a wonderful variety of human relationships and family structures that reflect life-giving values of love, mutuality, and equality.[32] In this chapter we have explored a few of the ways in which LGBTQ people structure their interpersonal and family relationships with the goal of understanding how you, as a pastoral caregiver, can support queer people in their interpersonal and family relationships. While the biblical record urges you to be a caregiver who is open to a variety of relationships and family structures, the ministry of pastoral care challenges you to provide excellent care for those who come to you for help in sustaining their relationships and their families.

Once again, the hallmarks of such care include an acceptance and celebration of LGBTQ persons and their sexuality; an eagerness to learn from queer people themselves about their relationships and their families; and a commitment to explore theologies of sexuality that creatively apply the healing wisdom of the Jewish and Christian faith traditions to the lived experience of queer people. As we know, caregivers in these faith traditions have often been anything but a source of healing or support for LGBTQ people. Fortunately, however, the growing acceptance and affirmation of queer people in many of our congregations is bringing about a revolution of positive pastoral care. Caring for LGBTQ people and their families may not always be easy but it is certainly a much-needed and rewarding ministry.

---

32. Mollenkott, *Sensuous Spirituality*, 194–97, lists forty "Diverse Forms of Family Mentioned or Implied in the Hebrew and Christian Scriptures."

# Epilogue
## Thank You and Welcome

WE BELIEVE THAT PASTORAL care with lesbian, bisexual, transgender, queer, and gay people of faith is a challenging, rewarding, and grace-filled experience. As we remarked in the Introduction, "What a time to be in ministry to us!" We now add, "What a gift pastoral care with queer folk can be for care receiver and caregiver alike!"

Clearly, there is an urgent need for compassionate and reality-based pastoral care for the many LGBTQ people who strive to embrace their gender identity, their sexual orientation, *and* their commitment to a spiritual life in a faith community—all in equal measure. No longer content to hide in the shadows of church or synagogue life, queer people of faith are standing up in increasing numbers and claiming their rightful place as children of God who are called to full membership in our communities of faith.

To ignore the pastoral care needs of LGBTQ people because they are LGBTQ is unjust; to insist that the sexual orientation, gender identity, and/or sexual expression of queer people is sinful or disordered is incompatible with the powerfully liberating message of the Scriptures; to offer pastoral care that is half-hearted or does not speak adequately to the lives and needs of LGBTQ persons is to deny them the love and support that all religions teach is due every person.

In this book we have attempted to provide a practical handbook for pastoral caregivers, especially those in training, who are called to work with LGBTQ people. While we do not claim to offer the last word on any aspect of LGBTQ pastoral care, we do hope that we have provided you, the reader, with some reliable guidance and thought-provoking questions. Most importantly, we have stressed the importance of listening, with an open mind and open heart, to the experiences of queer persons in your care so that you might know something of their lives and build with them a pastoral relationship of genuine respect, effective care, and mutual growth.

It is common knowledge that current debates concerning LGBTQ persons and queer sexuality threaten some denominations, churches, and synagogues with schism and outright dissolution. Your pastoral care with LGBTQ people is indispensable in this tumultuous time because it offers living testimony to Jewish and Christian beliefs that everyone is equal in God's sight. Moreover, your ministry can change peoples' hearts and contribute significantly, probably in ways never fully knowable, to building the beloved community that Martin Luther King, Jr., described so eloquently and that we, as committed believers, yearn for so deeply.

LGBTQ pastoral care is still a relatively new and developing ministry and those caregivers who work in this field are trail blazers. We have shared our ideas in this book as one way of giving back to the many people who have served us as companions and guides on our own journeys as queer people of faith. We are grateful for your time and attention to our efforts. If you have been a pastoral caregiver to LGBTQ people for a long or short period of time, in our own names and in the names of many, we say, "Thank you! We are honored to be colleagues with you in this vital work." If you are new to this particular ministry or preparing for it, we say, "Welcome to a fulfilling, exciting, and urgently needed field of pastoral care!"

# Appendix
## Sexual Rating Scales

RESEARCH HAS CONSISTENTLY SHOWN that human sexuality can be understood more accurately as a continuum rather than as a duality, as a fluid state rather than a static one. Without commenting on the numbers in each category nor the exactness of the boundaries, the following two scales show this continuum in a graphic way.

The Kinsey Scale[1]

The Kinsey Scale attempts to measure sexual orientation, from 0 (exclusively heterosexual) to 6 (exclusively homosexual). It was first published in *Sexual Behavior in the Human Male* (1948) by Alfred Kinsey, Wardell Pomeroy, and others; it also figured prominently in the complementary work *Sexual Behavior in the Human Female* (1953). Introducing the scale, Kinsey wrote:

> Males [this part of the study deals only with males] do not represent two discrete populations, heterosexual and homosexual. The world is not to be divided into sheep and goats. It is a fundamental of taxonomy that nature rarely deals with discrete categories. . . . The living world is a continuum in each and every one of its aspects.[2]

---

1. Kinsey Institute, "Kinsey Scale," is reproduced by permission of The Trustees of Indiana University on behalf of the Kinsey Institute. All rights reserved. Used with permission. Copyright © 2017.
2. Kinsey, *Sexual Behavior*, 639.

*Appendix*

While emphasizing the continuity of the gradations between exclusively heterosexual and exclusively homosexual histories, it has seemed desirable to develop some sort of classification which could be based on the relative amounts of heterosexual and homosexual experience or response in each history.... An individual may be assigned a position on this scale, for each period in his life.... A seven-point scale comes nearer to showing the many gradations that actually exist.[3]

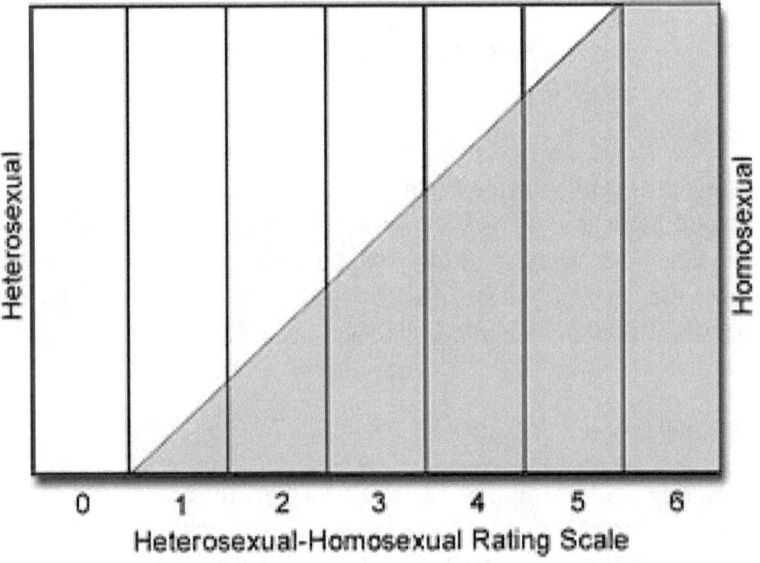

0- Exclusively heterosexual
1- Predominantly heterosexual, only incidentally homosexual
2- Predominantly heterosexual, but more than incidentally homosexual
3- Equally heterosexual and homosexual
4- Predominantly homosexual, but more than incidentally heterosexual
5- Predominantly homosexual, only incidentally heterosexual
6- Exclusively homosexual
X-No socio-sexual contacts or reactions

3. Kinsey, *Sexual Behavior*, 639 and 656.

## The Klein Sexual Orientation Grid[4]

The Klein Sexual Orientation Grid is a system for describing a person's sexual proclivities in a more detailed and informative way than previous methods. It was introduced by Dr. Fritz Klein (1932–2006) in his book *The Bisexual Option*.

The Klein Sexual Orientation Grid is shown in the table below. For each person, it sets out the seven component variables of sexual orientation, listed as A through G down the left side. The three columns indicate three different points at which sexual orientation is assessed: the person's past, their present, and their ideal. The person then receives a rating from 1 to 7 for each of the 21 resulting combinations, one rating for each empty box in the chart below. The meanings of the ratings are indicated just below the grid itself.

### The Klein Sexuality Grid

| | Variable | Past | Present | Ideal |
|---|---|---|---|---|
| A | Sexual Attraction | | | |
| B | Sexual Behavior | | | |
| C | Sexual Fantasies | | | |
| D | Emotional Preference | | | |
| E | Social Preference | | | |
| F | Heterosexual/Homosexual Lifestyle | | | |
| G | Self Identification | | | |

For Variables A to E:

1 = Other sex only
2 = Other sex mostly
3 = Other sex somewhat more
4 = Both sexes
5 = Same sex somewhat more
6 = Same sex mostly
7 = Same sex only

For Variables F and G:

1 = Heterosexual only
2 = Heterosexual mostly
3 = Heterosexual somewhat more
4 = Hetero/Gay-Lesbian equally
5 = Gay/Lesbian somewhat more
6 = Gay/Lesbian mostly
7 = Gay/Lesbian only

---

4. Klein, "Klein Sexual Orientation Grid," is reproduced by permission of the American Institute of Bisexuality, Inc.

## DEFINITIONS HELPFUL IN USING THE KLEIN SEXUAL ORIENTATION GRID:[5]

Past: Your life up to 12 months ago.

Present: The most recent 12 months.

Ideal: What do you think you would eventually like?

## THE VARIABLES TO CONSIDER IN USING THE KLEIN SEXUAL ORIENTATION GRID:

Sexual Attraction: To whom are you sexually attracted?

Sexual Behavior: With whom have you actually had sex?

Sexual Fantasies: Whom are your sexual fantasies about? (They may occur during masturbation, daydreaming, as part of real life, or purely in your imagination.)

Emotional Preference: Emotions influence, if not define, the actual physical act of love. Do you love and like only members of the same sex, only members of the other sex, or members of both sexes?

Social Preference: Social preference is closely allied with but often different from emotional preference. With members of which sex do you socialize?

Lifestyle Preference: What is the sexual identity of the people with whom you socialize?

Sexual Identity: How do you think of yourself?

Political Identity: Some people describe their relationship to the rest of society differently than their personal sexual identity. For instance, a woman may have a *heterosexual* sexual identity, but a *lesbian* political identity. How do you think of yourself politically?

Note that The Klein Sexual Orientation Grid takes into consideration the fact that many people change their orientation over time. Where a person is today is not necessarily where she or he was in the past—or, for that matter, where he or she will be or would like to be in the future. The concept of sexual orientation as an *ongoing dynamic process* is necessary if we are to understand a person's orientation properly in its entirety.

5. Klein, "Klein Sexual Orientation Grid."

Please note that although it is entirely possible for an individual to utilize The Klein Sexual Orientation Grid for the purposes of better determining self-identification through a process of self-assessment, if you are in the process of coming out as bisexual, the best option is to seek the guidance of a professional therapist who understands bisexuality.

# Resources

## ACTIVISM

de la Torre, Miguel. *Reading the Bible from the Margins*. Maryknoll, NY: Orbis, 2002.
Faderman, Lillian. *The Gay Revolution: The Story of the Struggle*. New York: Simon and Schuster, 2015.
Fetner, Tina. *How the Religious Right Shaped Lesbian and Gay Activism*. Minneapolis: University of Minnesota Press, 2008.
GLAAD. An LGBTQ Media Advocacy Organization: www.glaad.org.
Goss, Robert. *Jesus Acted Up: A Gay and Lesbian Manifesto*. San Francisco: HarperSanFrancisco, 1993.
Kramer, Larry. The *Tragedy of Today's Gays*. New York: Jeremy P. Tarcher/Penguin, 2005.
Kumashiro, Kevin. *Troubling Education: Queer Activism and Anti-Oppressive Pedagogy*. New York: RoutledgeFalmer, 2002.
Parents and Friends of Lesbians and Gays (P-FLAG): www.pflag.org.
Quesada, Uriel, Letitia Gomez, and Salvador Vidal-Ortiz, eds. *Queer Brown Voices: Personal Narratives of Latina/o LGBT Activism*. Austin: University of Texas Press, 2015.
Soulforce. "A network of friends learning nonviolence from Gandhi and King seeking justice for God's lesbian, gay, bisexual and transgendered children": www.soulforce.org.
White, Mel. *Religion Gone Bad: The Hidden Dangers of the Christian Right*. New York: Tarcher, 2006.

*Resources*

## ADOPTION: SEE PARENTING, ADOPTION; LGBTQ

## ADVANCED-CARE PLANNING: SEE LIFE, ADVANCED CARE, AND ESTATE PLANNING

Burda, Joan M. *Estate Planning for Same-Sex Couples*. 2nd ed. Chicago: American Bar Association, 2012.
Chapman, Melissa. "5 Estate Planning Tips LGBT Families Need To Follow In 2016." http://www.huffingtonpost.com/entry/5-estate-planning-tips-lgbt-families-need-to-follow_us_57864235e4b0e7c8734f3524.
Lawton, Andrew, Jocelyn White, and Erik Fromme. "End-of-Life and Advance Care Planning Considerations for Lesbian, Gay, Bisexual, and Transgender Patients." Fast Facts and Concepts #275. https://www.mypcnow.org/blank-nu7xp.
"Protect Yourself and Those You Love: A Step-by-Step Guide to Life & Estate Planning for LGBT Americans and Their Families." Human Rights Campaign (HRC). http://myplanwithhrc.org/wp-content/uploads/sites/5/2015/07/HRC_Life_and_Estate_Planning_Guide-REVISION-v4.pdf.
Stone, Carrie, and John G. Culhane. *Same Sex Legal Kit for Dummies*. Hoboken: J. Wiley & Sons, 2013.

## AGE: YOUTH, AND OLDER AGE

Big Brothers Big Sisters of America: www.bbbs.org.
Boykin Keith. *For Colored Boys Who Have Considered Suicide When the Rainbow Is Still Not Enough: Coming of Age, Coming Out, and Coming Home*. New York: Magnus, 2012.
Clunis, D. Merilee. *Lives of Lesbian Elders: Looking Back, Looking Forward*. New York: Haworth, 2005.
Cottrell, Susan. *"Mom, I'm Gay": Loving Your LGBTQ Child and Strengthening Your Faith*. Rev. ed. Louisville: Westminster John Knox, 2016.
Covenant House. A national outreach to kids who live on the streets. www.covenanthouse.org.
D'Augelli, Anthony R., and Charlotte J. Patterson, *Lesbian, Gay, Bisexual Identities over the Lifespan: Psychological Perspectives*. New York: Oxford University Press, 2005.
Flynn, Peggy. *The Caregiving Zone: A Unique Guide to Facing the Realities of Illness, Aging, Dying, and Death*. New York: iUniverse, 2006.
Kimmel, Douglas, ed. *Lesbian, Gay, Bisexual, and Transgender Aging: Research and Clinical Perspectives*. New York: Columbia University Press, 2006.
Kimmel, Douglas et al., eds. *Midlife and Aging in Gay America: Proceedings of the Sage Conference 2000*. New York: Harrington Park, 2001.
Lambda GLBT Community Services website has a useful article on teen suicide: www.lambda.org/youth_suicide.htm.
McDermott, Elizabeth, and Katrina Roen. *Queer Youth, Suicide and Self-Harm: Troubled Subjects, Troubling Norms*. Houndmills: Palgrave Macmillan, 2016.

Pacha, Kelsey. "Transitioning to Inclusion: A Guide to Welcoming Transgender Children and Their Families in Your Community of Faith." The Center for LGBTQ and Gender Studies in Religion (CLGS), 2015: https://clgs.org/multimedia-archive/transitioningyouthresource/.
Point Foundation provides financial support, mentoring, and hope to meritorious students who are marginalized due to sexual orientation, gender expression, or gender identity: https://pointfoundation.org/.
Remafedi, Gary, ed. *Death by Denial: Studies of Suicide in Gay and Lesbian Teenagers.* Boston: Alyson, 1994.
Ryan, Caitlin, and Donna Futterman. *Lesbian and Gay Youth: Care and Counseling.* New York: Columbia University Press, 1998.
Sanders, Cody J. *A Brief Guide to Ministry with LGBTQIA Youth.* Louisville: Westminster John Knox, 2017.
Stop A Suicide Today: Screening for Mental Health: www.stopasuicide.org/signs.html.
Suicide Awareness Voices of Education (SAVE): https://save.org/.

# AIDS: SEE HIV/AIDS

# BIBLE/BIBLICAL INTERPRETATION: SEE THEOLOGY AND BIBLICAL INTERPRETATION

# BISEXUAL RESOURCES: IDENTITY, RELATIONSHIPS, SEXUALITY, AND SPIRITUALITY

Alford-Harkey, Marie, and Debra W. Haffner. *Bisexuality: Making the Invisible Visible in Faith Communities.* Bridgeport, CT: Religious Institute, 2014.
Andrew, Elizabeth. *Swinging on the Garden Gate: A Spiritual Memoir.* Boston: Skinner, 2000.
Bisexual Resource Center: www.biresource.org.
Hutchins, Loraine, and Lani Kaahumanu, eds. *Bi Any Other Name: Bisexual People Speak Out.* 25th Anniversary ed. Riverdale, NY: Riverdale, 2015.
Kinsey Scale of Human Sexuality: www.kinseyinstitute.org/research/ak-hhscale.html.
Klein, Fred. *The Bisexual Option: A Concept of One Hundred Percent Intimacy.* New York: Priam, 1978.
Klein Sexual Orientation Grid: www.americaninstituteofbisexuality.org/thekleingrid.
Kolodny, Debra R., ed. *Blessed Bi Spirit: Bisexual People of Faith.* New York: Continuum, 2000.
Money, John. *Gay, Straight, and In-Between: The Sexology of Erotic Orientation.* New York: Oxford University Press, 1988.
Ochs, Robyn, and Sarah Rowley. *Getting Bi: Voices of Bisexuals around the World.* 2nd ed. Boston: Bisexual Resource Center, 2009.

## CELIBACY, LGBTQ

Goergen, Donald. *The Sexual Celibate*. New York: Seabury, 1974.
Isherwood, Lisa. *The Power of Erotic Celibacy: Queering Heteropatriarchy*. London: T&T Clark, 2006.
Schneiders, Sandra. *Selling All: Commitment, Consecrated Celibacy, and Community in Catholic Religious Life*. New York: Paulist, 2001.

## CHILDREN OF LGBTQ PARENTS

Garner, Abigail. *Families Like Mine: Children of Gay Parents Tell It Like It Is*. New York: HarperCollins, 2004.
Greenberg, Keith. *Zack's Story: Growing Up with Same-Sex Parents*. Minneapolis: Lerner, 1996.
Herman, Gabriela. *The Kids: The Children of LGBTQ Parents in the USA*. New York: New Press, 2017.
Howey, Noelle, and Ellen Samuels, eds. *Out of the Ordinary: Essays on Growing Up with Gay, Lesbian, and Transgendered Parents*. New York: St. Martin's, 2000.
Newman, Leslea. *Heather Has Two Mommies*. 10th Anniversary ed. Los Angeles: Alyson, 2000.
Willhoite, Michael. *Daddy's Roommate*. Los Angeles: Alyson, 1990.

## COMING OUT

Argent, Jay. *Coming Out: High School Boys Share Their Stories*. Self-published, 2017.
Austin, Jen. *Coming Out Christian: Finding Wholeness in Faith and Sexuality*. Dallas: Sources of Hope, 2006.
Bono, Chastity, and Billie Fitzpatrick. *Family Outing*. Boston: Little, Brown, 1998.
Borhek, Mary. *Coming Out to Parents: A Two-Way Survival Guide for Lesbians and Gay Men and Their Parents*. Cleveland: Pilgrim, 1993.
Buxton, Amity. *The Other Side of the Closet: The Coming-Out Crisis for Straight Spouses and Families*. Rev. ed. New York: J. Wiley, 1994.
de la Huerta, Christian. *Coming Out Spiritually: The Next Step*. New York: Jeremy P. Tarcher/Putnam, 1999.
Dickens, Joy, ed. *Family Outing: A Guide for Parents of Gays, Lesbians and Bisexuals*. London: P. Owen, 1995.
Glaser, C. *Coming Out to God: Prayers for Lesbians and Gay Men, Their Families and Friends*. Louisville: Westminster/John Knox, 1991.
Grever, Carol. *My Husband Is Gay: A Woman's Guide to Surviving the Crisis*. Freedom, CA: Crossing, 2001.
Griffin, Carolyn, and Marian Wirth. *Beyond Acceptance: Parents of Lesbians & Gays Talk About Their Experiences*. Rev. ed. New York: St. Martin's, 1996.
It Gets Better Project: https://itgetsbetter.org/?gclid=CjwKCAiA1O3RBR BHEiwAq5fD_Hc86wR_CpAmpsofS39Kz6A38rDTTS4d9YvXinIq_ D8ZCyG9WxKQDxoCvfIQAvD_BwE.

Likosky, Stephan, ed. *Coming Out: An Anthology of International Gay and Lesbian Writings.* New York: Pantheon, 1992.
Mattmann, Urs. *Coming In: Gays and Lesbians Reclaiming the Spiritual Journey.* Glasgow: Wild Goose, 2006.
New York Times. "Transgender Lives: Yours Stories": www.nytimes.com/interactive/projects/storywall/transgender-today.
O'Neill, Craig, and Kathleen Ritter. *Coming Out Within: Stages of Spiritual Awakening for Lesbians and Gay Men.* San Francisco: HarperSanFrancisco, 1992.
PFLAG. *Our Daughters and Our Sons: Questions and Answers for Parents of Gay, Lesbian and Bisexual People.* www.pflag.org/sites/default/files/Our%20Daughters%20And%20Sons.pdf.
———. *Our Trans Loved Ones*: www.pflag.org/sites/default/files/Our%20Trans%20Loved%20Ones.pdf.
Schimel, Lawrence, ed. *Found Tribe: Jewish Coming Out Stories.* Santa Fe, NM: Sherman Asher, 2002.
Tigert, Leanne, and Timothy Brown, eds. *Coming Out Young and Faithful.* Cleveland: Pilgrim, 2001.

## DISABLED: SEE OTHER-ABLED /DIFFERENTLY-ABLED/ PERSONS WITH DISABILITIES

## DIVERSITY

Bell, A., and M. Weinberg. *Homosexualities: A Study of Diversity among Men and Women.* New York: Simon and Schuster, 1978.
Religious Tolerance. A useful website for researching religious tolerance and diversity: www.religioustolerance.org.
Ward, Jane. *Respectably Queer: Diversity Culture in LGBT Activist Organizations.* Nashville: Vanderbilt University Press, 2008.

## DIVORCE: SEE SEPARATION/DIVORCE

## DRUGS AND ADDICTION

The "Anti-Meth Site" contains valuable information about crystal meth: http://www.kci.org/.
Drescher, Jack, Andrew J. Kolodny, and Milton L. Wainberg, eds. *Crystal Meth and Men Who Have Sex with Men: What Mental Health Care Professionals Need to Know.* New York: Haworth Medical, 2006.
Fawcett, David. *Lust, Men, and Meth: A Gay Man's Guide to Sex and Recovery.* Wilton Manors, FL: Healing Path, 2015.

Minor, Robert N. "When Religion Is an Addiction" (Fairness Project Lecture Series). Audio cassette. QuestLiving.com, 2006 (ASIN: B000FPE952).
Moore, Patrick. *Tweaked: A Crystal Memoir*. New York: Kensington, 2006.
Osborne, Duncan. *Suicide Tuesday: Gay Men and the Crystal Meth Scare*. New York: Carroll & Graf, 2006.
Ringwald, Christopher D. *The Soul of Recovery: Uncovering the Spiritual Dimension in the Treatment of Addictions*. New York: Oxford University Press, 2002.
Specter, Michael. "Higher Risk: Crystal Meth, the Internet, and Dangerous Choices about AIDS." *New Yorker Magazine*, 2005: https://facultystaff.richmond.edu/~bmayes/pdf/CMeth_AIDS.pdf.

## EDUCATION

Canadian Plains Research Center. *I Could Not Speak My Heart: Education and Social Justice for Gay and Lesbian Youth*. Regina: University of Regina Press, 2002.
GLSEN: The Gay, Lesbian & Straight Education Network: www.glsen.org.
Greenberg, Rabbi Steven. *Wrestling with God and Men: Homosexuality in the Jewish Tradition*. Madison: University of Wisconsin Press, 2004.
Hawley, John C., ed. *Expanding the Circle: Creating an Inclusive Environment in Higher Education for LGBTQ Students and Studies*. Albany: State University of New York Press, 2015.
Isay, Richard A. *Being Homosexual*. New York: Farrar Straus Giroux, 1989.
McNeill, John J. *The Church and the Homosexual*. 4th ed. Boston: Beacon, 1993.
"The Respect for All Project." Four Films: "It's Elementary: Talking About Gay Issues in School"; "That's a Family"; "Let's Get Real" (on bullying); and "Straightlaced" (on the pressure to conform to gender roles): https://groundspark.org/respect-for-all.

## ETHICS AND MORALITY

Balka, Christie, and Andy Rose, eds. *Twice Blessed: On Being Lesbian, Gay, and Jewish*. Boston: Beacon, 1989.
Batchelor, Edward, Jr. *Homosexuality and Ethics*. New York: Pilgrim, 1980.
Countryman, L. W. *Dirt, Greed, and Sex: Sexual Ethics in the New Testament and Their Implications for Today*. New ed. London: SCM, 2001.
Gula, Richard M. *Ethics in Pastoral Ministry*. New York: Paulist, 1996.
Hunt, Mary E. *Fierce Tenderness: A Feminist Theology of Friendship*. New York: Crossroad, 1991.
Jacobsen, Janet R., and Ann Pellegrini. *Love the Sin: Sexual Regulation and the Limits of Religious Tolerance*. Boston: Beacon, 2003.
Jordan, Mark D. *The Ethics of Sex*. Oxford: Blackwell, 2002.
———. *Telling Truths in Church: Scandal, Flesh, and Christian Speech*. Boston: Beacon, 2003.
Jung, Patricia Beattie, and Ralph Smith. *Heterosexism: An Ethical Challenge*. Albany: State University Press of New York, 1993.
Kolodny, Debra R., ed. *Blessed Bi Spirit: Bisexual People of Faith*. New York: Continuum, 2000.

Nelson, James B. *Embodiment: An Approach to Sexuality and Christian Theology.* Minneapolis: Augsburg, 1978.
Stuart, Elizabeth. *Just Good Friends: Towards a Lesbian and Gay Theology of Relationships.* London: Mowbray, 1995.
Weaver, Andrew, et al. *Counseling on Sexual Issues: A Handbook for Pastors and Other Helping Professionals.* Cleveland: Pilgrim, 2005.

## "EX-GAY" MINISTRIES

Besen, Wayne R. *Anything but Straight: Unmasking the Scandals and Lies Behind the Ex-Gay Myth.* New York: Harrington Park, 2003.
Human Rights Campaign. *Mission Impossible: Why Reparative Therapy and Ex-Gay Ministries Fail,* 1999: www.scribd.com/document/34297786/Mission-Impossible-Why-Reparative-Therapy-and-Ex-gay-Ministries-Fail-Mills.
Shidlo, Ariel, ed. *Sexual Conversion Therapy: Ethical, Clinical and Research Perspectives.* New York: Haworth Medical, 2001.

## FAITH-BASED LGBTQ-AFFIRMING RESOURCES

Affirmation: LGBT Mormons Families and Friends: www.affirmation.org.
Affirmation: United Methodists for Lesbian, Gay, Bisexual, and Transgender Concerns: www.umaffirm.org.
Al-Fatiha Foundation: An international organization that aims to support LGBTQ Muslims in reconciling their sexual orientation or gender identity with Islam. www.al-fatiha.org.
Association of Welcoming & Affirming Baptists: www.wabaptists.org.
AXIOS. Eastern and Orthodox Christian Gay Men and Lesbian Christians: www.qrd.org/qrd/www/orgs/axios.
Brethren Mennonite Council for Lesbian, Gay, Bisexual, and Transgender Interests: www.bmclgbt.org.
Catholic Apostolic Church in North America: www.cacina.org.
The Center for LGBTQ and Gender Studies in Religion (CLGS): www.clgs.org.
Christian Science Group for Lesbian, Gay, Bisexual and Transgender People, Their Friends & Supporters: http://www.nycsgroup.com.
Comstock, Gary David. *A Whosoever Church: Welcoming Lesbians and Gay Men into African American Congregations.* Louisville: Westminster John Knox, 2001.
Dignity Canada Dignité; Roman Catholic: www.dignitycanada.org.
Dignity USA. Lesbian, Gay, Bisexual & Transgendered Catholics: www.dignityusa.org.
Disciples LGBTQ+ Alliance: http://disciplesallianceq.org/.
Emergence International. A world-wide community supporting LGBT Christian Scientists: emergence-international.org.
Evangelicals Concerned. A national network of gay and lesbian evangelical Christians and friends: http://ecinc.org.
Friends [Quakers] for Lesbian & Gay Concerns: http://flgbtqc.quaker.org/.
Gay Christian Network: www.gaychristian.net.

Gay Spirit Visions. "Creating safe, sacred space for men who love men": http://gayspiritvisions.org/.

Integrity. A National Association of Lesbian and Gay Episcopalians and Their Friends: www.integrityusa.org.

Interweave. Unitarian Universalists: www.uua.org/offices/organizations/interweave.

Keshet. "A national organization that works for full LGBTQ equality and inclusion in Jewish life": www.keshetonline.org.

The Lesbian, Gay, Bisexual and Transgender Religious Archives Network. "A resource center and information clearinghouse for the history of LGBT religious movements." A project of The Center for LGBTQ and Gender Studies (CLGS): www.lgbtran.org.

Lutherans Concerned North America. See Reconciling Works below.

Metropolitan Community Churches: www.ufmcc.com.

More Light Presbyterians. www.mlp.org.

New Ways Ministry (Roman Catholic): www.newwaysministry.org.

Open and Affirming Coalition of the United Church of Christ: https://openandaffirming.org.

Quest: Pastoral Support for LGBT Catholics (United Kingdom): http://questgaycatholic.org.uk/.

Rainbow Sash Movement. Roman Catholic: www.rainbowsash.com/.

Reconciling Ministries Network of The United Methodist Church: http://www.rmnetwork.org/.

Reconciling Works/Lutherans for Full Participation. Advocates "for the full welcome, inclusion, and equity of lesbian, gay, bisexual, transgender, and queer (LGBTQ) Lutherans in all aspects of the life of their Church, congregations, and community": www.reconcilingworks.org.

The Reformation Project. "A Bible-Based, Gospel-Centered Approach to LGBTQ Inclusion": www.reformationproject.org.

Room for All. The Reformed Church in America: www.roomforall.com.

SDA Kinship International, Inc. Gay & Lesbian Support Group Seventh-Day Adventists. www.sdakinship.org.

United Church of Christ (UCC) Coalition for LGBT Concerns. See Open and Affirming Coalition above.

Unity Fellowship Church Movement. "Founded ... for openly gay and lesbian African Americans": http://ufcmlife.org.

Welcoming Community Network. Community of Christ: http://welcomingcommunitynetwork.org.

World Congress of Gay, Lesbian, Bisexual, and Transgender Jews: Keshet Ga'avah. glbtjews.org.

## FAMILIES, LGBTQ

Bernstein, Robert. *Families of Value: Personal Profiles of Pioneering Lesbian and Gay Parents*. New York: Marlowe, 2005.

Brynholf, Lyon K., and Archie Smith, Jr. *Tending the Flock: Congregations and Family Ministry*. Louisville, KY: Westminster John Knox, 1998.

Drucker, Jane. *Lesbian and Gay Families Speak Out*. New York: Insight, 1998.

Mezey, Nancy J. *LGBT Families*. Los Angeles: SAGE, 2015.
Straight Spouse Network. An "international organization that provides personal, confidential support and information to heterosexual spouses/partners, current or former, of gay, lesbian, bisexual or transgender mates and mixed-orientation or transgender/non-transgender couples for constructively resolving coming-out problems": www.straightspouse.org.
Weston, Kath. *Families We Choose: Lesbians, Gays, Kinship*. New York: Columbia University Press, 1991.

## FAMILIES (NON-LGBTQ) WITH LGBTQ MEMBERS

Cottrell, Susan. *"Mom, I'm Gay." Loving Your LGBTQ Child and Strengthening Your Faith*. Rev. ed. Louisville: Westminster John Knox, 2016.

## GAY MALE RESOURCES: IDENTITY, RELATIONSHIPS, SEXUALITY, AND SPIRITUALITY

Berzon, Betty. *Permanent Partners: Building Gay & Lesbian Relationships That Last*. New York: E. P. Dutton, 1988.
Boisvert, Donald L. *Out on Holy Ground: Meditations on Gay Men's Spirituality*. Cleveland: Pilgrim, 2000.
———. *Sanctity and Male Desire: A Gay Reading of Saints*. Cleveland: Pilgrim, 2004.
Clark, J. Michael. *Doing the Work of Love: Men and Commitment in Same-Sex Couples*. Harriman, TN: Men's Studies, 1999.
Driggs, John, and Stephen Finn. *Intimacy between Men: How to Find and Keep Gay Love Relationships*. New York: Plume, 1991.
Fellows, William. *Farm Boys: Lives of Gay Men from the Rural Midwest*. Madison: University of Wisconsin Press, 2001.
Fox, Matthew. *The Hidden Spirituality of Men: Ten Metaphors to Awaken the Sacred Masculine*. Novato, CA: New World, 2008.
Isay, Richard A. *Commitment and Healing: Gay Men and the Need for Romantic Love*. Hoboken, NJ: John Wiley and Sons, 2006.
Mancilla, Michael, and Lisa Troshinsky. *Love in the Time of HIV: The Gay Man's Guide to Sex, Dating, and Relationships*. New York: Guilford, 2003.
Nimmons, David. *The Soul Beneath the Skin: The Unseen Hearts and Habits of Gay Men*. New York: St. Martin's, 2002.
Roscoe, Will. *Queer Spirits: A Gay Men's Myth Book*. Boston: Beacon, 1995.
Yip, Andrew. *Gay Male Christian Couples: Life Stories*. Westport, CT: Praeger, 1997.

## HIV/AIDS

Ball, Susan C. *Voices in the Band: A Doctor, Her Patients, and How the Outlook on AIDS Care Changed from Doomed to Hopeful*, Ithaca: ILR, 2015.

Bartlett, John G., and Ann K. Finkbeiner. *The Guide to Living with HIV Infection.* Baltimore: Johns Hopkins University Press, 2006.
Connolly, Sean. *AIDS Pastoral Care: An Introductory Guide.* Grantsville: Arc, 1994.
Gebhardt, Daniel. *I Am This One Walking Beside Me: Meditations of an HIV Positive Gay Man.* Eugene, OR: Wipf and Stock, 2010.
Local resources: Use search engines and printed directories to find local AIDS services. Here are two examples: Chicago: APCN (AIDS Pastoral Care Network): https://www.achn.net/. Mississippi's AIDS Services Coalition: https://www.ascms.net/.
Messer, Donald E. *Breaking the Conspiracy of Silence: Christian Churches and the Global AIDS Crisis.* Minneapolis: Augsburg Fortress, 2004.

## HOMOPHOBIA/HETEROSEXISM

Blumenfeld, Warren J., ed. *Homophobia: How We All Pay the Price.* Boston: Beacon, 1992.
Pharr, Suzanne. *Homophobia: A Weapon of Sexism.* Little Rock, AR: Chardon, 1988.

## HOMOSEXUALITY

Jordan, Mark D. *The Silence of Sodom: Homosexuality in the Modern Catholicism.* Chicago: University of Chicago Press, 2000.
Oliveto, Karen, Kelly Turney, and Traci West. *Talking About Homosexuality: A Congregational Resource.* Cleveland: Pilgrim, 2005.
Sullivan, Andrew. *Virtually Normal: An Argument about Homosexuality.* New York: Vintage, 1995.

## IMMIGRANTS AND REFUGEES, LGBTQ

ILRC (Immigrant Legal Resource Center): www.ilrc.org/lgbt-immigrant-rights.
ORAM (Organization for Refuge, Asylum & Migration): www.oramrefugee.org.

## LESBIAN RESOURCES: IDENTITY, RELATIONSHIPS, SEXUALITY, AND SPIRITUALITY

Adelman, Marcy R., ed. *Midlife Lesbian Relationships: Friends, Lovers, Children, and Parents.* New York: Harrington Park, 2000.
Berzon, Betty. *Permanent Partners: Building Gay & Lesbian Relationships That Last.* New York: E. P. Dutton, 1988.
Clunis, D. Merilee, and G. Dorsey Green. *Lesbian Couples: A Guide to Creating Healthy Relationships.* Emeryville, CA: Seal, 2005.
Haley-Banez, Lynn. *Lesbians in Committed Relationships: Extraordinary Couples, Ordinary Lives.* New York: Harrington Park, 2002.

Laird, Joan, and Robert-Jay Green, eds. *Lesbians and Gays in Couples and Families: A Handbook for Therapists.* San Francisco: Jossey-Bass, 1996.

Marshall, Joretta L. *Counseling Lesbian Partners.* Louisville, KY: Westminster John Knox, 1997.

## LEGAL TOPICS; LGBTQ

American Civil Liberties Union (ACLU): www.aclu.org/issues/lgbt-rights.

Lambda Legal Defense and Education Fund: www.lambdalegal.org.

Mogul, Joey, L., Andrea J. Ritchie, and Kay Whitlock. *Queer (In)Justice: The Criminalization of LGBT People in the United States.* Boston: Beacon, 2011.

National Center for Lesbian Rights: www.nclrights.org.

Pinello, Daniel R. *America's War on Same-Sex Couples and Their Families.* Cambridge: Cambridge University Press, 2016.

Sember, Brette. *Gay and Lesbian Rights: A Guide for GLBT Singles, Couples and Families.* 2nd ed. Naperville, IL: Sphinx, 2006.

## LIFE, ADVANCED CARE, AND ESTATE PLANNING

Hanson, Holly. *The LGBT & Modern Family Money Manual: Financial Strategies for You and Your Loved Ones.* Los Angeles: Hanson, 2015.

Hertz, Frederick, and Emily Doskow. *A Legal Guide for Lesbian and Gay Couples.* 19th ed. Berkeley, CA: Nolo, 2018.

## MARRIAGE, WEDDINGS, COMMITMENT CEREMONIES; LGBTQ

Ayers, Tess, and Paul Brown. *The Essential Guide to Lesbian and Gay Weddings.* New York: Experiment, 2012.

Deakin, Michael. *Gay Marriage, Real Life: Ten Stories of Love and Family.* Boston: Skinner House, 2005.

Ellison, Marvin. *Same-Sex Marriage?: A Christian Ethical Analysis.* Cleveland: Pilgrim, 2004.

Jordan, Mark D. *Blessing Same-Sex Unions: The Perils of Queer Romance and the Confusions of Christian Marriage.* Chicago: University of Chicago Press, 2005.

Lewin, Ellen. *Recognizing Ourselves: Ceremonies of Lesbian and Gay Commitment.* New York: Columbia University Press, 1998.

Tigert, Leanne McCall, and Maren C. Tirabassi. *All Whom God Has Joined: Resources for Clergy and Same-Gender Loving Couples.* Cleveland: Pilgrim, 2010.

United Church of Christ Coalition for LGBT Concerns. *Blessing Ceremonies: Resources for Same-Gender Services of Commitment.* Holden, MA: United Church of Christ Coalition for LGBT Concerns, 1998.

Vines, Matthew. *God and the Gay Christian: The Biblical Case in Support of Same-Sex Relationships.* New York: Convergent, 2014.

## OLD(ER) AGE: SEE AGE: YOUTH, AND OLDER AGE

## OTHER-ABLED /DIFFERENTLY-ABLED/ LGBTQ PERSONS WITH DISABILITIES

Deaf Queer Resource Center: www.deafqueer.org.
Eisland, Nancy. *The Disabled God: Toward a Liberation Theology of Disability*. Nashville: Abingdon, 1999.
Sweeney, Eva. *Queers on Wheels*. A "resource guide for disabled people who want to explore their sexuality." Pasadena: Queers on Wheels, 2001.

## PARENTING, ADOPTION; LGBTQ

Clunis, D. Merilee, and G. Dorsey Green. *The Lesbian Parenting Book: A Guide to Creating Families and Raising Children*. 2nd ed. Seattle, WA: Seal, 1995.
COLAGE (Children of Lesbians and Gays Everywhere). "Unites people with lesbian, gay, bisexual, transgender, and/or queer parents into a network of peers and supports them as they nurture and empower each other to be skilled, self-confident, and just leaders in our collective communities": www.colage.org.
Family Equality Council. Mission "is to advance legal and lived equality for LGBTQ families, and for those who wish to form them, through building community, changing hearts and minds, and driving policy change": www.familyequality.org.
Friends In Adoption: www.friendsinadoption.org.
*Gay Parent: LGBTQ Magazine*: www.gayparentmag.com.
Glazer, Deborah F., and Jack Drescher, eds. *Gay and Lesbian Parenting*. New York: Haworth Medical, 2001.
Growing Generations. A "family building families through surrogacy and egg donation, driven by unparalleled safety and quality standards": www.growinggenerations.com.
Johnson, Suzanne, and Elizabeth O'Connor. *For Lesbian Parents: Your Guide to Helping Your Family Grow Up Happy, Healthy, and Proud*. New York: Guilford, 2001.
Lev, Arlene. *The Complete Lesbian and Gay Parenting Guide*. New York: Berkley, 2004.
Martin, April. *The Lesbian and Gay Parenting Handbook: Creating and Raising Our Families*. New York: Harper Perennial, 1993.
Seyda, Barbara. *Women in Love: Portraits of Lesbian Mothers and Their Families*. New York: Bulfinch, 1998.
Strah, David, and Susanna Margolis. *Gay Dads: A Celebration of Fatherhood*. New York: Tarcher, 2003.
Symons, Johnny. *Daddy and Papa*. "A Film about Gay Fathers in America." 2002: www.daddyandpapa.com.
Toevs, Kim, and Stephanie Brill. *The Essential Guide to Lesbian Conception, Pregnancy and Birth*. Los Angeles: Alyson, 2006.

## PASTORAL CARE AND MINISTRY

AAPC (American Association of Pastoral Counselors): www.aapc.org.
ACPE (Association for Clinical Pastoral Education): www.acpe.edu.
CASC (Canadian Association for Spiritual Care): www.spiritualcare.ca.
Clinebell, Howard. *Basic Types of Pastoral Care and Counseling: Resources for the Ministry of Healing and Growth.* Nashville: Abingdon, 1984.
———. *Ecotherapy: Healing Ourselves, Healing the Earth.* Minneapolis: Fortress, 1996.
Countryman, L. William, and M. R. Ritley. *Gifted by Otherness: Gay and Lesbian Christians in the Church.* Harrisburg PA: Morehouse, 2001.
David, J. A. *Pastoral Care for the Mentally Ill.* Australia: Universal, 2001.
Doehring, Carrie. *The Practice of Pastoral Care.* Rev. ed. Louisville: Westminster John Knox, 2015.
Friedman, Rabbi Dayle A., ed. *Jewish Pastoral Care: A Practical Handbook from Traditional and Contemporary Sources.* 2nd ed. New York: Jewish Lights, 2005.
Gerkin, Charles V. *An Introduction to Pastoral Care.* Nashville: Abingdon, 1997.
Graham, Larry Kent. *Care of Persons, Care of Worlds: A Psychosystems Approach to Pastoral Care and Counseling*, Nashville, TN: Abingdon, 1992.
———. *Discovering Images of God: Narratives of Care among Lesbians and Gays.* Louisville, KY: Westminster John Knox, 1997.
———. "Prophetic Pastoral Caretaking: A Psychosystemic Approach to Symptomatology." *Journal of Psychology and Christianity* 8:1 (1989) 49–60.
Johnson, W. Brad, and William L. Johnson. *The Pastor's Guide to Psychological Disorders and Treatments.* Binghamton, NY: Haworth, 2000.
Kessler, David, and Elizabeth Kubler-Ross. *On Grief and Grieving: Finding the Meaning of Grief through the Five Stages of Loss.* New York: Scribner, 2005.
Kirkwood, Neville A. *Pastoral Care to Muslims: Building Bridges.* Binghamton, NY: Haworth, 2002.
Kujawa-Holbrook, Sheryl A., and Karen B. Montagno, eds. *Injustice and the Care of Souls: Taking Oppression Seriously in Pastoral Care.* Minneapolis: Fortress, 2009.
Lartey, Emmanuel Yartekwei. *In Living Color: An Intercultural Approach to Pastoral Care and Counseling.* 2nd ed. London: Jessica Kingsley, 2003.
Marshall, Joretta L. "Caring When It Is Tough to Care." *Religion Online*: www.religion-online.org/article/caring-when-it-is-tough-to-care/.
Stone, Howard W. *Theological Context for Pastoral Caregiving: Word in Deed.* New York: Haworth Pastoral, 1996.
Switzer, David K. *Pastoral Care of Gays, Lesbians, and Their Families.* Minneapolis: Fortress, 1999.
Way, Peggy. *Created by God: Pastoral Care for All God's People.* Atlanta: Chalice, 2005.
Winston, Binford. *The Pastoral Care of Depression.* Binghamton, NY: Haworth, 1997.

## PASTORAL/RELIGIOUS LEADERSHIP

Alpert, Rebecca T., and Sue Levi Elwell. *Lesbian Rabbis: The First Generation.* New Brunswick, NJ: Rutgers University Press, 2001.
Holmen, R. W. *Queer Clergy: A History of Gay and Lesbian Ministry in American Protestantism.* Cleveland: Pilgrim, 2013.

## PEOPLE/COMMUNITIES OF COLOR; RESOURCES

Boykin, Keith. *Beyond the Down Low: Sex, Lies, and Denial in Black America.* New York: Carroll & Graf, 2005.
Chacaby, Ma-Nee, and Mary Louise Plummer. *A Two-Spirit Journey: The Autobiography of a Lesbian Ojibway-Cree Elder.* Winnipeg: University of Manitoba Press, 2016.
*De Colores: Lesbian and Gay Latinos: Stories of Strength, Family & Love.* A film by Peter Barbosa: https://vimeo.com/2303777.
Douglas, Kelly Brown. *Sexuality and the Black Church: A Womanist Perspective.* Maryknoll, NY: Orbis 1999.
Gilley, Brian Joseph. *Becoming Two-Spirit: Gay Identity and Social Acceptance in Indian Country.* Lincoln, NE: University of Nebraska Press, 2006.
Griffin, Horace. *Their Own Received Them Not: African American Lesbians & Gays in Black Churches.* Cleveland: Pilgrim, 2006.
Human Rights Campaign. *Guía de Recursos Para Salir Del Clóset,* 2004: www.hrc.org/resources/guia-de-recursos-para-salir-del-closet.
———. *Resource Guide to Coming Out for African Americans,* 2004: https://www.hrc.org/resources/resource-guide-to-coming-out-for-african-americans.
Jacobs, Sue-Ellen, Wesley Thomas, and Sabine Lang, eds. *Two-Spirit People: Native American Gender Identity, Sexuality, and Spirituality.* Urbana: University of Illinois Press, 1997.
King J. L. *Coming Up from the Down Low: The Journey to Acceptance, Healing, and Honest Love.* New York: Three Rivers, 2006.
———. *On the Down Low: A Journey Into the Lives of "Straight" Black Men Who Sleep with Men.* New York: Broadway, 2004.
Kirkwood, Neville A. *Pastoral Care to Muslims: Building Bridges.* New York: Haworth, 2002.
Lightsey, Pamela. *Our Lives Matter: Womanist Queer Theology.* Eugene, OR: Pickwick, 2015.
Montilla, R. Esteban, and Ferney Medina. *Pastoral Care and Counseling With Latinos/as.* Minneapolis: Fortress, 2006.
Poling, James Newton. *In Living Color: An Intercultural Approach to Pastoral Care and Counseling.* London: Jessica Kingsley, 2003.
Smith, Archie, Jr., and Ursula Riedel-Pfaefflin. *Siblings by Choice: Race, Gender, and Violence.* St. Louis: Chalice, 2004.
*Two Spirits.* A film by Lydia Nibley, 2011: http://www.pbs.org/independentlens/films/two-spirits/.
Way, Peggy. *Created by God: Pastoral Care for All God's People.* St. Louis: Chalice, 2005.
Williams, Walter L. *The Spirit and the Flesh: Sexual Diversity in the American Indian Culture.* Boston: Beacon, 1992.
Wimberly, Edward P. *Claiming God, Reclaiming Dignity: African American Pastoral Care.* Nashville: Abingdon, 2003.

## POLYAMORY

Anapol, Deborah. *Polyamory: The New Love Without Limits: Secrets of Sustainable Intimate Relationships.* Rev. ed. San Rafael, CA: IntiNet Resource Center, 1997.

Open Love ("a New York-based organization that serves the polyamorous community by coordinating a variety of educational and social events for its members, and by fostering a public climate in which all forms of consensual adult relationship choices are respected and honored"): http://openloveny.com/.

Unitarian Universalists for Polyamory Awareness: www.uupa.org.

## PSYCHOLOGY

Bradshaw, John. *Healing the Shame that Binds You.* Rev. ed. Deerfield Beach, FL: HCI, 2005.

Burke, Mary, et al. *Religious and Spiritual Issues in Counseling: Applications Across Diverse Populations.* New York: Brunner-Routledge, 2005.

Campbell, Robert J. *Psychiatric Dictionary.* New York: Oxford University Press, 2009.

Collie, Robert M. *The Obsessive-Compulsive Disorder: Pastoral Care for the Road to Change.* Binghamton, NY: Haworth Pastoral, 2000.

Erickson, Erik. *Childhood and Society.* New York: W.W. Norton, 1993.

Fowler, James. *Stages of Faith: the Psychology of Human Development.* San Francisco: HarperSanFrancisco, 1995.

Green, Sheila. *The Psychological Development of Girls and Women: Rethinking Change in Time.* Florence, KY: Routledge, 2003.

Hill, Clara. *Helping Skills: Facilitating Exploration, Insight, and Action.* Washington: American Psychological Association, 2004.

Hopke, Robert H. *Jung, Jungians and Homosexuality.* Boston: Shambala, 1989.

Lee, Wanda M. L. *An Introduction to Multicultural Counseling.* Philadelphia: Accelerated Development, 1999.

Potter-Efron, Ron, and Patricia Potter-Efron. *Letting Go of Anger: The Eleven Most Common Anger Styles and What to Do about Them.* Berkeley: New Harbinger, 2006.

———. *Letting Go of Shame: Understanding How Shame Affects Your Life.* San Francisco: Harper & Row, 1989.

## RELATIONSHIPS, LGBTQ

Balka, Christie, and Andy Rose, eds. *Twice Blessed: On Being Lesbian, Gay, and Jewish.* Boston: Beacon, 1989.

Goss, Robert, and Amy Strongheart, eds. *Our Families, Our Values: Snapshots of Queer Kinship.* New York: Harrington Park, 1997.

Heyward, Carter. *Touching Our Strength: The Erotic as Power and the Love of God.* San Francisco: Harper & Row, 1989.

Johnson, Robert. *A Study in the Contrast of Homoerotic and Homosexual Relationships* (audio cassette tape). Los Angeles: C. G. Jung Institute.

Shneer, David, and Caryn Aviv. *Queer Jews.* New York: Routledge, 2002.

Stiers, Gretchen. *From This Day Forward: Commitment, Marriage, and Family in Lesbian and Gay Relationships.* New York: St. Martin's, 1999.

Stuart, Elizabeth. *Just Good Friends: Towards a Lesbian and Gay Theology of Relationships.* London: Mowbray, 1995.

## RURAL LIVING, LGBTQ

Gray, Mary L., Colin R. Johnson, and Brian J. Gilley, eds. *Queering the Countryside: New Frontiers in Rural Gay Studies*. New York: NYU Press, 2016.

Murray, Tom. "Farm Family: In Search of Gay Life in Rural America." A documentary film: www.imdb.com/title/tt0409954/.

Smith, James Donald, and Ronald J. Mancoske, eds. *Rural Gays and Lesbians: Building on the Strengths of Communities*. Binghamton, NY: Haworth, 1997.

## SEPARATION/DIVORCE

American Psychological Association. "Are Same-sex Marriages Different from Heterosexual Marriages?" www.apa.org/topics/divorce/same-sex-marriage.aspx.

Green, Jesse. "From 'I Do' to 'I'm Done': With Newfound Rights, Newfound Fears. The Peculiar Mechanics—and Heartbreak—of Gay Divorce." *New York Magazine* (Feb. 24, 2013). http://nymag.com/news/features/gay-divorce-2013-3/index1.html.

Logan, Colleen. *When Gay Parents Divorce: A Practitioner's Guide for Understanding and Working with Blended and Reconstructed LGBT Families*. New York: Routledge, 2017.

Sember, Brette McWhorter. *The Complete Gay Divorce*. Franklin Lakes, NJ: Career, 2005.

## SEXUALITY, LGBTQ

Bornstein, Kate. *My Gender Workbook: How to Become a Real Man, a Real Woman, the Real You, or Something Else Entirely*. New York: Routledge, 1998.

Corwin, Gail. *Sexual Intimacy for Women: A Guide for Same-Sex Couples*. Berkeley: Seal, 2010.

Henry J. Kaiser Family Foundation and MTV. "It's Your Sex Life." "Public information partnership to support young people in making responsible decisions about sexual health": www.kff.org/its-your-sex-life.

Kinsey Scale of Human Sexuality: www.kinseyinstitute.org/research/ak-hhscale.html.

Klein Sexual Orientation Grid: www.americaninstituteofbisexuality.org/thekleingrid.

Nelson, James B. *Embodiment: An Approach to Sexuality and Christian Theology*. New ed. Minneapolis: Augsburg Fortress, 1979.

Newman, Felice. *The Whole Lesbian Sex Book: A Passionate Guide for All of Us*. 2nd ed. San Francisco: Cleis, 2004.

Rahman, Quazi, and Glenn Wilson. *Born Gay: The Psychobiology of Sex Orientation*. London: Peter Owen, 2005.

Silverstein, Charles, and Felice Picano. *The Joy of Gay Sex*. 3rd ed. New York: HarperCollins, 2003.

Weaver, Andrew J. et al. *Counseling on Sexual Issues: A Handbook for Pastors and Other Helping Professionals*. Cleveland: Pilgrim, 2006.

Winks, Cathy. *The Good Vibrations Guide to Sex: The Most Complete Sex Manual Ever Written*. 3rd ed. Pittsburgh: Cleis, 2002.

# SPIRITUALITY

Edman, Elizabeth. *Queer Virtue: What LGBT People Know About Life and Love and How It Can Revitalize Christianity.* Boston: Beacon, 2016.
Ellison, Marvin, and Kelly Brown Douglas. *Sexuality and the Sacred: Sources for Theological Reflection.* 2nd ed. Louisville: Westminster John Knox, 2010.
Empereur, James L. *Spiritual Direction and the Gay Person.* New York: Continuum, 1998.
Fortunato, John E. *Embracing the Exile: Healing Journeys of Gay Christians.* New York: Seabury, 1983.
Glaser, Chris. *Reformation of the Heart: Seasonal Meditations by a Gay Christian.* New York: Westminster John Knox, 2001.
Helminiak, Daniel A. *Sex and the Sacred: Gay Identity and Spiritual Growth.* New York: Harrington Park, 2006.
Johnson, Toby. *Gay Perspective: Things Our Homosexuality Tells Us About the Nature of God and the Universe.* Los Angeles: Alyson, 2003.
———. *Gay Spirituality: The Role of Gay Identity in the Transformation of Human Consciousness.* Los Angeles: Alyson, 2000.
McNeill, John. *Both Feet Firmly Planted in Midair: My Spiritual Journey.* New York: Westminster John Knox, 1998.
Pepper, Michal Anne. *Reconciling Journey: A Devotional Workbook for Lesbian and Gay Christians.* Cleveland: Pilgrim, 2003.
Thompson, Mark. *Gay Soul: Finding the Heart of Gay Spirit and Nature.* San Francisco: HarperSanFrancisco, 1990.

# THEOLOGY AND BIBLICAL INTERPRETATION

Adler, Rachel. *Engendering Judaism: An Inclusive Theology and Ethics.* Philadelphia: Jewish Publication, 1998.
Bellis, Alice Ogdon, and Terry L. Hufford. *Science, Scripture, and Homosexuality.* Cleveland: Pilgrim, 2002.
Cheng, Patrick S. *Radical Theology: Introduction to Queer Theology.* New York: Seabury, 2011.
———. *Rainbow Theology: Bridging Race, Sexuality, and Spirit.* New York: Seabury, 2013.
de la Torre, Miguel. *Reading the Bible from the Margins.* Maryknoll, NY: Orbis, 2002.
Ellison, Marvin. *Sexuality and the Sacred: Sources for Theological Reflection.* 2nd ed. Louisville: Westminster John Knox, 2010.
Goss, Robert E., and Mona West, eds. *Take Back the Word—A Queer Reading of the Bible.* Cleveland: Pilgrim, 2005.
Helminiak, Daniel A. *What the Bible Really Says about Homosexuality.* San Francisco: Alamo Square, 2000.
Hornsby, Teresa. *Transgender, Intersex, and Biblical Interpretation.* Atlanta: SBL, 2016.
Jimmerson, Ellin Sterne, ed. *Rainbow in the Word: LGBTQ Christians' Biblical Memoirs.* Eugene, OR: Wipf and Stock, 2017.
Johnson, Jay Emerson. *Peculiar Faith: Queer Theology for Christian Witness.* New York: Seabury, 2014.

Lightsey, Pamela. *Our Lives Matter: Womanist Queer Theology.* Eugene, OR: Pickwick, 2015.

Martin, Colby. *Unclobber: Rethinking Our Misuse of the Bible on Homosexuality.* Louisville: Westminster John Knox, 2016.

Rogers, Jack. *Jesus, the Bible, and Homosexuality: Explode the Myths, Heal the Church.* Louisville, KY: Westminster John Knox, 2006.

Stuart, Elizabeth. *Gay & Lesbian Theologies: Repetitions With Critical Difference.* London: Ashgate, 2003.

Stuart, Elizabeth, et al. *Religion Is a Queer Thing: A Guide to the Christian Faith for Lesbian, Gay, Bisexual, and Transgendered Persons.* Cleveland: Pilgrim, 1998.

Talvaccia, Kathleen, et al, eds. *Queer Christianities: Lived Religion in Transgressive Forms.* New York: NYU Press, 2015.

Tigert, Leanne McCall. *Coming Out While Staying In: Struggles and Celebrations of Lesbians, Gays, and Bisexuals in the Church,* Cleveland: United Church, 1996.

## TRANSGENDER RESOURCES: IDENTITY, RELATIONSHIPS, SEXUALITY, AND SPIRITUALITY

Althaus-Reid, Marcella, and Lisa Isherwood. *Trans/Formations: Controversies in Contextual Theology.* Oxford: SCM Press, 2009.

Beardsley, Christina, and Michelle O'Brien. *This Is My Body: Hearing the Theology of Transgender Christians.* London: Darton, Longman, and Todd, 2017.

Boenke, Mary, ed. *TransForming Families: Real Stories About Transgender Loved Ones.* Imperial Beach, CA: Walter Trook, 1999.

Brill, Stephanie A., and Lisa Kenney. *The Transgender Teen: A Handbook for Parents and Professionals Supporting Transgender and Non-Binary Teens.* Jersey City: Cleis, 2016.

Conover, Pat. *Transgender Good News.* Silver Springs, MD: New Wineskins, 2002.

Cook, Ann Thompson. *Made in God's Image: A Resource for Dialogue About the Church and Gender Differences.* Washington, DC: Many Voices, 2004.

Dzmura, Noach. *Balancing on the Mechitza: Transgender in Jewish Community.* Berkeley: North Atlantic, 2010.

Hornsby, Teresa. *Transgender, Intersex, and Biblical Interpretation.* Atlanta: SBL, 2016.

Human Rights Campaign. "Explore Transgender." www.hrc.org/explore/topic/transgender.

Institute for Welcoming Resources/National Gay and Lesbian Task Force. "transACTION." "A curriculum designed to help churches and institutions address this issue of understanding and welcome by providing step-by-step training about the needs, apprehensions, and fears of transgender people, as well as the wealth of gifts and graces they bring, while responding to the concerns of the church or religious institution": www.uccresources.com/products/transaction-a-transgender-curriculum-for-churches-and-religious-institutions?variant=924312593.

Krieger, Irwin. *Counseling Transgender and Non-Binary Youth: The Essential Guide.* Philadelphia: Jessica Kingsley, 2017.

Kukla, Elliot, and Reuben Zellman. "Making Your Jewish Community Trans-Friendly." TransTorah: http://transtorah.org/PDFs/Trans_Friendly_Community.pdf.

Lev, Arlene. *Transgender Emergence: Therapeutic Guidelines for Working with Gender-Variant People and Their Families.* New York: Haworth Clinical Practice, 2004.
Mollenkott, Virginia Ramey. *Omnigender: A Trans-Religious Approach.* Cleveland: Pilgrim, 2001.
Mollenkott, Virginia Ramey, and Vanessa Sheridan. *Transgender Journeys.* Cleveland: Pilgrim, 2003.
National Center for Transgender Equality: www.nctequality.org.
PFLAG. *Our Trans Loved Ones.* www.pflag.org/ourtranslovedones.
Sheridan, Vanessa. *Crossing Over: Liberating the Transgendered Christian.* Cleveland: Pilgrim, 2001.
Tanis, Justin. *Transgendered: Theology, Ministry, and Communities of Faith.* Cleveland: Pilgrim, 2003.
Tigert, Leanne McCall, and Maren C. Tirabassi. *Transgendering Faith: Identity, Sexuality, and Spirituality.* Cleveland: Pilgrim, 2004.
Transgender Law Center: www.transgenderlawcenter.org.
United Church of Christ and Filmworks, Inc. *Call Me Malcolm: One Man's Struggle With Faith, Love and Gender Identity.* 2004. www.ucc.org/lgbt_callmemalcolm.

## VIOLENCE

Fortune, Marie. M. *Sexual Violence: The Sin Revisited.* Boston: Pilgrim, 2005.
Futures Without Violence. Providing "programs, policies, and campaigns that empower individuals and organizations working to end violence against women and children around the world": www.futureswithoutviolence.org.
GLBTQ Domestic Violence Project: www.glbtqdvp.org.
Meyer, Doug. *Violence against Queer People: Race, Class, Gender, and the Persistence of Anti-LGBT Discrimination.* New Brunswick: Rutgers University Press, 2015.
Miles, Al. *Domestic Violence: What Every Pastor Needs to Know.* Minneapolis: Fortress, 2011.
Miles, Al, and Marie M. Fortune. *Violence in Families: What Every Christian Needs to Know.* Minneapolis: Augsburg Fortress, 2002.
National Coalition Against Domestic Violence (NCADV): www.ncadv.org.
Women Organized to Make Abuse Nonexistent, Inc. (WOMAN): A "community-based, multi-service agency, serving survivors of domestic violence in San Francisco and the larger Bay Area": www.womaninc.org.

## WELCOMING CONGREGATION RESOURCES

Alexander, Marilyn, and James Preston. *We Were Baptized Too: Claiming God's Grace for Lesbians and Gays.* Louisville: Westminster John Knox, 1996.
Beck, Luane. *God and Gays: Bridging the Gap.* A film that explores sexuality and spirituality through the eyes of people wanting a relationship with the religion that rejects them. www.godandgaysthemovie.com/about.html.
Center for LGBTQ and Gender Studies in Religion (CLGS). *An Expansive Welcome: A Resource for LGBTQI+ Affirming Communities Engaging Intersectional Work.* 2018. https://clgs.org/multimedia-archive/expanding-your-welcome/.

Flunder, Yvette. *Where the Edge Gathers: Building a Community of Radical Inclusion.* Cleveland: Pilgrim, 2005.

Glück, Robert, ed. *Homosexuality and Judaism: A Reconstructionist Workshop Series.* Wyncote, PA: Reconstructionist, 1993.

Hanway, D. G. *A Theology of Gay and Lesbian Inclusion: Love Letters to the Church.* New York: Haworth Pastoral, 2006.

Heskins, Jeffrey. *Face to Face: Gay And Lesbian Clergy on Holiness and Life Together.* Grand Rapids, MI: Eerdmans, 2006.

Jewish Reconstructionist Movement. "JRF Homosexuality Report and Inclusion of GLBTQ Persons." https://archive.is/aAXT.

*Kulanu (All of Us): A Program for [Jewish] Congregations Implementing Gay and Lesbian Inclusion*: http://www.rabbinicalassembly.org/sites/default/files/public/social_action/inclusion/kulanu-inclusion-resource-guide.pdf.

Law, Eric. *Inclusion: Making Room for Grace.* St. Louis: Chalice, 2000.

Martin, James. *Building a Bridge: How the Catholic Church and the LGBT Community Can Enter Into a Relationship of Respect, Compassion, and Sensitivity.* New York: HarperCollins, 2017.

Mattmann, Urs. *Coming In: Gays and Lesbians Reclaiming the Spiritual Journey.* Glasgow: Wild Goose, 2006.

Oliveto, Karen, ed. *Enfold: A Reconciling Congregation Explores What It Means to Welcome All People.* San Francisco: Bethany United Methodist Church, 1997.

Oliveto, Karen P., et al. *Talking About Homosexuality: A Congregational Resource.* Cleveland: Pilgrim, 2005.

Pacha, Kelsey. *Transitioning to Inclusion: A Guide to Welcoming Transgender Children and Their Families in Your Community of Faith,* 2015: https://clgs.org/multimedia-archive/transitioningyouthresource/.

Schlager, Bernard. *With Open Arms: Gay Affirming Ministries in* [San Francisco] *Bay Area Faith Communities.* 2003. https://clgs.org/multimedia-archive/with-open-arms-gay-affirming-ministries-in-bay-area-faith-communities/.

Shneer, David, and Caryn Aviv. *Queer Jews.* New York: Routledge, 2002.

Tigert, Leanne McCall. *Coming Out While Staying In: Struggles and Celebrations of Lesbians, Gays, and Bisexuals in the Church,* Cleveland: United Church, 1996.

UUA Office of Bisexual, Gay, Lesbian, and Transgender Concerns. *Living the Welcoming Congregation.* Boston: UUA, 2004.

———. *The Welcoming Congregation Handbook: Resources for Affirming Bisexual, Gay, Lesbian, and/or Transgender People.* Boston: UUA, 1999.

Waun, Maurine. *More Than Welcome: Learning to Embrace Gay, Lesbian, Bisexual and Transgendered Persons in the Church.* St. Louis: Chalice, 1999.

## WORKPLACE ISSUES

Friskopp, Annette, and Sharon Silverstein. *Straight Jobs, Gay Lives: Gay and Lesbian Professionals, the Harvard Business School, and the American Workplace.* New York: Simon & Schuster, 1996.

Kingsley, Jessica. *Transgender Employees in the Workplace: A Guide for Employers.* London: Jessica Kingsley, 2018.

Sheridan, Vanessa. *The Complete Guide to Transgender in the Workplace*. Santa Barbara: Praeger/ABC-CLIO, 2009.

## WORSHIP RESOURCES; LGBTQ

Duncan, Geoffrey, ed. *Courage to Love: Liturgies for the Lesbian, Gay, Bisexual and Transgender Community*. Cleveland: Pilgrim, 2002.
Glaser, Chris. *Coming Out to God: Prayers for Lesbians and Gay Men, Their Families and Friends*. Louisville, KY: Westminster John Knox, 1991.
Kittredge, Cherry, and Zalmon Sherwood. *Equal Rites: Lesbian and Gay Worship, Ceremonies, and Celebrations*. Louisville, KY: Westminster/John Knox, 1995.
Ritualwell.org: Ceremonies for Jewish Living: www.ritualwell.org.
Stuart, Elizabeth. *Daring to Speak Love's Name: A Gay and Lesbian Prayer Book*. London: Hamish Hamilton, 1992.
Turney, Kelly, ed. *Shaping Sanctuary: Proclaiming God's Grace in an Inclusive Church*. Chicago: Reconciling Congregation, 2000.
United Church of Christ Coalition for LGBT Concerns. *Blessing Ceremonies: Resources for Same-Gender Services of Commitment*. Holden, MA: 1998.

## YOUTH, LGBTQ: SEE AGE: YOUTH, AND OLDER AGE

# Bibliography

Alford-Harkey, Marie, and Debra W. Haffner. *Bisexuality Making the Invisible Visible in Faith Communities*. Bridgeport, CT: Religious Institute, 2014.
American Psychological Association. "Report of the American Psychological Association Task Force on Appropriate Therapeutic Responses to Sexual Orientation: Research Summary." August 2009. https://www.apa.org/pi/lgbt/resources/therapeutic-response.pdf.
———. "Resolution on Appropriate Affirmative Responses to Sexual Orientation Distress and Change Efforts." n.d. http://www.apa.org/about/policy/sexual-orientation.aspx.
Anderson-Minshall, Diane. "HIV Survivors Face Their Own Vietnam." *The Advocate*, August 29, 2016. www.advocate.com/current-issue/2016/8/29/hiv-survivors-face-their-own-vietnam.
Balka, Christie, and Andy Rose, eds. *Twice Blessed: On Being Lesbian, Gay, and Jewish*. Boston: Beacon, 1989.
Ball, Susan C. *Voices in the Band: A Doctor, Her Patients, and How the Outlook on AIDS Care Changed from Doomed to Hopeful*. Ithaca, NY: ILR, 2015.
Bearak, Max, and Darla Cameron. "Here are the 10 Countries where Homosexuality May Be Punished by Death." *Washington Post*, June 16, 2016. https://www.washingtonpost.com/news/worldviews/wp/2016/06/13/here-are-the-10-countries-where-homosexuality-may-be-punished-by-death-2/?utm_term=.4e6bb17c9acf.
Belile, Jacki. "Building Well-Coming Communities of Faith." *Chicago Theological Seminary Register* 92.2 (Summer 2002) 4–5.
Bellis, Alice Ogden, and Terry L. Hufford. *Science, Scripture, and Homosexuality*. Cleveland: Pilgrim, 2002.
Boorstein, Michelle. "I'm Gay and I'm a Priest, Period." *The Washington Post*, January 31, 2016. https://www.washingtonpost.com/local/social-issues/im-gay-and-im-a-priest-period/2016/01/31/ab09c83e-bfb6-11e5-83d4-42e3bceea902_story.html?noredirect=on&utm_term=.064c92831b52.
Boykin, Keith. *Beyond the Down Low: Sex, Lies, and Denial in Black America*. New York: DaCapo, 2006.
Boyle, Sally M. *Embracing the Exile: A Lesbian Model of Pastoral Care*. Dundas, Ontario: Artemis 1995.
Bradshaw, John. *Healing the Shame that Binds You*. Rev. ed. Deerfield Beach, FL: Health Communications, Inc., 2005.

Bressert, Steve. "Gender Dysphoria Symptoms." PsychCentral, August 16, 2017. www.psychcentral.com/disorders/gender-dysphoria-symptoms.

Brill, Stephanie A., and Lisa Kenney. *The Transgender Teen: A Handbook for Parents and Professionals Supporting Transgender and Non-Binary Teens*. Jersey City: Cleis, 2016.

Brown, Taylor N. T., and Jody L. Herman. "Intimate Partner Violence and Sexual Abuse Among LGBT People: A Review of Existing Research." The Williams Institute, November 2015. https://williamsinstitute.law.ucla.edu/wp-content/uploads/Intimate-Partner-Violence-and-Sexual-Abuse-among-LGBT-People.pdf.

Burke, Mary, et al. *Religious and Spiritual Issues in Counseling: Applications Across Diverse Populations*. New York: Brunner-Routledge, 2005.

Campbell, Robert J. *Psychiatric Dictionary*. New York: Oxford University Press, 1989.

CARA. "Fact Sheet: Hispanic Catholics in the U.S." n.d. http://cara.georgetown.edu/staff/webpages/Hispanic%20Catholic%20Fact%20Sheet.pdf.

Centers for Disease Control and Prevention. "HIV in the United States: At A Glance." October 11, 2017. www.cdc.gov/hiv/statistics/overview/ataglance.html.

———. "Pre-exposure Prophylaxis (or PrEP)." October 11, 2017. www.cdc.gov/actagainstaids/basics/prep.html.

The Child Welfare Information Gateway. "Mandatory Reporters of Child Abuse and Neglect." https://www.childwelfare.gov/topics/systemwide/laws-policies/statutes/manda/.

Chung, Andrew. "U.S. Top Court Rejects 'Gay Conversion' Therapy Ban Challenge." *Reuters*, May 1, 2017. http://www.reuters.com/article/us-usa-court-gayconversion/u-s-top-court-rejects-gay-conversion-therapy-ban-challenge-idUSKBN17X1SJ.

Clebsch, William A., and Charles R. Jaekle. *Pastoral Care in Historical Perspective*. New York: Jason Aronson, 1994.

Clinebell, Howard. *Basic Types of Pastoral Care and Counseling*. Nashville: Abingdon, 1984.

———. *Ecotherapy: Healing Ourselves, Healing the Earth*. New York: Haworth, 1996.

Coleman, Eli. "Developmental Stages of the Coming Out Process." In *A Guide to Psychotherapy with Gay and Lesbian Clients*, edited by John C. Gonsiorek, 31–43. New York: Harrington Park, 1985.

Columbia Law School. "What Does the Scholarly Research Say about the Wellbeing of Children with Gay or Lesbian Parents?" http://whatweknow.law.columbia.edu/topics/lgbt-equality/what-does-the-scholarly-research-say-about-the-wellbeing-of-children-with-gay-or-lesbian-parents/.

Congregation for the Doctrine of the Faith. "Letter to the Bishops of the Catholic Church on the Pastoral Care of Homosexual Persons." The Roman Curia, October 1, 1986. http://www.vatican.va/roman_curia/congregations/cfaith/documents/rc_con_cfaith_doc_19861001_homosexual-persons_en.html.

Costa-Roberts, Daniel. "8 Things You Didn't Know About Truvada." *PBS News Hour*, April 12, 2015. https://www.pbs.org/newshour/health/8-things-didnt-know-truvadaprep.

Countryman, L. William, and M. R. Ritley. *Gifted by Otherness: Gay and Lesbian Christians in the Church*. Harrisburg, PA: Morehouse, 2001.

Davis, Julia. "Evolution of an Epidemic: 25 Years of HIV/AIDS Media Campaigns in the U.S." The Henry J. Kaiser Family Foundation, June 2006. https://kaiserfamilyfoundation.files.wordpress.com/2013/01/7515.pdf.

# Bibliography

De La Torre, Miguel. *Reading the Bible From the Margins*. Maryknoll, NY: Orbis, 2002.
Drescher, Jack. "The Closet: Psychological Issues of Being In and Coming Out." *Psychiatric Times*, October 1, 2004. www.psychiatrictimes.com/articles/closet-psychological-issues-being-and-coming-out.
Drescher, Jack, et al., eds. *Crystal Meth and Men Who Have Sex with Men: What Mental Health Care Professionals Need to Know*. New York: Haworth Medical, 2007.
Duin, Julia. "Gay Bishop Dismisses Anglican Report." *Washington Times*, October 11, 2004. http://www.washingtontimes.com/national/20041010-113559-1206thtm.
Empereur, James L. *Spiritual Direction and the Gay Person*. New York: Continuum, 1998.
Erikson, Erik. *Childhood and Society*. New York: W. W. Norton, 1993.
———. *The Life Stages Completed: Extended Version*. New York: W. W. Norton, 1998.
Fawcett, David. *Lust, Men, and Meth: A Gay Man's Guide to Sex and Recovery*. Wilton Manors, FL: Healing Path, 2015.
FBI. "Latest Hate Crime Statistics Released: Annual Report Sheds Light on Serious Issue." November 14, 2016. https://www.fbi.gov/news/stories/2015-hate-crime-statistics-released.
Fellows, William D. *Farm Boys: Lives of Gay Men from the Rural Midwest*. New ed. Madison: University of Wisconsin Press, 2001.
Flynn, Peggy. *The Caregiving Zone: A Unique Guide to Facing the Realities of Illness, Aging, Dying, and Death*. New York: iUniverse, Inc., 2006.
Fowler, James. *Stages of Faith: The Psychology of Human Development*. San Francisco: HarperSanFrancisco, 1995.
Gadoua, Renée K. "Are Catholic High Schools Supporting Their LGBT Students?: Gay-Straight Alliances Are a Way to Show LGBT Teens God's Love. How Do They Fare in Catholic High Schools?" *U.S. Catholic*, February 2016. http://www.uscatholic.org/articles/201602/are-catholic-high-schools-supporting-their-lgbt-students-30565.
Gates, Gary J. "In US, More Adults Identifying as LGBT." Gallup, January 11, 2017. http://news.gallup.com/poll/201731/lgbt-identification-rises.aspx.
Gessen, Masha. "The Gay Men Who Fled Chechnya's Purge." *The New Yorker*, July 3, 2017. http://www.newyorker.com/magazine/2017/07/03/the-gay-men-who-fled-chechnyas-purge.
Goergen. Donald. *The Sexual Celibate*. New York: Seabury, 1974.
Goss, Robert E. "Queering Procreative Privilege: Coming Out as Families." In *Our Families, Our Values: Snapshots of Queer Kinship*, edited by Robert E. Goss and Amy Adams Squire Strongheart, 3–20. New York: Haworth, 1997.
Graham, Larry Kent. *Care of Persons, Care of Worlds: A Psychosystems Approach to Pastoral Care and Counseling*. Nashville: Abingdon, 1992.
———. *Discovering Images of God: Narratives of Care Among Lesbians and Gays*. Louisville: Westminster John Knox, 1997.
———. "Prophetic Pastoral Caretaking: A Psychosystemic Approach to Symptomatology." *Journal of Psychology and Christianity* 8.1 (1989) 49–60.
Gray, Mary L., et al., eds. *Queering the Countryside: New Frontiers in Rural Gay Studies*. New York: NYU Press, 2016.
Green, Sheila. *The Psychological Development of Girls and Women: Rethinking Change in Time*. Florence, KY: Routledge, 2003.

Greenberg, Steven. *Wrestling with God and Men: Homosexuality and the Jewish Tradition.* Madison: University of Wisconsin Press, 2004.
Gula, Richard M. *Ethics in Pastoral Ministry.* New York: Paulist, 1996.
Haggas, Stuart. "Racism and the Gay Scene." GMFA, June 3, 2015. https://www.gmfa.org.uk/fs148-racism-and-the-gay-scene.
Halkitis, Perry N., et al. "The Meanings and Manifestations of Religion and Spirituality Among Lesbian, Gay, Bisexual, and Transgender Adults." *Journal of Adult Development* 16 (2009) 250–62.
Harm Reduction Coalition. "Principles of Harm Reduction." http://harmreduction.org/about-us/principles-of-harm-reduction/.
Helminiac, Daniel. *What the Bible Really Says about Homosexuality.* San Francisco: Alamo Square, 2000.
Heyward, Carter. *Touching Our Strength: The Erotic as Power and the Love of God.* San Francisco: HarperSanFrancisco, 1989.
Hobbes, Michael. "Together Alone: The Epidemic of Gay Loneliness." *Huffington Post*, March 2, 2017. http://highline.huffingtonpost.com/articles/en/gay-loneliness/.
Holpuch, Amanda. "Trans Children Allowed to Express Identity 'Have Good Mental Health'." *The Guardian*, February 26, 2016. https://www.theguardian.com/society/2016/feb/26/crucial-study-transgender-children-mental-health-family-support.
Hopke, Robert H. *Jung, Jungians and Homosexuality.* Boston: Shambala, 1989.
Human Rights Campaign. "Policy and Position Statements on Conversion Therapy." www.hrc.org/resources/policy-and-position-statements-on-conversion-therapy.
Hunt, Mary E. *Fierce Tenderness: A Feminist Theology of Friendship.* New York: Crossroad, 1991.
Institute of Welcoming Resources. "Christian/Denominationally-Based LGBT Organizations." http://www.welcomingresources.org/links.htm#religious.
Isay, Richard. *Being Homosexual.* New York: Farrar Straus Giroux, 1989.
Jacobs, Sue-Ellen, Wesley Thomas, and Sabine Lang, eds. *Two-Spirit People: Native American Gender Identity, Sexuality, and Spirituality.* Urbana: University of Illinois Press, 1997.
Jacobson, J. R., and A. Pellegrini. *Love the Sin: Sexual Regulation and the Limits of Religious Tolerance.* Boston: Beacon, 2003.
James, S. E., et al. "2015 U.S. Transgender Survey." National Center for Transgender Equality, December 2016. https://transequality.org/sites/default/files/docs/usts/USTS-Full-Report-Dec17.pdf.
Johnson, Robert. "A Study in the Contrast of Homoerotic and Homosexual Relationships" (audio cassette tape). Los Angeles: C. G. Jung Institute. No date.
Jung, Patricia Beattie, and Ralph Smith. *Heterosexism: An Ethical Challenge.* Albany: State University Press of New York, 1993.
King, J. L., and Courtney Carreras. *Coming Up from the Down Low: The Journey to Acceptance, Healing, and Honest Love.* New York: Harmony, 2006.
King, J. L., and Karen Hunter. *On the Down Low: A Journey into the Lives of "Straight" Black Men Who Sleep with Men.* New York: Harlem Moon/Broadway Books, 2005.
Kinsey, Alfred. *Sexual Behavior in the Human Male.* Rev. ed. Bloomington: University of Indiana Press, 1998.
Kinsey Institute at Indiana University. "The Kinsey Scale." www.kinseyinstitute.org/research/publications/kinsey-scale.php.

Klein, Fritz. *The Bisexual Option: A Concept of One Hundred Percent Intimacy.* New York: Priam, 1978.

———. "The Klein Sexual Orientation Grid." The American Institute of Bisexuality. www.americaninstituteofbisexuality.org/thekleingrid.

Kosnik, Anthony, et al. *Sexual Morality: New Directions in Catholic Thought.* New York: Paulist, 1996.

Kramer, Larry. *The Tragedy of Today's Gays.* New York: Tarcher, 2005.

Krieger, Irwin. *Counseling Transgender and Non-Binary Youth: The Essential Guide.* London: Jessica Kingsley, 2017.

Lee, Wanda M. L. *An Introduction to Multicultural Counseling.* Philadelphia: Accelerated Development Group, 1999.

Levinson, Daniel. *The Seasons of a Man's Life.* Reissue. New York: Ballantine, 1986.

The LGBT Issues Committee of the Group for the Advancement of Psychiatry (GAP). "The Declassification of Homosexuality by the American Psychiatric Association." In "LGBT Mental Health Syllabus: The History of Psychiatry & Homosexuality." http://www.aglp.org/gap/1_history/#declassification.

Marshall, Joretta L. "Caring When It Is Tough to Care." Religion Online, n.d. http://www.religion-online.org/article/caring-when-it-is-tough-to-care/.

———. *Counseling Lesbian Partners.* Louisville: Westminster John Knox, 1997.

McLeod, Saul. "Erik Erikson's Stages of Psychosocial Development." *Simply Psychology,* Updated May 3, 2018. https://www.simplypsychology.org/Erik-Erikson.html.

Meir, Vered. "Resources for Transgender Jews, Their Families, Friends, Communities, and Allies." Stanford Berman Jewish Policy Archive, January 1, 2009. https://www.bjpa.org/search-results/publication/7792.

Mental Health America. "Bullying and LGBT Youth." n.d. http://www.mentalhealthamerica.net/bullying-and-gay-youth.

Minor, Robert N. *When Religion Is an Addiction.* St. Louis: HumanityWorks!, 2007.

Mollenkott, Virginia R. *Sensuous Spirituality: Out From Fundamentalism.* New York: Crossroad, 1992.

Money, John. *Gay, Straight, and In-Between: The Sexology of Erotic Orientation.* New York: Oxford University Press, 1988.

Moore, Patrick. "Clarity About Crystal." *Advocate,* August 14, 2006. https://www.advocate.com/politics/commentary/2006/08/14/clarity-about-crystal.

———. *Tweaked: A Crystal Memoir.* New York: Kensington, 2006.

Morris-Young, Dan. "US Priests' Group Calls Vatican Vocations Document 'Insulting.'" *National Catholic Reporter* April 20, 2017. https://www.ncronline.org/blogs/ncr-today/us-priests-group-calls-vatican-vocations-document-insulting.

Movement Advancement Project. "Conversation Therapy Laws." http://www.lgbtmap.org/equality-maps/conversion_therapy.

Murphy, Caryle. "Lesbian, Gay and Bisexual Americans Differ From General Public in Their Religious Affiliations." Pew Research Center, May 26, 2015. http://www.pewresearch.org/fact-tank/2015/05/26/lesbian-gay-and-bisexual-americans-differ-from-general-public-in-their-religious-affiliations/.

Murray, T. Joe, dir. *Farm Family: In Search of Gay Life in Rural America.* Film, 2004. www.imdb.com/title/tt0409954/.

National Center for Lesbian Rights. "Born Perfect Campaign." http://www.nclrights.org/our-work/bornperfect/.

National Center for Transgender Equality (NCTE). "Teaching Transgender: A Guide to Leading Effective Trainings." January 15, 2009. http://www.transequality.org/issues/resources/teaching-transgender-guide-leading-effective-trainings.

The National Coalition Against Domestic Violence (NCADV). "National Statistics." www.ncadv.org/learn-more/statistics.

Nelson, James B. *Embodiment: An Approach to Sexuality and Christian Theology*. New ed. Minneapolis: Augsburg Fortress, 1979.

Niemöller, Martin. "First They Came." https://en.wikipedia.org/wiki/First_they_came_.

Nimmons, David. *The Soul Beneath the Skin: The Unseen Hearts and Habits of Gay Men*. New York: St. Martin's, 2002.

O'Brien, Tim. *The Things They Carried*. New York: Broadway, 1998.

Oliveto, Karen, et al. *Talking About Homosexuality: A Congregational Resource*. Cleveland: Pilgrim, 2005.

Ontario Consultants on Religious Tolerance. "Bisexuality—The Least Common and Most Misunderstood of the Three Sexual Orientations." http://www.religioustolerance.org/bisexuality.htm.

The Open and Affirming Coalition of the United Church of Christ. www.openandaffirming.org/about.

Parson, Fairley. "Finding Common Ground: Intergenerational Programs Connect LGBT Elders, Youth." *Aging Today* 35.3 (May–June 2014). https://www.openhouse-sf.org/finding-common-ground.

Patterson, Eric. "The Effects of Crystal Meth Use." DrugAbuse.com, n.d. https://drugabuse.com/library/the-effects-of-crystal-meth-use/.

Peck, Jane, and Jeanne Gallo. "JPIC: A Critique from a Feminist Perspective." *The Ecumenical Review* 41.4 (October 1989) 573–81.

Peregoy, J., et al. "Society Identity, and Meaning: Alcohol and Other Drug Prevention/Interventions for Mental Health Professionals Working With Gay, Lesbian, Bisexual, and Transgendered Clientele." *VISTAS Online* 51 (2006) 229–32. http://www.counseling.org/docs/default-source/vistas/social-identity-and-meaning-alcohol-and-other-drug-prevention-interventions-for-mental-health-professionals-working-with-gay-lesbian-bisexual-and-transgendered-clientele.

Peter, Laurence. "Chechen Police 'Kidnap and Torture Gay Men'—LGBT Activists." *BBC News*, April 11, 2017. http://www.bbc.com/news/world-europe-39566136.

Peterson, Nicholas. "The Health and Rights of Transgender Youth." Advocates for Youth, November 2013. www.advocatesforyouth.org/component/content/article/2282-the-health-and-rights-of-transgender-youth.

Pew Research Center. "America's Changing Religious Landscape." May 12, 2015. http://www.pewforum.org/2015/05/12/americas-changing-religious-landscape/.

Pharr, Suzanne. *Homophobia: A Weapon of Sexism*. Little Rock, AR: Chardon, 1998.

Phend, Crystal. "Psychosis Common in Meth Addicts." MedPageToday, January 9, 2013. https://www.medpagetoday.com/psychiatry/addictions/36783.

Plaskow, Judith. "Toward a New Theology of Sexuality." In *Twice Blessed: On Being Lesbian, Gay, and Jewish*, edited by Christie Balka and Andy Rose, 141–51. Boston: Beacon, 1989.

Pullin, Zachary. "Two Spirit: The Story of a Movement Unfolds." *Native Peoples*, May–June 2014. http://www.nativepeoples.com/Native-Peoples/May-June-2014/Two-Spirit-The-Story-of-a-Movement-Unfolds/.

Ringwald, Christopher D. *The Soul of Recovery: Uncovering the Spiritual Dimension in the Treatment of Addictions*. New York: Oxford University Press, 2002.

Rodriguez, Mathew. "After Party: Why Does Crystal Meth Still Attract Gay Men?" *POZ Magazine*, April 4, 2016. www.poz.com/article/party.

Rogers, Jack. *Jesus, the Bible, and Homosexuality: Explode the Myths, Heal the Church*. Louisville: Westminster John Knox, 2006.

Rudy, Kathy. *Sex and the Church: Gender, Homosexuality, and the Transformation of Christian Ethics*. Boston: Beacon, 1997.

Ryan, Caitlin, and Donna Futterman. *Lesbian and Gay Youth: Care and Counseling*. New York: Columbia University Press, 1998.

Salas, Antonio. "My Journey of Deliverance." Unpublished Paper.

Schlager, Bernard. "With Open Arms: Gay Affirming Ministries in Bay Area Faith Communities," 2003. https://clgs.org/multimedia-archive/with-open-arms-gay-affirming-ministries-in-bay-area-faith-communities/.

Schmider, Alex. "2016 Was the Deadliest Year on Record for Transgender People." GLAAD, November 9, 2016. https://www.glaad.org/blog/2016-was-deadliest-year-record-transgender-people.

Scoggs, Robin. *The New Testament and Homosexuality*. Philadelphia: Fortress 1983.

Shidlo, Ariel, ed. *Sexual Conversion Therapy: Ethical, Clinical and Research Perspectives*. New York: Haworth Medical, 2001.

Sloane, Craig. "The Perfect Storm: Gay Men, Crystal Meth and Sex: Cultural Considerations for Gay Affirming Treatment." NAADAC, n.d. www.naadac.org/assets/2416/craig_sloane_-_naadac_handouts.pdf.

Smid, Rev. John J. "Love in Action." https://web.archive.org/web/20110721221302/http://www.loveinaction.org.

Smith, Archie, Jr., and Ursula Riedel-Pfaefflin. *Siblings By Choice: Race, Gender, and Violence*. St. Louis: Chalice, 2004.

Smith, Gregory A., and Alan Cooperman. "The Factors Driving the Growth of Religious 'Nones' in the U.S." Pew Research Center, September 14, 2016. http://www.pewresearch.org/fact-tank/2016/09/14/the-factors-driving-the-growth-of-religious-nones-in-the-u-s/.

Smith, James Donald, and Ronald Mankoske, eds. *Rural Gays and Lesbians: Building on the Strengths of Communities*. New York: Haworth, 1997.

Spahr, Janie. "Profile." LGBT Religious Archives Network, November 2002. www.lgbtran.org/Profile.aspx?ID=1.

"Standards of Care (SOC) for the Health of Transsexual, Transgender, and Gender Nonconforming People." The World Professional Association for Transgender Health, Inc. https://www.wpath.org/media/cms/Documents/Web%20Transfer/SOC/Standards%20of%20Care%20V7%20-%202011%20WPATH.pdf.

Stop a Suicide Today. "Learn to Act." http://stopasuicide.org/learn-to-act.php.

Stuart, Elizabeth. "Just a Perfect Blendship: Friendship and Sexuality." In *Our Families, Our Values: Snapshots of Queer Kinship*, edited by Robert E. Goss and Amy Adams Squire Strongheart, 163–81. New York: Harrington Park, 1997.

Suicide Awareness Voices of Education (SAVE). "Warning Signs of Suicide." https://save.org/about-suicide/warning-signs-risk-factors-protective-factors/.

Sweeney, Eva. *Queers on Wheels*. Pasadena, CA: CreateSpace, 2001.

Sylvestre, Berlin. "HPV: The Health Crisis We're Not Talking About." *Advocate*, January 5, 2017. https://www.advocate.com/current-issue/2017/1/05/hpv-health-crisis-were-not-talking-about.

Tamashiro, Dustin. "Coming Out." In *glbtq: An Encyclopedia of Gay, Lesbian, Bisexual, Transgender, and Queer Culture*, edited by Claude J. Summers. http://www.glbtqarchive.com/ssh/coming_out_ssh_S.pdf.

Tanis, Justin. *Trans-Gendered: Theology, Ministry, and Communities of Faith*. Cleveland: Pilgrim, 2003.

Tigert, Leanne M. *Coming Out While Staying In: Struggles and Celebrations of Lesbians, Gays, and Bisexuals in the Church*. Cleveland: United Church, 1996.

———. "Trouble Behind the Door." *Open Hands* 12.1 (Summer 1996) 8–9.

Tolbert, Mary Ann. "Marriage and Friendship in the Christian New Testament: Ancient Resources for Contemporary Same-Sex Unions." In *Authorizing Marriage?: Canon, Tradition, and Critique in the Blessing of Same-Sex Unions*, edited by Mark D. Jordan et al., 41–51. Princeton: Princeton University Press, 2006.

Turney, Kelly, ed. *Shaping Sanctuary: Proclaiming God's Grace in an Inclusive Church*. Chicago: Reconciling Congregation Program, 2000.

Unitarian Universalist Association. "Planning Guide for *Our Whole Lives* Facilitator Training." 2015. http://www.uua.org/re/owl/planning-guide.

Unitarian Universalists for Polyamory Awareness. www.uupa.org.

The United Methodist Church. "Commission on a Way Forward Issues Status Report." June 26, 2017. http://www.umc.org/news-and-media/commission-on-a-way-forward-issues-status-report.

Villarosa, Linda. "America's Hidden H.I.V. Epidemic." *New York Times Magazine*, June 6, 2017.

Weaver, Andrew, et al. *Counseling on Sexual Issues: A Handbook for Pastors and Other Helping Professionals*. Cleveland: Pilgrim, 2006.

WebMD. "Preventing HIV and Other STDs With Safe Sex." https://www.webmd.com/hiv-aids/safe-sex-preventing-hiv-aids-stds#1.

Weston, Kath. *Families We Choose: Lesbians, Gays, Kinship*. New York: Columbia University Press, 1991.

Williams, Walter L. *The Spirit and the Flesh: Sexual Diversity in the American Indian Culture*. Boston: Beacon, 1992.

Wilson, D. Mark. "'I Don't Mean to Offend, but I Won't Pretend' Experiences of Family Life for Gay Men Within an African American Church." In *Tending the Flock: Congregations and Family Ministry*, edited by K. Brynolf Lyon and Archie Smith, Jr., 145–72. Louisville: Westminster John Knox, 1998.

Wilson, Nancy L. *Our Tribe: Queer Folks, God, Jesus, and the Bible*. San Francisco: HarperSanFrancisco, 1995.

# Index

Abby, 215–17
abuse
　by parents, 40–41
　reporting, xiv
　sexual, 95
addiction, xx, 90–93
　origin of, as spiritual challenge, 93, 93n28
　sexual, 95
　shame leading to, 34, 127
adolescence, coming out resembling, 142–43, 145–46
adoption, 212
advanced planning. See end-of-life concerns
affirming attitudes, xviii–xix, 40, 137, 178–79
　change demanded for, 154–55
　in congregations, 51n12, 77, 121, 153–77
　in sermons, 50, 77, 105, 137
　and spaces for youth, 106, 110
African American LGBTQ people, 62, 69
AIDS liturgies, 169, 172
　See also HIV/AIDS
Alice, 218–20
alienation, 51–52, 135
allies, 36–37
　at Pride, 44
alternative insemination, 212
anger, 74–76
　channeling, 44, 75–76
　hidden, 75
　at religion, 32–33, 117

anxiety disorders, 89–90
April, 213–14
arrogance, avoiding, 4–5, 20–21
Asian American LGBTQ people, 63–64
assisted living, 115–16
　partner separation and, 42, 114, 116–17
assumptions, questioning, 70–71, 85
attraction, 228

Ball, Susan, 84
bathrooms and locker rooms, 103, 166
beginner's mind, 64
Belile, Jackie, 153
"beloved community," 224
berdache. See Two-Spirit
the Bible, xiii, 119, 120, 221, 223
　friendship in, 183–84
　hospitality in, 184
　transgender readings of, 219
biphobia, 81
bipolar disorder, 90
birth control, 95
bisexuality, 55–56, 70, 101–2, 200–203, 225–26
　and coming out as bi, 131, 132, 141, 229
　definition of, xxii
　disbelief in, 131, 132
　Klein Grid and, 229
　resources about, 203
blindness, 95
bodies, celebration of, 186–87, 189

261

"Born This Way" (Lady Gaga), 130
boundaries, 13–17, 71
　definition of, 13
　emotional/spiritual, 16–17
　extending, 13
　physical/sexual, 14–15
　transference and, 19
Boyle, Sally, 191
Buddhism, 174, 206–7
bullying, 104, 108–10, 111

care receivers
　appearance of, avoiding comments on, 15
　asking for help from, 48
　believing, 25
　definition of, xxi
　expecting judgment from caregivers, 70
　feelings of, respecting, 6–7, 15, 21–22
　internalized homophobia of, 12–13, 74, 114, 135–36, 149, 187
　people of color as, 61–68
　struggling with orientation or identity, 72
caring intimacy, 3–4
　authentic, 5–6
　and avoiding fear and arrogance, 4–5
case studies, 191–210
Catholicism
　homosexuality and, 97
　in Latinx communities, 62–63
Cecil, 200–202
celibacy, 53, 181, 208–10
　resources about, 210
The Center for LGBTQ and Gender Studies in Religion (CLGS), 35n21, 124–25
Chechnya, 75
checklist for pastoral caregivers, 70–72
children
　abuse suffered by, 40–41
　adoption of, 212
　alienation suffered by, 135
　custody of, 131, 132
　film resources for, 110
　in queer families, 211–20
　transgender, 218–20
　*See also* youth
Children of Lesbians and Gays Everywhere (COLAGE), 215
choice, xv–xvi, 118–20
chosen family. *See* families, chosen
chronic illness, 87
Clare, 215–17
Clebsch, William A., 38
Clinebell, Howard, xx, 38, 39, 55
the closet
　as destructive, 127–28, 144
　and double lives, 67, 126
　pre-coming out, 134–37
　"safety" of, 29, 41, 127, 151
　*See also* coming out; liberation
Coleman, Eli, xx, 133–34, 143, 148, 150
coming out, xx, 29, 124–52
　*vs.* being outed, 130, 139
　as bisexual, 131, 132, 141, 229
　caregiver aiding in, 29
　by caregivers, 23–25, 54–55
　daily, 124–25
　definition of, xxii, 125
　discernment and, 138–39
　discrimination and, 132, 136, 141, 151
　diverse ways of, 128–30
　elders, 114–15
　later in life, 114, 128
　as liberation, 151–52
　as ministry, 54–55
　to oneself, 125, 137
　as pastoral care opportunity, 132–33
　reasons for, 126
　regret and, 114–15
　resources for, 125n1
　as rite of passage, 130–32
　role-playing scenarios, 141
　as a spiritual journey, 151–52
　stories, 24–25, 114–15, 126, 131, 137, 142
　support during, 139–40
　surprise at, 46–47

# Index

as transgender, 25, 41, 125, 126, 149
as unpredictable, 130–31, 138, 141–42
worship services, 167
youth, 104, 106–8
*See also* coming out, stages of
coming out, stages of, 133–50
  coming out (2nd stage), 134, 137–42
  exploration, 134, 142–47
  first relationships, 134, 147–50
  integration, 134, 150
  pre-coming out, 134–37
Coming Out Day, 176
communication, fostering, 35–36, 55–56, 105
communities of care, xx, 153–77
community-building, 185–86
*compadres*, 63
competence in LGBTQ issues, 46–48
confidence, 46
confidence, developing, 144–45
confidentiality, 17–18, 103
confrontation, 49
Confucianism, 63
congregations
  affirming, 51n12, 77, 121, 153–77
  apologizing for, 39
  backlash from, 156
  as communities of care, xx, 153–77
  definition of, xxi
  disagreement within, 158–59
  diversity of, 163, 164
  educating, 77, 156–59, 171–72, 175
  and LGBTQ communities, alliances between, 174–76
  LGBTQ people integrated in, 153, 164–74
  LGBTQ people leaving, 51–52
  offering meeting space, 176
  parents supported by, 213–20
  pastoral care provided by, 1
  seeking safe, 193
  sex education and, 94
  support groups in, 171
  surveying, on LGBTQ issues, 158
  transforming, 155–56, 160–62, 166

withdrawal from, 127–28, 198–99, 200
wounds inflicted by, xi, 32, 34, 39–40, 51–52, 57, 70, 79, 153–54, 221
connection, fostering, 35–36, 55–56
contact between LGBTQ and non-LGBTQ people, 36, 55–56
content and process, 21–22
contraception, 95
conversion therapy. *See* "ex-gay" ministries
counter-transference, 19–20
Covenant House, 31n17
creativity
  anger channeled into, 76
  closets stifling, 127
  fostering, 33–34
  in pastoral care, 69
crisis, pastoral care in times of, 73–123
crystal meth, 91–93
"curing" homosexuality, 70
custody of children, 131, 132

Damon, 215–17
deafness, 95–96
death, facing, 117
death penalty, 74, 75n3
defensiveness, 19, 21, 40
de la Torre, Miguel, 97
dementia, 116
denominations
  advocacy groups of, 172–74
  curricula of, 158
  *See also* non-affirming denominations
depression, 88–89
  the closet leading to, 127, 128
  signs of, 89
Derek, 203–5
development, 56–57
  in coming out, 143–47
  faith, 57
  of interpersonal skills, 143–44
  social, 56, 57, 58
dignity, 116–17
disabilities, physical, 95–96

discrimination, 33–34, 79–82
  coming out and, 132, 136, 141, 151
  legal protections from, 32, 121, 176
  religious, xi, 32, 34, 70, 79, 153–54
  working to end, 175, 176
diversity, congregational, 163, 164
divorce
  after coming out, 131, 132
  child custody and, 131, 132
  ritualizing, 169
Dixie, 192–95
domestic violence, 99–101
  resources on, 100–101
  stereotypes about, 99, 100
double lives, 67, 69
double stress, 66–68
"the down low," 69
dress codes, 103
drugs, 90–93, 146–47
dualism, 186

eating disorders, 127
education
  bullying affecting, 109
  of caregivers, 71, 172, 189–90
  of congregations, 77, 156–59, 171–72, 175
  on HIV/AIDS, 84, 85
  on progressive religion, 175
  resources for, 157–58, 191
  sex, 94, 216–17
  on transgenderism, 103
elders, 114–17
  coming out, 114–15
  dignity of, 116–17
  and end-of-life issues, 117
  and integration, 115–16
  loss faced by, 114–15
  as mentors, 116
  retiring, 115
  sexual expression of, 116
  transgender, 114
Ella, 218–20
embodiment, 186–87, 189
emotions
  and emotional preference, 228
  negative, 73–79

  and sexuality, connection between, 16
  *See also* transference
empathy, 41–42
Empereur, James, 51
employment discrimination, 131, 132
empowerment, friendship leading to, 182–83
end-of-life concerns, 117, 206–8
  resources about, 208
Erikson, Erik, 56, 115n55, 134
ethnicity, 61–68, 69
  and inter- and intra-ethnic issues, 68
  stereotypes of, 64, 65–66
exclusion, xvii, 2–3, 33–34, 53, 63
  language as tool of, 165–66
  and self-exclusion, 117
  as spiritual violence, 77
"ex-gay" ministries, xx, 118–22
  as anti-science, 119
  definition of, 118
  dissuading people from, 121
  harm caused by, 120–21
  legal prohibition of, 121, 126n3
  pastoral care and, 120–22
ex-lovers, friendship with, 183
Exodus, 151–52, 187
experimentation, 145–46
exploration, 142–47

faith
  development of, 57
  new perspectives on, 163
  overcoming homophobia, 137
families, chosen, 117, 210–20
  definition of, 210
  friendship essential to, 210–11
  resources about, 212, 215, 216
families of origin
  centrality of, in Latinx communities, 63
  coming out to, 46–47, 108, 141–42
  definition of, 210
  educating, 106, 142
  end-of-life planning and, 206–7
  illness and, 87
  involving, for youth, 107

## Index

reconciliation with, 169
rejection by, 29–30, 31, 63–64
of transgender people, 218–20
wounds inflicted by, 40–41, 210
fantasies, 228
fear, 76
  in caregiver, 4–5, 20–21
  of rejection, 76
feminism, 28–29, 165
fidelity, 194–95, 204, 205
film resources for children, 110
"flaunting it," 98
flexibility, 9
fluidity, sexual, xv, 228
Fowler, James, 57
frailty, 117
friendship, 182–84, 185
  in the Bible, 183–84
  as egalitarian, 183
  with ex-lovers, 183
  sex as part of, 204–5
  traditional philosophies of, 182n3
functions of pastoral care, 38–72
  healing, 39–42
  sustaining, 43–46

Gallo, Jeanne, 29
"gay agenda," 79
"gay bashers," 97
gay people
  couples, resources for, 206
  definition of, xxii
  as parents, 213–18
Gay Pride. *See* Pride
Gay-Straight Alliances, 106, 110
gender dysphoria, 88
gender fluidity, 165–66, 167
gender identity
  as a gift, xvii
  ignorance about, 25
  *vs.* mental illness, 88
  sexual orientation and, 25, 71
genderqueer, definition of, xxii
gender-reassignment surgery, xxii, 49, 72, 104, 196
gender roles, 70, 72
  ethnicity and, 64–65

gender transitions, rituals marking, 167–68
generational gaps, 35
generativity, 115, 115n55, 188–89
gifts of God, LGBTQ people as, xii–xiii, 223
God
  co-creating with, 189
  imitation of, 3–4
  liberation and, 151–52
  love of, xii–xiii
  relationships modeled on, 18
Goergen, Donald, 209
Goss, Robert, 182, 189
grace, 68–69
Grace, J., 150
Graham, Larry Kent, 26, 38, 127, 192, 192n14
Greenberg, Steven, 28, 54–55
grief, 34
  AIDS and, 86
guidance, 46–51
  competence in LGBTQ issues and, 46–48
  confrontation as, 49
  definition of, 46
  moral, 49–50
  public, 48
  spiritual direction as, 50–51

Hall, Warren, 24
handicaps, 95–96
harassment, 104, 108–10, 111
harm reduction, 91, 91n22
hate crimes, 96
hatred, 16–17
healing, 39–42
  definition of, 39
hearing impairment, 95–96
heterosexism, 11–13, 66–68, 135
  definition of, 11–12
  internalized, 12–13
  unconscious, 164
Heyward, Carter, 186, 204–5
HIV/AIDS, 31, 34, 82–86
  intergenerational issues and, 35
  PTSD and, 83
  relationships and, 45

HIV/AIDS *(continued)*
  resources for understanding, 83–84
  stereotypes related to, 85
  treatment of, 82, 84–85
holiness, xvi, xviii
homelessness, 31, 131
homophobia, 11–13, 66–68
  care receivers expecting, 70
  definition of, 11
  faith liberating from, 137
  and fear of being "tainted," 46
  internalized, 12–13, 74, 114, 135–36, 149, 187
  sexism linked with, 28–29
homosexuality
  affirming, xix
  the Catholic Church on, 97
  as innate, 101, 118–20
  not a mental illness, 87–88, 126, 126n3
hospitality, 164, 184–86
  sexual ethic of, 184–85, 202
HPV, 86
Hunt, Mary, 182, 182n3, 183, 205

identity
  celibacy and, 208–9
  development and, 56
  ethnic, 67–68
  exclusion because of, 53
  friendship and, 209
  wholeness and, xvii
illness, xx, 46, 82–90
  access of relatives and, 86
  chronic, 87
  guilt and, 85, 86
  mental, 87–90
  pastoral visits and, 87
  suicide and, 49
  *See also* HIV/AIDS
"I'm Coming Out" (Diana Ross), 130
incarnation, 186–87
inclusion, hospitality as, 184–85
inclusive language, 164–66
inclusive rituals, 164, 167–74
  resources for, 169–70
inclusive space, 164, 166, 185

The Institute of Welcoming Resources, 216
integration, 115–16, 115n55, 134, 150
interconnectedness. *See* psychosystems
intergenerational issues, 35, 116
the internet, 113
interpersonal skills, 143–44
intersectional oppressions, 30, 31, 61–68, 80–82
intimacy
  and arrested development, 56, 57, 127
  caring, 3–6
  coming out and, 126
Isaiah, xii
Islam, 173
isolation, 77–78, 213–14

Jaekle, Charles R., 38
Jared, 196–97
Jesus
  friendship and, 183, 185
  liberation by, 187
Johnson, Robert, 3–4
José, 213–14
joy, 151
Judaism, 126n3, 196–97
  advocacy groups in, 173
Jung, Patricia Beattie, xix
justice work, 32, 42, 44, 163–64, 175, 176
  and prophetic pastoral care, 59–60

King, J. L., 69
Kinsey, Alfred, 225–26
Kinsey Rating Scale, xv, 225–26
Klein Sexual Orientation Grid, xv, 227–29
  aids in understanding, 228
  bisexuality and, 229
Kundtz, David, xxi

labels, xvi, xxi–xxii
Latinx LGBTQ people, 62–63
legal protections, 32, 33–34, 121
  lack of, 33–34, 80
  working for, 176

*See also* discrimination
Lenore, 192–95
lesbians
  covenantal relationships between, 194–95
  definition of, xxii
  resources for, 194
LGBTQ, definition of, xxi
LGBTQ communities, alliances with, 174–76
LGBTQ people, xi–xii, xiv–xv
  celebrating, 221
  of color, 30, 31, 61–68, 169
  experience of, discounted, 33
  as gifts of God, xii–xiii, 223
  handicapped, 95–96
  in heterosexual-appearing marriages, 70
  holistic view of, 122–23
  as leaders in the congregation, 169, 171
  listening to, 159
  meeting, importance of, 36, 55–56
  over-sexualization of, 14
  as parents, 213–18
  persecution of, 74–75, 75n3, 153–54
  prejudice and intolerance among, 81–82, 81n7
  programs for, 175
  rural, support for, 43
  in sermons, 50, 77, 105, 137
  systems affecting, 26–36
  *See also* elders; youth
liberation
  coming out as, 151–52
  congregational participation as, 162
  shared, 187–88
lifestyle preference, 228
limitations, acknowledging, 21, 71
Lionel, 203–5
listening, importance of, 159
loneliness, 67, 76, 77–78, 127
love
  of friends, 182–84
  queer relationships generating, 188–89
"love the sinner, hate the sin," 16–17

Luke, 218–20

mandated reporting, xiv
manic depression, 90
Marissa, 211–12
marriage
  dethroning, 183, 184
  discernment regarding, 192–95
  planning, 193
  preparation courses, 195
  resources for, 195
  "straight," 70
marriage equality, 32, 44–45, 168–69
Marshall, Joretta, 20, 50, 121–22, 178, 194–95
Mary Margaret, 208–9
medical care, partners separated for, 42, 114, 116–17
meeting space for support groups, 176
mental illness, 87–90
  bullying and, 109
  gender identity *vs.*, 88
  homosexuality misidentified as, 87–88, 126, 126n3
mentoring, 112–13, 116
  resources for, 112n53, 113
meth, 91–93
Metropolitan Community Churches (MCC), 184, 203
Michael, 213–14
minister, definition of, xxi
minority
  definition of, 61
  positive aspects of being in, 67–68
minority stress, 80–81
monogamy, 194–95
Moore, Patrick, 93n28
morality, xix
  changing, xviii, xviiin9
  guidance in, 49–50, 146, 201–2
  in polyamory, 198, 200
  self-discovery of, 9, 34
mutual care, 1, 82

names, chosen, 103, 117
Native Americans, 64
Nelson, James, xix
Niemöller, Martin, 37

Nimmons, David, 96, 185
non-affirming denominations
  coming out in, 23–24
  openness in, 11, 179, 190, 224
  public disagreement with, 77
nonbinary people, 165–66, 167
the "nones," 52–53
non-monogamy, 180, 201–2, 203–5
noticing, 58, 77–78, 108
nurturing, 55–58
  development and, 56–58
  noticing as part of, 58

obsessive-compulsive disorder (OCD), 89–90, 95
older age. See elders
online challenges, 113
openness, 9–11, 35–36, 72, 122, 133, 221, 223–24
  in non-affirming denominations, 11, 179, 190, 224
  as transformative, 9–10
open relationships. See non-monogamy
oppression
  intersections of, 30, 31, 61–68, 80–82
  self-love despite, 32
otherness, 52
"Our Whole Lives," 216–17
outing, 17–18, 130

parenthood
  biological vs. adoptive, 211–12
  resources about, 212, 215
  support for, 213–14
partners and spouses, separation of, 42, 114, 116–17
passive-aggressive behavior, 75, 75n5
pastoral care, xiii–xv, xviii–xix
  definition of, xiv, 1
  denial of, 2–3
  functions of, xx, 38–72
  goals of, 27–28, 37, 192
  guiding, 46–51
  healing, 39–42
  location of, 27
  "negative" emotions in, xx

  nurturing, 55–58
  omission in, 48–49
  vs. pastoral counseling, xiv
  postponing, 6–7
  power inequalities in, 14, 15, 19
  prophetic, 58–61
  reasons for seeking, 1–2
  reconciling, 51–55
  referral and, 6–7, 8
  as a relationship, xix, 1–37
  skills for, 2, 133, 138
  sustaining as, 43–46
  sustaining the work of, 10–11
  vignettes, 191–210
pastoral caregiver
  assumptions of, 70–71, 85
  checklist for, 70–72
  as closeted, 23–24
  coming out, 23–25, 54–55
  dealing with negative emotions, 6, 8, 19–20
  definition of, xxi
  education of, 71, 172, 189–90
  fear and arrogance in, 4–5, 20–21
  LGBTQ, 22–25
  pastoral care for, 23–24
  presence of, 67
  qualifications of, 2
  straight, 25–26, 78
  testing, 2–3, 4–5
  transformed by caregiving, 24–25
  unresolved issues of, 20, 178–79
pastoral counseling vs. pastoral care, xiv
the "pastoral solution," 53–55, 72
pastoral theology
  definition of, xiii–xiv
  vs. systematic theology, 10
pastoral visitation, 87, 117
patriarchy, 183, 186
Peck, Jane, 29
people of color, 30, 31, 61–68, 169
PEP (Post-Exposure Prophylaxis), 85
persecution, 74–75, 75n3, 153–54
PFLAG, 36n22, 44
physicality, 186–87
Plaskow, Judith, 186
political identity, 228

polyamory, 197–200, 211
  definition of, 199
  resources on, 198
pornography, 113
power, fair balance of, 30–31
prejudice, 11–13, 15
PrEP (Pre-Exposure Prophylaxis), 84–85
presence of pastoral caregiver, 67
Pride, 43
  allies participating in, 44
  worship services celebrating, 168, 172, 176
principles, xii–xix
process and content, 21–22
procreativity, 188–89
"promiscuity," 184, 201–2, 204–5
pronouns, 103, 117
prophetic pastoral care, 38, 58–61
psychology, xiv, 159
psychosystems, 26–36
  competing values of, 26–27
  definition of, 26
  healing, 42
PTSD, 83
public guidance, 48

queer, definition and usage of, xvi, xxii
queer culture, 36
"queer for a day" exercise, 78
queer theologians, 181, 184

racism, 66–68, 81n7
rating scales, xv, xxi, 225–29
reconciliation, 51–55
  definition of, 51
  "ongoing," 54–55
  sacrament of, 53
referral, 6–7, 8, 71
  list of resources for, 8
  mental illness and, 88, 89, 95, 112
  for young people, 112
rejection, 6–7, 76
  by families of origin, 29–30, 31, 63–64
relationships, xx, 44–45, 178–221
  challenges to, 148, 149–50

embodiment celebrated in, 186–87
ethics of, 34n19, 145, 146, 188, 191, 200–202, 204–5
first, after coming out, 134, 147–50
friendship, 182–84, 187
gender roles and, 70, 72, 149
as generative, 188–89
hospitality, 184–86
liberation shared in, 187–88
new models of, 179, 180
pastoral care for, 189–210
starting, 143–44
understanding, 180–91
visibility of, 148–49
religion
  anger at, 32–33, 117
  and "ex-gay" ministries, 118–22
  opening up, 35
  race, ethnicity, and, 61, 62–66
  and religious prejudice, xi, 32, 34, 39–40, 70, 79, 153–54
  vs. science, 119
  spirituality separated from, 52–53
  violence stoked by, 96–97
religious orders, 208–9
respect, 71–72
retirement, 115
rituals, inclusive, 164, 167–74
Robinson, Gene, 152
role-playing for coming out, 141
Rudy, Kathy, 201–2
Ryan, Caitlin, 106

sacraments, 40
  reconciliation, 53
Salas, Antonio, 151
sanctification. *See* nurturing
Schlager, Bernard, xxi
scrutiny, being under, 44
self-acceptance, 32, 74
self-awareness, 20, 71, 82, 178–79
self-care, 86
  modeling, 82
self-worth, 40, 43, 127
  fostering, 43–44, 74, 144–45
  not based on sexual conquests, 145–47

sermons, LGBTQ people in, 50, 77, 105, 137
service to others, 185–86
sex, 94–95
  addiction, 95
  boundaries and, 14–15
  emotional boundaries and, 16
  ethical, 34n19, 145, 146, 188, 200–202, 204–5
  goodness of, 94
  hospitality and, 184–85, 202
  importance of discussing, 50, 144–45, 146, 202
  meaningful, 201–2
  negativity, xviii
  safer, 94–95
  and sexual abuse, 95
  substance abuse and, 146–47
  taboo on discussing, 50, 85
  unprotected, drug use and, 93
  *See also* relationships
sexism, 28–29
sexual behavior, 228
sexual conversion therapy. *See* "ex-gay" ministries
sexual identity
  definition of, xxii, 228
  and political identity, 228
  presuming, 22
sexuality
  expression of, as choice, xv–xvi
  "flaunting," 98
  as a gift, xvii, 94, 186–87
sexual orientation
  age and, 106, 107, 107n47, 135, 135n10
  definition of, xxii
  discernment of, in pastoral care, 192n14
  as dynamic process, 228
  gender identity and, 25, 71
  as innate, 118–21, 122–23
shame, 34, 73–74, 86
  definition of, 74
sin, definition of, 17
singleness, 180–81
skills for caregivers, 2, 133, 138
Smid, John J., 120

Smith, Archie, 68
Smith, Ralph, xix
social media, 113
social preference, 228
solidarity, 36–37
Spahr, Janie Adams, 24
"spiritual but not religious," 52–53
spiritual direction, 50–51
stereotypes, ethnic, 64, 65–66
the straight voice, power of, 36–37
stress, 79–82
  on children, 64
  intersections of, 66–68
  mental illness and, 88
  and PTSD, 83
  reduction, 82
  types of, 79
Stuart, Elizabeth, 183, 187
substance abuse, 90–93, 146–47
suicide, 127, 135
  illness and, 49
  signs of, 111–12
  youth and, 111–12
support groups, 186, 213–14, 219, 220
  congregational, 171
  pastoral caregivers in, 24
  for youth, 131, 139, 196
surgery, gender-reassignment, xxii, 49, 72, 104, 196
surveys, congregational, 158
sustaining, 43–46
  definition of, 43
Sweeney, Eva, 95
systematic *vs.* pastoral theology, 10
systems, 26–36
  competing values of, 26–27
  healing, 42

Tanis, Justin, 166n8, 219
Taoism, 63
terminology, xxi–xxii, 71
Tigert, Leanne, 51
touching, 15
tradition, xiii
transference, 18–21
  and counter-transference, 19–20
  definitions of, 18, 19
  positive, 20

transformation, congregational, 155–56, 160–62, 166
Transgender Day of Remembrance, 168, 172, 176
transgender people, 102–4, 196–97
　coming out, 25, 41, 125, 126, 149
　definition of, xxii, 125n2
　faith and, 218–20
　families of origin and, 218–20
　ignorance about, 25, 71, 72
　inclusive language and, 165–66, 167
　inclusive space and, 166
　medical care for, 114
　names and pronouns of, 103, 166n8
　resources for, 196, 197, 219–20
　sexual orientations of, 25, 71
　surgery and, xxii, 49, 72, 104, 196
　violence against, 97
transphobia, 11, 66
　among gay people, 13
　care receivers expecting, 70
transsexual, definition of, xxii
The Trevor Project, 112n52
truth, living out, 127
Turney, Kelly, 167n9
Two-Spirit, 64

UCC Coalition for LGBT Concerns, 216
Unitarian Universalists for Polyamory Awareness (UUPA), 199, 199n17

values
　clarification of, 33, 145
　mutual understanding of, 31–33
vignettes, 191–210
violence, xx, 74, 75, 76, 96–101
　anti-trans, 97, 168
　domestic, 99–101
　emotional and spiritual, 77
　religion stoking, 96–97
visibility
　in congregations, 162–63
　of LGBTQ relationships, 148–49
visual impairment, 95
Vivian, 206–7

weddings. *See* marriage
welcome, 153–54, 155–64, 215–17
　*vs.* affirmation, 154
　clearly stating, 160–62
　and diversity, 163, 164
　as educated, 156–59
　statements of, 160–62, 171, 174–75
　stories of, 177
　as transformative, 155–56, 162–64
　and welcoming taskforce, 158
Wilson, D. Mark, 62
Wilson, Nancy, 184–85
women, 30
　feminism and, 28–29
World Professional Association for Transgender Health, Inc., 196, 196n16
worship
　coming out celebrated in, 167
　gender transition marked in, 167–68
　inclusive rituals for, 167–74
　Pride celebrated in, 168, 172, 176
　resources, 169–70
　unconscious biases in, 165
　welcoming, 40, 154
woundedness, 39–42
　faith communities inflicting, xi, 32, 34, 39–40, 51–52, 57, 70, 79, 153–54, 221
　families of origin inflicting, 40–41, 210

Yolanda, 197–200
youth, 104–13
　affirming spaces for, 106, 110
　bullying and harassment of, 104, 108–10, 111
　coming out, 104, 106–8, 131, 132
　education of, 109
　mentoring, 112–13, 116
　needs of, 104
　online challenges of, 113
　questions of, 104–5
　suicide risk of, 111–12
　supporting, 105–6, 109–10, 132

www.ingramcontent.com/pod-product-compliance
Lightning Source LLC
Chambersburg PA
CBHW030821230426
43667CB00008B/1321